URBAN DANGER

Life in a
Neighborhood
of Strangers

URBAN DANGER

Life in a Neighborhood of Strangers

SALLY ENGLE MERRY

Temple University Press, Philadelphia

Temple University Press, Philadelphia 19122
© 1981 by Temple University. All rights reserved
Published 1981
Printed in the United States of America

Library of Congress Cataloging in Publication Data

Merry, Sally Engle.
Urban danger.

Bibliography: p.
Includes index.
1. Urban anthropology—Case studies.   2. Public
housing—Massachusetts—Boston—Case studies.
3. Crime and criminals—Massachusetts—Boston—
Case studies.   4. Urban renewal—Massachusetts—
Boston—Case studies.   5. Ethnopsychology—Case
studies.   I. Title.
GN395.M47   307.7'6   81-1237
      ISBN 0-87722-219-3   AACR2

To
Paiche and Joshua

CONTENTS

ACKNOWLEDGMENTS

Many people contributed to this book in a variety of ways. Professor David Jacobson encouraged me to investigate the uncertainties and discontinuities of urban social life and urbanites' strategies for coping with these situations. His stimulating ideas and guidance contributed both to the research and to the analysis of the data in many ways. The Center for Studies of Metropolitan Problems of the National Institute of Mental Health generously supported this research with a predoctoral dissertation grant (no. 1 F31 MH05088-01). Wellesley College granted me leave from teaching responsibilities to complete the book. Professor Ulf Hannerz in a sense inspired this book by his insightful and provocative paper on the management of danger in which he urged anthropologists to tackle the analysis of fleeting as well as enduring relationships. Subsequent conversations with Prof. Hannerz have amplified my understanding of urban social life. For fruitful and thought-provoking guidance during my graduate training at Brandeis University, I am grateful to Professors Robert Hunt, Marguerite Robinson, and Alex Weingrod. The editors of *Law and Society Review, Human Organization*, and *Urban Affairs Quarterly* have kindly allowed me to include materials previously published in their journals. The editorial staff at Temple University Press, particularly Michael Ames and Michael Fisher, have provided valuable insight and editorial assistance in the creation of the book.

I am particularly indebted to the residents of the community I studied for their tolerance of my endless questions, their good-natured acceptance of my research, and their keen insight into the dynamics of the society around them. In the interest of preserving their anonymity, I will not mention anyone by name, but acknowledge their tremendous collective contribution. I only hope that I have presented all perspectives fairly and that this book may help others to understand the difficulties they face and their strength in handling them. The research benefitted greatly from several skilled research assistants: Patricia Annez, Charles Brown, Stella Chin, Ira Goldenberg, and Vinton Wong. Lisanne Crowley contributed significantly to Chapter 7 through her careful and thoughtful research into historical and cross-cultural aspects of danger. Above all, my husband was a continuing source of support and encouragement, both in his willingness to join me in the experience of inner-city living and, along with our young son, in his tolerance of my periods of distraction and absence during the writing of this book.

Wellesley, Mass.   Sally Engle Merry
December 1980

URBAN DANGER

Life in a
Neighborhood
of Strangers

CHAPTER 1

Introduction

In a small, ethnically diverse neighborhood enmeshed in the vast sprawl of a major American city the residents have developed their own strategies for coping with the danger that surrounds them. One young Chinese woman never returns home alone on foot after dark. When she arrives by car, she honks her horn to alert her parents and then dashes the twenty feet to her door. A white man cautiously packs his suitcases into his car under cover of darkness before he leaves for a trip to escape being noticed by potential burglars. A middle-aged black woman sneaks surreptitiously from her home at 6:00 A.M. to do her laundry before the neighborhood youths gather in the laundromat to visit and smoke. She is anxious not to leave her home vacant, even for a few minutes, as an invitation to the burglars she constantly fears. Yet, in the same neighborhood, a young black woman moves freely, visiting neighbors late at night with no thought of danger. Young men rendezvous in dark secluded hallways even though they are aware that they risk being mugged. A Chinese man reputed to possess marvelous skill in Chinese martial arts is studiously avoided by youths choosing profitable and safe robbery victims. He walks through the project without fear. And an adult black man declares that his neighborhood is very safe because he knows everyone and everyone knows him.

All of these people face the same hazards, yet their attitudes, fears, and modes of coping vary enormously. Why do they respond so differently to the same risks? Why are some residents afraid of crime, and others unafraid? These questions lead to larger questions: How do urbanites in general conceptualize and manage danger? How do they decide which people and locations are dangerous and which are safe? Does their sense of danger simply reflect neighborhood crime rates? Urban residents must continually decide what situations they consider dangerous, but rarely have access to accurate statistics about when and where crimes occur. Through a detailed ethnographic examination of the perceptions of danger and coping strategies developed by residents of an urban neighborhood, I try in this book to answer some of these questions. In the process, I formulate a theory about the multifaceted meanings of danger and the features of urban social systems that spark a sense of danger. Further, employing cross-cultural and historical data, I analyze the social conditions that foster widespread concern about urban danger.

THE FEAR OF CRIME

The turbulent decade of the mid-1960s to the mid-1970s witnessed a tremendous outpouring of research on the American public's fear of crime (McIntyre 1967; National Crime Commission 1967, 1968; Boggs 1971; Erskine 1974; Hindelang 1974; DuBow, McCabe, and Kaplan 1979). Survey researchers investigated whether Americans were afraid to walk in their neighborhoods at night, whether they thought crime rates were rising, and whether they viewed crime as a major social problem (McIntyre 1967; Erskine 1974). The results clearly indicated that concern about crime and fear for personal safety were significant factors in the lives of many Americans. Throughout the period, concern about crime fluctuated, rising in response to racial violence, political assassinations, war protests, campus unrest, or purely criminal activities, and falling in periods of relative calm, while fear for personal safety in the streets rose gradually but inexorably (Erskine 1974: 131–132). The poor, the less educated, and blacks consistently reported the most fear of walking in their own neighborhoods (Erskine 1974: 131), but in a 1972 survey, 41 percent of a diverse sample of Americans reported that they were afraid of walking alone at night close to their homes (Hindelang 1974: 103). Among female respondents, 58 percent expressed such fears, and of those living in cities having a population over one million, 53 percent said they were afraid at night. Clearly, crime and the fear of crime are major problems for Americans (National Crime Commission 1967; Conklin 1975; DuBow, McCabe, and Kaplan 1979).

Sociologists argue that the fear of crime actually contributes to the incidence of crime, that fear of crime breaks down neighborhood cohesion, undermines neighborly sociability and concern for others, and instills distrust and suspicion in their place (McIntyre 1967: 41; National Crime Commission 1967; Fowler and Mangione 1974; Wilson 1975; Conklin 1975; DuBow, McCabe, and Kaplan 1979: 24–26). As community solidarity weakens, informal social controls atrophy. Residents are less willing to intervene to stop a crime, to help a stranger, or to question and drive out intruders. They become more afraid to venture from their homes. As a result, there are fewer people on the streets, less surveillance of street life, and less chance of effective intervention (Jacobs 1961; Newman 1973). The crime rate climbs. As Wilson argues, "By disrupting the delicate nexus of ties, formal and informal, by which we are linked with our neighbors, crime atomizes society and makes of its members mere individual calculators estimating their own advantage, especially their own chances for survival amidst their fellows. Common undertakings become difficult or impossible, except for those motivated by a shared desire for protection" (Wilson 1975: 21). Newman adopts this theory in arguing that characteristics of building design that promote social interaction and foster a sense that space is semi-private facilitate surveillance of public spaces and encourage collective responsibility for intervening in crime incidents, thus reducing crime (1973; see also Yancey 1971; Jacobs 1961).

The relationship of the fear of crime to the crime rate is not only of theoretical interest but also has an important implication for law enforcement policies: If fear of crime is not related to the crime rate, then the psychological costs of crime will not be diminished by reducing the incidence of crime. Some anomalies in the survey findings suggest that the relationship is neither simple nor direct. For example, the fear of crime focuses on the threat of violent attack by a stranger, but the chances of being killed in a car accident are ten times higher than those of being murdered by a stranger, and the risk of death from an accidental fall is three times as great. In 1973, 5 million people were injured in car accidents and 24 million were hurt in accidents at home, 4 million of whom suffered temporary or permanent disability, but only 400,000 robbery victims were injured, and 550,000 persons were hurt in incidents of aggravated assault (Silberman 1978: 6). Despite these awesome statistics, we do not live in fear of our automobiles, nor do home accidents make front-page reading in the newspapers (Silberman 1978: 6). There are more deaths from inadequate emergency medical service than from crimes of violence, but crime evokes far more anxiety than first-aid services (McIntyre 1967: 40).

Furthermore, fear of crime focuses on violent acts committed by strangers, yet most crimes of violence are committed by people who know their victims (National Crime Commission 1967: 87; McIntyre 1967: 40). The risk of serious attack from spouses, family members, friends, and acquaintances is almost twice as great as the risk of attack from strangers on the street (National Crime Commission 1967: 87). An analysis of criminal homicides reported to the police in Philadelphia between 1948 and 1952 indicated that only 12.2 percent were committed by strangers (Wolfgang, "Patterns of Criminal Homicide," cited by National Crime Commission 1967: 81). National figures reflect the same pattern: in 1965, 31 percent of all murders occurred within the family, and 48 percent resulted from conflicts between acquaintances, of which 38 percent were the result of lovers' quarrels or drinking situations (National Crime Commission 1967: 81). Killings resulting from robbery, sexual assault, or gangland activities and other felonies constituted another 16 percent, and 5 percent had unknown causes. A contemporary study of assaults and rapes in the District of Columbia indicated a similar pattern for these crimes (National Crime Commission 1967: 81). Almost two-thirds of rape victims were attacked by people with whom they were at least acquainted. Fourteen percent were relatives, family friends, or boyfriends of the victim and 39 percent were acquaintances or neighbors. Only 25 percent of aggravated assault victims were not acquainted with their assailants, while 21 percent were relatives of the assailant. In 20 percent of the cases, the victim and offender had had trouble with each other before.

Those individuals who are most afraid of crime are often not those most likely to be victims of crimes. For example, nationwide, women fear crime more than men, yet have lower rates of victimization than men for crimes other than rape (Conklin 1975: 8). A 1966 victimization survey revealed that women over sixty years old, who tend to be very afraid of crime, were only one-sixth as likely as young men in their twenties to experience crimes of homicide, rape, robbery, aggravated assault, burglary, larceny over fifty dollars, and auto theft, yet young men in their twenties are characteristically much less frightened (Hindelang et al. 1973: 170; Hindelang 1974: 103). A 1967 study of Washington, D.C., found that anxiety about crime was higher for women than men, although women were not more victimized (McIntyre 1967: 38). Nor does the experience of victimization itself significantly increase the fear of crime in most cases (McIntyre 1967; Boggs 1971; Hindelang 1974; Fowler and Mangione 1974: 9; DuBow, McCabe, and Kaplan 1979: 18–19). These surveys indicate that virtually no effects appear for victimization in the aggregate although slight increases in fear accompany experience with violent crimes.

Contrary to expectations, those who live in areas with the highest crime rates do not necessarily express the greatest fear of crime. A 1967 survey of Washington, D.C., found that the average level of concern about crime was lower in a black district with one of the highest rates of crime in the city than in another black precinct that had less crime, according to police statistics (McIntyre 1967: 38). Two years later, a survey of Baltimore, Maryland, found that, when fear was defined as the expectation of being the victim of one of eight different crimes, 21 percent of the residents of high-crime areas had a low level of fear, while an almost equal share, 19 percent, of people in relatively low-crime areas expressed the highest level of fear (Furstenberg 1971: 601). In a Boston study of three housing projects in a high-crime area, half the respondents felt their environment was fairly safe or very safe, while the other half felt the environment was moderately unsafe or very unsafe (Clay 1972).

Finally, urbanites typically perceive their own neighborhood to be much safer than the surrounding city, even when the neighborhood has a high crime rate. The familiarity of the neighborhood appears to impart to it an aura of safety. A nationwide survey in 1967 found that 60 percent of respondents believed that their own neighborhood was safer than the surrounding community, and only 14 percent thought it was more dangerous (McIntyre 1967: 38). A 1967 Washington study found that even in precincts with average or higher crime rates, only 20 percent of respondents thought their chances of being beaten were greater in the local neighborhood than in other parts of the city (McIntyre 1967: 38–39). A 1975 Detroit survey reported that 52 percent of respondents think their neighborhood is less dangerous than the average in Detroit, while only 9 percent think it is more dangerous (Survey Research Center 1975). Similar findings come from other cities and more recent studies (DuBow, McCabe, and Kaplan 1979: 4). Even in a small city such as Edmonton, Canada, with a population of half a million, 17 percent of the people interviewed were afraid of crime in the city while only 7 percent were afraid of crime in their own neighborhoods (Hartnagel 1979: 189). The sense of safety provided by familiarity extends even to users of mass transit: those who express the greatest fear are often those who use it least (DuBow, McCabe, and Kaplan 1979: 38).

Urbanites typically hold outsiders responsible for the local crime rate, even though some evidence suggests that certain crimes, such as homicide, aggravated assault, and residential burglary, tend to occur within the neighborhood of residence (Boggs 1965: 907–908; Conklin 1975: 30–33). Even in Zürich and Stuttgart, two-thirds of residents surveyed thought that people outside their neighborhoods were responsible for local crimes (Clinard 1978: 21).

Similar anomalies between rates of victimization and fear of crime appear in "Dover Square," the neighborhood described in this book. Dover Square is a small housing project in an area undergoing extensive urban renewal. The project has a diverse ethnic composition. In 1975–1976, about half the families (52 percent) were Chinese, one-quarter (27 percent) black, one-tenth (12 percent) white, and a small fraction (6 percent) Hispanic. It was constructed in the mid-1960s using federal housing subsidies to provide good housing for low-to-moderate-income families. "Dover Square" is not the real name of this community. I have disguised its real identity and location in order to protect the privacy of the people of the neighborhood. According to 1976 police statistics, the area had the highest per capita rate of robberies and assaults in the city. In 1969, it was ranked third in rate of robberies, fourth in assaults, and eighth in residential burglaries among the eighty-one neighborhoods in the city. Yet, in a survey of 101 residents, representative in age, sex, and ethnicity, 75 percent said they did not think the project was dangerous, 18 percent said it was fairly dangerous, and only 7 percent said it was very or extremely dangerous. Fifty-six percent said they were afraid to walk around their neighborhood alone at night, but 53 percent of residents of large cities nationwide expressed the same fear (Hindelang 1974: 103).

Those who expressed the most fear were not always those most likely to be victimized. A victimization survey of two-thirds of the three hundred households revealed that almost half (48 percent) had experienced a robbery, burglary, or assault against one of their members. Only 36 percent of the households had experienced no victimization. Yet each ethnic group responds differently to these high rates of victimization. The Chinese residents express the greatest fear and are most likely to raise the crime issue in discussions. In the attitude survey of 101 residents, only 18 percent of the Chinese respondents said the project was not at all dangerous, in comparison to 33 percent of the whites and 65 percent of the blacks. Rates of victimization support neither the prevailing Chinese fear of crime nor the blacks' lack of concern, however. Rates of robbery, burglary, and assault are roughly the same for blacks and Chinese but are almost twice as high for white families. Clearly, variations in levels of fear in Dover Square depend neither on the neighborhood crime rate nor on actual probability of victimization.

DEFINING DANGER

Despite the insights provided by their wealth of data, survey research on the fear of crime has become a quagmire of conflicting definitions. Different surveys have used different questions to evaluate the concept, tapping a wide variety of related but analytically distinct phenomena, such as sense of importance of crime as a political and social issue, perception that rates of crime have increased or decreased, fear for personal safety, perceptions of risk, judgments about neighborhood crime rates, attitudes toward the causes of crime, and types of preventive behavior (DuBow, McCabe, and Kaplan 1979: 1–2). Above all, surveys have assumed that the fear of crime is a continuous variable that can be measured. (For an overview of the survey literature and a discussion of these problems, see DuBow, McCabe, and Kaplan 1979.)

One useful clarification was Furstenberg's distinction between the fear of victimization and concern about crime as a public issue. The former described the level of fear for personal safety, the latter reflected political and social attitudes toward rapid social change, efforts to eliminate racial injustice, and social and political unrest. These political opinions seemed to bear little relation to the personal fear of crime (Furstenberg 1971). It seems useful to differentiate between attitudes toward the crime problem at a general, impersonal level and attitudes towards the way crime impinges on one's own life, and it seems useful to separate cognitive judgments or assessments about the extent and seriousness of crime and emotional reactions to these assessments (see DuBow, McCabe and Kaplan 1979: 1–7).

Personal reactions to crime have three components: cognitive, emotional, and behavioral. The cognitive component, which I term danger, is a judgment that a situation contains personal risks, based on cues in the environment and on past experience with these cues. These anticipations are learned, shared, and refined through experience. They incorporate estimations of the risks associated with particular locations, kinds of people, and times of day, and the vulnerability of the observer.

The emotional component refers to feelings about danger. Although the emotional response usually is fear, fear is not the only response to danger. Some individuals find danger exciting, thrilling, even pleasurable. Others, because they believe that they have effective strategies for coping, respond to danger only with greater caution.

The behavioral component describes the strategies individuals adopt to cope with the danger they perceive. Unwillingness to venture outside alone after dark, for example, is a behavioral response to a judgment of danger. The residents of Dover Square employ a wide variety of both defensive and offensive strategies, and feel more or less afraid depending on whether they feel powerless or masterful in handling the hazards that surround them.

These components of the reaction to crime are analytically distinct from the actual hazards presented by the environment. Crime rates are the measure commonly adopted to assess hazards, but are hardly accurate guides to the volume of crime (see Pepinsky 1980). Further, our understanding of the fear of crime is repeatedly hindered by the assumption that crime alone is perceived as hazardous. Some studies suggest that uncivil and disreputable behavior such as drunkenness, teenage rowdiness, untidiness, and indecency, which signal social breakdown and moral decay, may be as threatening as victim-oriented crimes (Wilson 1975: 23–25; DuBow, McCabe, and Kaplan 1979: 8). A 1968 survey of Missouri residents found that 55 percent of the respondents felt it was the character of the residents that made a neighborhood unsafe, while an additional 14 percent blamed general moral decline (Boggs 1971: 324).

Danger, which I define as the individual's cognitive reaction to crime, has three characteristics. First, it is a cognitive assessment of cues that lead an individual to anticipate harm in a situation. These cues are structured into spatial, temporal, and personal cognitive maps that define the places, times, and categories of persons who are likely to be safe or dangerous. The decision that a situation is or is not dangerous depends on the intersection of these maps. To understand the fear of crime, it is much less useful to ask how afraid an individual feels than it is to explore the content of his or her cognitive maps and the frequency with which he or she encounters situations these maps define as dangerous. Chapter 5 further elaborates the notion of danger as a set of cognitive maps.

A second characteristic of danger is that it encompasses a wide variety of harm, not just the risk of crime, injury, or loss of property. Nor are all crimes perceived as dangerous. Larceny (simple theft of property without personal confrontation or violence), auto theft, and even assault, when the parties know one another, frequently are not considered dangerous. Many years ago Rainwater catalogued the range of human and non-human dangers lower-class slum dwellers face: poisons, poor plumbing, inadequate heat, violence, theft, symbolic violence to the self—in the form of shaming, verbal insult, and exploitation—and moral danger in the form of more attractive and exciting alternatives to a stable, family-centered way of life (1966, 1970). In Dover Square, residents similarly see danger in such diverse phenomena as the deterioration in neighborhood social status, personal insults, intrusions of culturally alien populations, assaults on order and morality, and threats to self-respect and one's sense of belonging in the community.

A third characteristic of danger is that it is a cultural construct, imposed on a particular environment and learned as part of an understanding about the way the world functions. Notions of danger appear to be embedded in belief systems shared within social groups and responsive to individual and group experiences and cultural values. The process of forming attitudes about which kinds of people, which places, and which times of day and night are safe or dangerous and the cues that are useful to identify such categories is one facet of the elaborate process through which the individual becomes a member of a culture. He integrates communications from other people and from the mass media, past experiences, and general cultural stereotypes. He thus acquires cultural skills for survival in the city. Harm itself is culturally defined and shared. Definitions of insult, humiliation, degradation, and even serious bodily injury are part of an individual's cultural repertoire.

Two examples from remote societies illustrate this point. The Saulteaux Indians, living in isolated forest settlements in Canada, do not fear wolves or bears but consider snakes, toads, and frogs dangerous (Hallowell 1938: 252–255). Although these creatures are among the most harmless inhabitants of the forest, they are perceived as dangerous because they are linked to powerful supernatural forces. They can serve as emissaries for sorcerers, exert malevolent magical powers, and act as omens of ill fortune. Further, the Indians believe there are monster frogs and toads inhabiting the forest. The Azande farmers of East Africa, on the other hand, fear the man who is quarrelsome, spiteful, and dirty, the person who defecates in others' gardens and eats house rats, since they believe these qualities signal witchcraft, the power to inflict misfortunes, wasting diseases, and death on others, even without intention (Evans-Pritchard 1937: 52). Although the cues the Saulteaux and Azande learn for danger and the kinds of harm they fear differ greatly from those of American urbanites, the underlying process is very similar.

Although danger as I define it is a cognitive assessment of personal risk alone, it incorporates more general social understandings about who and what is dangerous. It draws on shared images of what kinds of persons are violent, immoral, and inclined to commit crimes, and where such persons are likely to appear. In Zürich, Switzerland, for example, one survey found substantial agreement about the three sections of the city that were dangerous, attributing their terrors with some unanimity to the presence of prostitutes, drunks, foreign workers, young people, and tourists in these areas (Clinard 1978: 26). Historically, American national leaders have bewailed the dangers of foreign immigration, labeling immigrants dangerous because of their alleged radicalism, their apparent unwillingness to assimilate, and the risks of "racial mongrelization" (Higham 1955). Nineteenth-century American and European urbanites were preoccupied with the problem of the "dangerous classes," the ranks of the urban poor outside respectable society, who were viewed as bereft of morals, education, and the desire to work, and carried the threat of both revolution and criminal activity (Brace 1872; Tobias 1967; Chevalier 1973; Monkkonen 1975). In Dover Square, as in these historical situations, fear of the stranger, of the morally repugnant, of the culturally unfamiliar, and of the disorderly blend into an undifferentiated sense of danger, which has been given the rubric "the fear of crime." Chapter 7 explores such cross-cultural and historical conceptions and develops a theory of the conditions under which urban danger emerges as a major social issue, amplifying the analysis of the Dover Square situation.

This conception of danger suggests that the question of the rational basis for the fear of crime, which has preoccupied many researchers, is inappropriate and perhaps impossible to answer. The rationality of a fear can only be judged in comparison to the "real" risks that evoke it, but if these risks are cultural constructs that vary between social groups and situations, then we must take into account the whole range of culturally defined harm that awakens fear. What one group considers a mortal danger, such as the Anglo-Saxon fear that their political traditions would be diluted in the wave of foreign immigration, may appear to others to be an irrational fear (Higham 1955). Even the meaning of violence and of the loss of property differs greatly from one situation to another. Violence at the hand of a stranger is usually perceived as dangerous, but an assault in the context of a fight with a known enemy or neighbor is rarely viewed this way. Loss of property is less dangerous for the rich man than for the poor one, who faces immediate privation. A burglary that does not result in the loss of property can seem dangerous because a place that once seemed safe and inviolable has been invaded, and a sense of security has been irretrievably lost. In order to understand when and why people fear crime, it is thus essential to examine what they mean by danger, how they develop and solidify their temporal, spatial, and personal cognitive maps, and what strategies they develop to manage the dangers they perceive.

This book proposes the thesis that crime serves as an idiom for expressing and legitimating the fear of the strange and the unknown. Such fears often focus on populations that are racially, culturally, and economically distinct. Members of a dominant group may denounce a subordinate group for its criminality rather than denounce it for the real threat it poses to the perpetuation of the existing social order and continued elite dominance of that order. Concern about crime thus justifies and reinforces hostility that stems from class conflict and racial and ethnic differences. Discussions of danger often focus on aspects of the dangerous group's social life that are perceived as bizarre and immoral, such as the Irish tendency to live with pigs in nineteenth-century London (Engels 1845: 104–107) or the Chinese proclivity for opium in nineteenth-century America (Miller 1969). In Dover Square, fear of crime similarly serves as an idiom for expressing racial and ethnic hostilities. I am arguing not that a person's fear of crime is unrelated to a realistic assessment of the threat of attack, but that the sense of danger often cannot be accounted for just by examining the risk of criminal victimization and is often culturally channeled into existing racial, ethnic, and class conflicts.

My intensive study of a single neighborhood, involving a year and a half of participant observation of only three hundred families, explores the different ways people in a high-crime environment think and talk about danger. Further, it makes it possible to analyze the connections between their ideas and their personal experiences, their cultural familiarity with "street life" and crime, and the extent and structure of their social networks within and outside the neighborhood. On the other hand, such a research strategy has obvious limitations. The scope is narrow—a single neighborhood—and the neighborhood itself may be unique, even bizarre. It certainly is not a community, in the sense of a cohesive, integrated social system; rather it is a series of distinct, non-overlapping social networks occupying the same geographical space. Comparison with other urban ethnographies, however, suggests that although this neighborhood has certain unusual features, it is not atypical in attitudes toward danger or in strategies for coping with crime (e.g., Suttles 1968, 1972; Rainwater 1966, 1970; Hannerz 1969; Liebow 1967; Valentine 1978). Small-scale ethnographic research can provide a valuable complement to large-scale surveys since it can elicit new variables or questions that can then be examined in larger populations. My approach also makes possible a comparison between the way ordinary residents perceive and manage danger and the attitudes and strategies of local residents who actually commit crimes. Thus, this research should provide a new set of questions and concepts for further testing in a field rich with large-scale research but relatively poor in small-scale, intensive studies.

The remainder of this chapter discusses the methodology of this study and the particular problems of ethnography in an urban setting. Chapters 3 and 4 describe the social structure of the project and the nature of the social networks that bind and divide the residents. Detailed portraits of four families in Chapter 3, including the family of a youth steeped in the lore of local crime, provide a way of exploring the diverse social and cultural worlds of Dover Square residents. Chapter 4 focuses on how the distinct ethnic groups relate to one another, the nature of the boundaries to social relationships in the project, and the role of these boundaries and cultural differences in maintaining relations between strangers within the project. Chapter 5 analyzes the way these ethnic and social groups conceptualize danger, the way cognitive maps are created and revised, and the kinds of harm that are feared by different ethnic and social groups. Chapter 6 delineates the strategies residents develop to manage their hazardous environment, describing offensive as well as defensive postures and the techniques of those who commit crimes as well as those who try to avoid them. This chapter illuminates the critical role of knowledge of local social identities and familiarity with the cultural milieu in developing effective strategies that diminish the awareness of danger.

In Chapter 7, a cross-cultural and historical survey of attitudes toward danger provides further evidence that danger has always had multifaceted, complex meanings. Themes of disorder, fear of rapid social change, difficulties of coping with alien, culturally different populations, and fear of strangers reappear in very different places and settings. I argue that awareness of danger springs from certain features of the social structure of the large, industrial, heterogeneous city and develop a theory to account for the conditions under which danger becomes a major political and social issue. The final

chapter attempts to determine the generality of these findings by comparing this study with other urban ethnographic
work in similar neighborhoods and explores their relevance
to the nature of social life in the city.

RESEARCH METHODS

During eighteen months of participant observation in Dover
Square, from March 1975 to September 1976, I endeavored to
become part of the social life of the project. I spent more
than one hundred hours in the homes of two Chinese families, three black families, and one white family, observing patterns of social interaction, listening to discussions of attitudes
toward danger, crime, and more general issues, and asking
about cognitive models of the project and the world. In addition, I became good friends with two Chinese college students, three black youths in their early twenties, a black
woman in her forties, and a white man in his sixties who
spent much of his life visiting in the local laundromat. For
several months I spent three or four days a week lounging
with the group of local black youths who are involved in
crime, talking to both males and females and participating in
their activities. From this group I learned about strategies of
robbery, burglary, and techniques for handling the police. Although I was initially regarded with some suspicion as a spy
for the police or the management of the project, over time I
became more familiar, which allayed suspicion. I was always
careful to avoid questioning them about specific criminal incidents, however, and refrained from cataloguing in any detail the past activities of these youths. These contacts enabled
me to explore the cognitive worlds of a few individuals in
each of the separate social groups in the project and observe
their regular patterns of social life, their friendship networks,
and their disputes and conflicts.

The urban setting provided some special obstacles to
ethnographic research. Anthropologists who work in cities
typically gravitate to ethnic neighborhoods because it is
there, I suspect, that the traditional skills and methods of the
anthropologist are most appropriately and easily employed.
Other parts of cities pose far greater difficulties, as I dis-

covered in studying a community that possesses none of the characteristics of the urban village (see Foster and Kemper 1974). In Dover Square I was unable to establish an identity and reputation that spread to all residents of the project. I repeatedly had to present myself as if I were a stranger to each ethnic group in the project and even to each smaller group of friends and kinsmen within each ethnic group. I never felt as if I were part of a "community," but only that I was known in a few networks and to a large number of individuals.

There were no public gathering places, so I was unable to observe informal interaction in public settings, nor were there any effective political organizations through which I might introduce myself. Residents do participate in a variety of voluntary associations, religious groups, and social service institutions, but no group serves more than a fraction of the total population of the project. This fragmentation meant there were simply too many groups and they were too dispersed to allow me to observe all the social activities of project residents. Thus, it was virtually impossible for me to observe informal interaction in natural settings, which is a key aspect of participant observation, because most residents engaged in informal interaction only outside the project or inside their homes.

A central problem in my research was to overcome the identity of a stranger. My first strategy was to use network connections. After contacting a few leaders of the black and white communities, to whom I was introduced by the head of a local settlement house where they had worked, I interviewed them in a semi-formal way. I then asked them to introduce me to other members of their social networks. By attending the small tenant meetings they held, talking with them on repeated occasions, and helping them to organize against rent increases and inadequate maintenance, I was able to expand these contacts into more personal, enduring relationships. Their networks, however, were sharply circumscribed by ethnic boundaries, and I was rarely able to use network connections to cross ethnic boundaries.

Through the same settlement house, I also met a young Chinese-American woman who had been active in a community group in Chinatown, to which the core of the middle-class white leadership also belonged. These contacts, however, only introduced me to the small number of politically active people in the project, most of whom were white, either middle-class whites who had or were planning to move out or long-time Syrian-Lebanese residents of the adjacent neighborhood.

I also contacted a young American Chinese student who had taken a college course from me in a nearby university. Since he already knew me as a teacher, he was willing to introduce me to two young American Chinese childhood friends of his who lived in the project. Both agreed to be interviewed, but only reluctantly, and both refused to introduce me to other members of their networks, a problem that I frequently encountered among Chinese residents. One of them, a young woman, was willing to introduce me to a friend, a young black woman who worked with her as a cashier in the supermarket, but not to her Chinese friends or acquaintances. I hired one of these young American Chinese students as a research assistant, and gradually became better acquainted with him and his family.

The young black woman introduced me to a leader of the black teenage group that socialized in the playground, and after several long discussions with him about his life and his attitudes toward crime, he began to trust me and to introduce me to his friends. Many of the members of the group dropped by his house regularly or lounged in the playground or in front of the laundromat. Only in this group did the anthropological enterprise develop as expected. After several months of "hanging around," having been introduced by the leader, I became generally known and accepted by the group. Even peripheral members, whom I had never met, knew who I was and did not, as far as I could tell, suspect me of being a spy or wonder what I wanted. They trusted me more quickly and were more willing to talk openly on first meeting than people to whom I appeared a complete stranger, without a personal introduction.

Through the leaders of the tenants' association I met another young American Chinese woman with whom I worked closely for two summers and sporadically during the intervening year. Through frequent visits to her home, I became friendly with her parents and brother and sister, as well as with those relatives who dropped by regularly. Her sister got married during this period, so I was able to observe the wedding, and to some extent, the mobilization of support for the wedding. But I still was unable to use this family's social networks for access to other members of the Chinese community.

Consequently, I had to fall back on a more formal mechanism of data-gathering: knocking on doors and interviewing residents. Working with my American Chinese assistant as interpreter, I was able to interview a large number of Chinese residents. This strategy was not ideal, but was the best way to make contact with an otherwise inaccessible population. The social interactions of the Chinese families in the project occur, for the most part, either inside their homes or outside the project, so I had to talk to them at home. I was not a complete stranger to them since well over half knew either my assistant or her family. Often an interview began by their asking her who she was and where she lived, if they had not already recognized her. When they learned she was related to a family they knew in the project, they became visibly friendlier and more relaxed. Often someone would greet us at the door suspiciously, but after identifying my assistant and her family, would invite us in and offer us tea and oranges, a traditional small gesture of hospitality. Occasionally, people would agree to talk to us without recognizing my assistant, but in the course of the discussion would discover her identity. Suddenly, tea or oranges would appear. I am convinced that far fewer people would have consented to talk to us had they not been able to place my assistant within a family they knew. In the part of the project closest to her home, we had a noticeably higher rate of response and willingness to talk than in the section furthest from her home, where both she and her family were not well known. Several people confessed that they would never have admitted a strange white woman to their house, and would have hesitated to let in even a strange Chinese woman, but accepted us because they recognized my assistant and knew her family.

In interviews with blacks, whites, and English-speaking

Chinese, I discovered that even if I were a stranger to the person I wanted to interview, I would not be treated like a stranger if I indicated that I knew something about their friends, the project, or the issues and scandals within their ethnic group. People who began by speaking in very general terms about a project problem or personality became far more specific when I indicated that I already knew a good deal about the problem or person. By mentioning the names of other people I had met, whom they knew, I convinced them I was not really a stranger to their social world, even though I was a stranger to them. Although not a friend, I was a friend of a friend. The fact that I lived three blocks away also made me less of a stranger. Former long-term residents of the neighborhood I lived in were particularly warm toward me after hearing where I lived. These facts located me in a known social system and rendered my actions more accountable. Using both this approach and that of working with an American Chinese resident, I had a surprisingly low rate of refusal. Only about 5 percent of those who were home refused to open their doors or talk to me. In comparison, in a study of a middle-income neighborhood in Manhattan, 60 percent of the households at which a female stranger asked to make a phone call refused her admission (Milgram 1970). My higher rate of acceptance suggests that the reluctance to trust a stranger can be counteracted by locating the stranger in a known social world.

Still, because of the diverse nature of the project, I remained a stranger to many of the people I encountered. Despite the fact that the project was only the size of a small village, I continually had to explain myself and my purpose and, aside from the black youth group, never felt I was part of a community that knew and accepted me. The boundaries between networks and the anonymity of members of different ethnic groups did prove to have one advantage, however. Even after several months of publicly lounging with the black youth group, who are widely viewed as criminals by Chinese residents, the Chinese people I talked to did not appear to be any more suspicious of me than previously, nor did they appear to recognize me as someone they had seen before. I suspect they paid no attention to the individual identities of either the black youths or myself, and thus, seeing me out of context, did not remember me as the person they had seen associating with a suspicious group. But, overall, the research experience was probably less personally satisfying than that of the anthropologist who feels himself included in and accepted by a local community. Even at the end of the research, I was still a stranger to many residents who were not incorporated into any of the local networks I had contacted.

Inevitably, I had to rely on more formal data-gathering techniques than are necessary in a village study. I formally interviewed community leaders, the project owner, the manager, local youth leaders, and leaders of the surrounding ethnic communities. Helped by two young Chinese-speaking research assistants who lived in the project, I conducted semi-formal, open-ended interviews with more than two hundred residents, about victimization experiences, attitudes toward crime, and strategies of coping, and I was able to establish more enduring relationships with a few of these people. Then, with the help of five research assistants, three of whom lived in the project and two of whom were local college students, I administered a closed-ended questionnaire to a sample of 101 individuals, roughly representative of the project's population in terms of age, sex, length of residence, and ethnic background. The intensive participant observation generated hypotheses that the questionnaire, used at the end of the research period, was designed to test.

The difficulties I encountered in creating and administering this questionnaire, even after a year of fieldwork and extensive contacts in the neighborhood, are instructive. Even with people I knew well, as soon as we began the formal questionnaire, they felt an obligation to put the "best face" on things. The questionnaire seemed somehow a public statement, even though I assured everyone anonymity. Many people de-emphasized the danger and scariness of their environment when asked to give their "official" position, perhaps because they did not want to admit publicly that they were forced to live in an environment they considered dangerous. Individuals who earlier had described in great detail the precautions they took and regaled me with stories of crimes they had heard about claimed that they did not perceive the project as dangerous. I felt that answers to closed-ended questions were flat and over-simplified in contrast to the complexity and subtlety of the reactions I received in less structured situations. People who were otherwise delighted to talk for hours about similar subjects often seemed bored. Even though I knew the community well and had a good idea of what was important and what to ask, some questions were too complex for some of the respondents, particularly with translation problems. The use of interpreters in interviews with members of the Chinese community presented the possibility of distortion of the data, but since I did not speak Chinese, I had no other means of gaining access to the adult population, most of whom were born in China and spoke little, if any, English. My interpreters, however, provided me with useful insights into the local social structure and the Chinese perspective on crime, as well as careful and attentive translations. I was fortunate to have the assistance of an intelligent young woman, born in Hong Kong and educated in the United States, who was fluent in both English and Cantonese. She worked with me off and on for two years and became interested in the research itself. I was also assisted by an American-born Chinese college student who spoke Toishanese, the local dialect of the older rural immigrants. Even with all these limitations, however, my formal research clearly provided directly comparable data on a complex topic. People differed in patterned ways in their responses, and probably the "public front" problem affected all respondents similarly.

Urban fieldwork inevitably poses a unit of analysis problem that, although shared by traditional anthropological studies of villages and communities, is more intractable in the city. Since urban patterns of social relationships are often not geographically determined, focusing on a geographical unit is useful for some purposes, but does not necessarily demarcate a single, complete social system. I based my research on a geographical unit because I was interested in finding out how urbanites deal with their neighbors in precisely those situations in which their neighbors do not belong to their social system. Other urban anthropologists have chosen to study either locally rooted social systems or occupants of social roles such as civil servants, migrants, or homeless alcoholics. I began by investigating a much larger area, commonly perceived as a single neighborhood, that contains approximately 22,000 people. I quickly discovered that, if I was interested in mapping the social networks that bind and divide the neighborhood residents, this unit was far too large. Furthermore, this neighborhood was very heterogeneous and contained numerous small social systems, which would have been difficult to analyze. Consequently, I focused on a much smaller and more limited community, a housing project. Clearly, a housing project is not itself a social system, but it became my unit of analysis for two reasons. First, I was interested in the effect of housing policies on the social organization of housing projects. Second, after the first few months of my research, in which I attempted to study the entire community surrounding the project, I concluded that the project residents generally resembled the residents of the surrounding community in terms of ethnicity and class. Thus, the project appeared to be an arbitrarily bounded site in which residents were required to deal with neighbors who are strangers in the same way that they had to in the larger community.

Since I was interested in relations between strangers, I wanted to get to know all the ethnic groups in the project. This posed new difficulties because I had to adjust my style of behavior and attitudes as I focused on each different group. Each ethnic group had its own attitudes about what was appropriate behavior, for example, the appropriate ways to express aggression and sexuality, show friendship, organize the family and family relationships, and manage conflicts. Further, each ethnic group had its own distinct attitudes about other groups, about crime and who is responsible for it, and about solutions to the crime problem. The Chinese residents, for instance, hold the blacks in the project responsible for all the crime and believe that blacks engage in crime because they are bad people who never learned right from wrong. The Chinese do not distinguish between those blacks who are driven to crime by family problems or personal difficulties and those who are simply interested in money, nor can the Chinese accept that there are blacks who are not at all involved in crime. On the other hand, most blacks and many whites believe that it is not just the blacks who live in the project who commit crimes, but also outsiders. Unlike the Chinese, they are aware of family problems driving some of the local youths to crime and realize that some youths are enticed into criminal activities by the influence of local leaders.

I found that I was unable to switch easily from working with the Chinese—for whom I had to tone down my aggressiveness and support their perception that the blacks were constantly victimizing them unfairly and without cause—to working with blacks and Syrian-Lebanese whites, who were, by and large, more assertive and aggressive in interpersonal relations, more expressive of feelings, more gregarious, and more sympathetic toward the youths committing crime. In order to overcome the difficulty of adjusting to each group's style of behavior, I focused for several months at a time on each group alone, thus acclimating myself to different sets of attitudes and norms of social relationships.

The white leaders of the tenants' association and the black youths were most accessible, perhaps because of my similarity in age and interests to both groups. The Chinese residents were generally suspicious and afraid, although only with people they defined as strangers. The blacks displayed very little racial hostility toward me, despite the massive racial tensions in the city during much of the research period. Although there are not extensive social contacts or friendships between whites and blacks in this neighborhood, it is one in which the two races live together without overt racial hostility.

I encountered one final problem that is, I suspect, typical of research on relatively sophisticated urban populations in the United States. Some members of the community, in particular the Syrian-Lebanese whites, saw me as another university-affiliated researcher who would gather data by using them as subjects and then disappear, with no benefit to them. They described their feelings of being exploited by previous researchers who had talked to them, including some who had paid them for their time. Although this feeling was not widespread, it may reflect an awareness of their position in the class system vis-à-vis a university researcher, and reveal their resentment about their own lack of social mobility. These attitudes were expressed most frequently by white families who observed other white families moving out as the composition of the project's population changed, but were themselves financially unable to leave. I encountered these attitudes much less often among Chinese and blacks. The black youths perceived me as a person writing a book, a syndrome that was familiar to them, since many "street" blacks have recently written accounts of their lives (e.g., Beck 1967). Although a few expected I would make a great deal of money from the book and resented me for this, most expressed little hostility. One of the young men began carrying a briefcase in imitation of the one I carried when administering questionnaires, in order to look like an educated person or researcher. The anthropologist seems to be in a different position studying his own society than he is when he does research in other societies. It appears that those who see the researcher in terms of class distinctions are more likely to feel resentment than those who see the researcher in terms of ethnicity. I expect that resentment toward the researcher is greater when the social and cultural distance between subject and researcher is not so great.

Thus, urban research presents difficulties not present in the small-scale, village research traditional among anthropologists. The methods of anthropology, however, provide a much deeper and fuller insight into the complexity of urban social systems than is possible using the survey methods more often employed to study urban communities. The local area is an important unit of analysis in cities, since geographical location affects the personal and social lives of urbanites, even if it does not encompass their social world. The very disjunction between geographical location and social world poses some of the most interesting questions for urban anthropology, since it highlights those aspects of urban social life that are most distinctive and, for many urbanites, most problematic.

My experience in the research site provides support for one hypothesis of my study: the connection between familiarity and danger. When I first moved into the larger, multiethnic neighborhood (which I call here "James Hill") that surrounds Dover Square and that also has a high crime rate, I felt quite nervous and uneasy, particularly when walking the streets alone at night. I felt tense in the city, was conscious of being more relaxed while away from it, and felt a surge of uncertainty and uneasiness when I returned after some time away. Although I had visited inner-city neighborhoods before, I had never lived in one. I felt oppressed by the need for continual vigilance against theft: the need to lock car doors and house doors and never to leave an attractive item unprotected even for a minute. During the first months of my research, I did not even go into Dover Square.

After a few months of living in James Hill, however, I found myself adjusting to the environment and enjoying the heterogeneity and variety of scenes in the neighborhood. I became friends with several neighbors and community leaders, which significantly reduced my feelings of isolation and vulnerability. Although none of these people ever intervened to help me in a crime incident, my awareness that they lived nearby substantially reduced my fear. I felt safe walking the street in front of my house alone at night, although I continued to feel uneasy walking on other, less familiar James Hill streets at night. I became accustomed to locking doors, concealing tempting items I left in the car overnight, and never leaving property unattended. Once these actions became habitual, they were no longer oppressive. I also became aware of informal surveillance in the neighborhood. When the backdoor lock on my car broke temporarily, a resident shouted at some children who had opened the door and were investigating the contents of the car. One day, after I had lived in the neighborhood for about a year, the proprietor of the corner store noticed a local drug addict, whom I had met in Dover Square, approach me and ask for money. The next day the store owner warned me that the boy was no good, an addict, and would continue to take money from me or rob me. Twice fires occurred on the street and some neighbors immediately called the fire department. One night a man ran down the street chasing two robbers, shouting for help, and within minutes six police cruisers had arrived, tipped off by several phone calls from residents. Since it appeared that other residents observed the street and responded to unusual events and that the city services were adequate, my feelings of uneasiness and isolation diminished. (Dover Square residents were generally not treated to such efficient service from the police and fire department, however.) After a few months, I knew more of my neighbors in James Hill than I had when I had lived in suburban communities for much longer periods of time.

During the first months I lived in James Hill I also felt uncomfortable and uneasy watching the alcoholics lounge on the street corners, sleep in the streets, and fight with one another. After several months, I learned that they would never molest or bother me, beyond occasionally asking for money, and did not pose a threat to my person, only to my sense of order and propriety.

My feelings about Dover Square followed a similar progression. On my first visits, I was struck by the trash, the unkempt appearance of the project, and its maze-like tunnels, walkways, and courtyards. I was frequently confused by the twists and turns of the project. After an evening interview early in the research, the couple I was talking to offered to walk me to the edge of the project, an offer that I accepted gratefully. Again, after becoming familiar with the layout of the project and becoming friendly with some of its residents, I felt much less afraid, even at night. I regularly used the project laundromat and supermarket with no concern for my safety, although, after I became aware of the frequency of purse-snatching, I stopped carrying a purse.

Another significant shift in my awareness of danger occurred when I became friends with the black youth group. I suddenly found that I did not consider the project dangerous at all, even at night, and resumed carrying a purse. The laundromat, now staffed by people I knew and occupied by a group of youths I knew, seemed like a familiar, safe place. As I walked through the project, I frequently encountered people I knew, and felt very relaxed and at home.

One further observation, however, suggests this familiarity that reduces fear fades quickly. After I stopped the research itself and began the analysis and writing phase, I continued to go to the project for visits and to use the laundromat and supermarket. As my visits became less frequent, however, I felt less safe and less comfortable in the laundromat and project grounds. Some of my original uneasiness returned. Although I never felt as frightened as I had in the initial phases of the research, I had lost the comfortable, safe feeling I experienced in the middle of the research period.

Finally, an incident on my street confirmed for me the truth of one argument of this book: that the simple experience of victimization does not necessarily generate fear. After I had lived in James Hill for two and a half years, I was robbed one night as I walked alone up the steps to my house. As I turned my back to the street to put my key in the door, a voice behind me demanded all my money. I turned to see a young man, his hand held inside his jacket, either holding a gun or pretending to. He appeared more nervous than I and waited while I searched my purse for my wallet, and gave him the total contents—35 cents. He turned and walked down the steps into a waiting car, leaving me shaken but not really frightened.

Two minutes later, several of my neighbors and friends walked by and we discussed the incident. Although they had not intervened, clearly they might have. I found that I was no more afraid after this incident than before, only more wary of turning my back to the street without checking first to see who was there. My subsequent interaction with the police also supports my argument that they are relatively ineffective in crimes between strangers. Although they came and took a detailed report, I could say only that a young man in a green car robbed me, which left me with a strong awareness of the futility of reporting the incident without having any identifying information. I heard nothing further from the police. Thus, in my experience, familiarity with people and places overcame an initial sense of danger and even the experience of victimization did not lead to a resurgence of fear.

CHAPTER 2

The Setting

Dover Square is a neighborhood of contrasts. On a typical summer morning, one sees an elderly Chinese grandmother, dressed in severe black pants and blouse, taking two small children wtih cropped black hair for a walk, while a young Chinese man in a suit and tie, carrying a briefcase, walks to his late-model Volkswagen to leave for work. A middle-aged black woman carries countless bags of groceries home from the store. Young black men in silk shirts watch her as they lounge around a radio playing disco music. Later, a group of black teenagers sits and talks in an elegant, ornate 1950s Jaguar. Nearby, an older black man carefully washes his purple Cadillac. A black mother in a simple cotton housedress sits outside her door on a milk crate watching her grandchildren play and talking with her daughters who live in other apartments in the project. Elderly white women sit outside their doors in folding chairs, hoping to catch some sun in the quiet period of the morning, before the teenagers are around. In one corner, several homeless, alcoholic white men sit staring vacantly into the street, their worn collars pulled around their ears. Others sleep in the few grassy patches. A middle-aged white man saunters into the laundromat in search of a friend with whom he can while away the morning fantasizing about his long-ago aborted career in medicine and the important people he still claims to know, attempting to differentiate himself from the surroundings he finds so humiliating. A small knot of Puerto Rican men stand over the open hood of an aging car, discussing intently in Spanish how to fix a re-

calcitrant carburetor. The diversity of an entire city is com-
pressed into a small neighborhood.

Dover Square is located in the center of a major North-
eastern city at the juncture of a Chinese and a white ethnic
neighborhood. This is an aging port city, and many parts of
the central city reflect decades of use by one immigrant
group after another. The city has traditionally served as a first
stop for a wide variety of immigrants, particularly the British,
Irish, Italian, Syrians, Portuguese, Chinese, and Puerto Ricans,
as well as black migrants from the rural South. The mix of
ethnic and racial groups in Dover Square and the adjacent
neighborhood, to which I have given the fictitious name
James Hill, is unusual in this city of tight, closed ethnic neighborhoods, intense ethnic politics, and strong ethnic loyalties.
Even after generations in the United States, many individuals in this city still identify themselves primarily in terms of
their ethnicity. Furthermore, this is a city that has been torn
by violent and emotional racial conflicts over school de-
segregation, which have pitted one ethnic and racial group
against another and driven neighborhoods into headlong
confrontations.

The brunt of the racial tensions bypassed this neighborhood, however. The most intense conflicts occurred in 1974
and 1975 and had begun to ebb by the time of this study. The
first years of busing did not affect this neighborhood directly,
but, by 1976, a few blacks were being bused to white neighborhoods away from the racially mixed local school. Further,
Dover Square and James Hill have long been neighborhoods
with unusual tolerance between black and white. Perhaps
this is because the area as a whole has never become the ex-
clusive "turf" of one or another of these ethnic groups, but
has served as a kind of tidal plain where groups intermingle
as one moves in and another out. A few groups of Irish Catholic whites randomly attacked black youths in the project
and took marauding trips through Chinatown, but by and
large these frictions eddied around James Hill and Dover
Square. During one morning of intense anxiety in the city,
when a bomb that exploded in a downtown courthouse was
blamed on these racial tensions, I was able to carry on a calm
discussion about the city's racism in the project laundromat

with a white, an Hispanic, a militant black, and several other project residents.

This city has placed tremendous emphasis on urban redevelopment in the 1960s and 1970s. In the 1960s it began three neighborhood-wide urban renewal programs and pursued a vigorous policy of downtown reconstruction. The beginnings of gentrification, the return of the professional elites to the city, in the late 1960s and 1970s was heralded by the city government as a major accomplishment for the city and a shining hope for the future. An astronomical rise in the property values of some gentrifying areas testifies to the success of this development and its promise for city tax revenues.

Inevitably, these changes have come at the expense of older ethnic neighborhoods, which have been destroyed in order to make way for the homes and businesses of the rich. Both James Hill and Chinatown have been victims of this transition, but other neighborhoods have suffered a similar fate. Much of Chinatown's housing has been destroyed to make way for expressways and a major hospital complex. James Hill was one of the three neighborhoods slated for urban renewal, and vast amounts of city and federal money have been poured into the area to create parks, new recreational facilities, improved streets and street lighting, improved low-income housing, and subsidies for home improvements by homeowners. The crowning achievement was replacing the cracked and broken concrete sidewalks with brick sidewalks in an effort to recapture the nineteenth-century charm of the area—an extremely expensive project. As a result, the political divisions that have plagued much of the rest of the city, between those who seek historic restoration that will attract wealthy suburbanites back into the city and those who wish to preserve existing working-class and ethnic neighborhoods, have been replicated in James Hill. Staggering increases in property values that follow restoration have thrown the private sector behind the efforts of the city government. The gradual transformation of most of the downtown neighborhoods that have attractive architecture and appealing locations seems inevitable.

This transformation has occurred intensively in James

Hill and Dover Square. James Hill's Victorian brick townhouses clustered around tree-shaded squares close to downtown have attracted young professionals willing to gamble on
a somewhat unorthodox urban neighborhood. Professionals,
particularly architects, began to buy up the old houses in the
middle 1960s, investing heavily in renovation and restoration, assisted by generous, low-interest government loans.
Though the proportion of professionals has increased substantially in the last fifteen years, the area has not yet "turned
around" in the sense of becoming an entirely elite enclave.
There still are signs of poverty and decay: alcoholics on street
corners in the summer, sidewalks and streets covered with
refuse, and a crime rate near the highest in the city. Parked
along the streets are late-model Mercedes sedans, deteriorating 1964 Chevrolets, ornate, new Cadillacs owned by pimps,
and long black sedans. Neighborhood stores range from inexpensive used furniture emporiums to elegant antique
shops full of Victoriana. Clean-cut businessmen in three-
piece suits rub shoulders with disheveled, unshaven alcoholics and groups of young black teenagers "hanging-out" on
streetcorners.

Because the urban renewal of James Hill was intended
to be a participatory process in which neighborhood residents were to have an active role and effective veto power,
the neighborhood has been torn by political factionalism and
conflict during the development process. This approach to
urban renewal has divided the neighborhood into two distinct class-based interest groups, irreconcilably opposed on
issues such as how much low-income housing should be provided for traditional poorer residents, whether park investment should go to playgrounds or to the restoration of historic fountains, and whether the city should invest in brick
sidewalks or in the modernization of the deteriorating public
housing project in the area. Hostilities coalesce along class
rather than ethnic lines, with the low-income blacks, Hispanics, and Chinese in one alliance led by educated, liberal
whites, and the white gentrifying homeowners in another.

James Hill has never been a stable, homogeneous neighborhood. Originally settled by the economic and social elite
who wished to escape the congested inner city in the 1860s

and 1870s, it soon deteriorated into a lodging-house district for rural factory workers and a few Irish immigrants. The elite fled to more distant neighborhoods and were quickly shuttled in and out of the city by the new and expanding net of streetcars. In the first half of the twentieth century, the area became a densely populated district of white ethnics, including small enclaves of Irish, Italian, Syrian-Lebanese, Greeks, Portuguese, and blacks. A single street often housed up to one hundred children. The area attracted some early settlement houses to ease the slum conditions and encourage the residents to pursue education and adopt Victorian moral codes.

The 1950s, 1960s, and 1970s witnessed a rapid ethnic transition. The explosive growth of the suburbs during the 1950s robbed white ethnic urban communities of their young families with children; increasing numbers of professionals moved in to replace them. At the same time, three new waves of immigrants arrived: Hispanics from Puerto Rico, blacks from the rural South, and those Chinese who, after emigrating from Hong Kong, had been unable to find housing in the shrinking area of Chinatown itself. (For Chinese immigrants James Hill was, and still is, a temporary, first step before they are able to move into Chinatown itself or to an inexpensive suburb.) As an indicator of the extent of the transition in this community, one white James Hill family pointed out the paradox that they were the first white family to move onto their street in the 1960s and had purchased their house from the first black man to move onto the street fifty years earlier. The area is now a kaleidoscope of races and cultures, but preserves some homogeneity from block to block. One end is predominantly white and Chinese, the center is Hispanic, and the other end blends into the neighboring black community, the core of the city's black population. I will refer to this black neighborhood by the pseudonym Winslow. In 1970, the area was 47 percent white, 39 percent black, 14 percent other—largely Chinese and 6 percent Hispanic. And a city survey in 1980 showed that James Hill had become 40 percent white, 25 percent black, 21 percent Oriental, and 14 percent Hispanic. It is still a center of the city's skid-row population.

Dover Square is afflicted by the same uncertainties about its identity and direction as have convulsed the rest of James Hill. When tenants first moved in, they considered the move a social step up, but now the project appears to be sliding downhill, becoming another public housing slum. Tenants who once pointedly described Dover Square as a "development" now call it a "project." It was constructed on the rubble of decaying tenement houses razed in the urban renewal of the 1960s. The area had been a stable, working-class neighborhood of Irish, Italians, and Syrian-Lebanese, with an active settlement house and vigorous community life. Many residents put up intense resistance to moving, a few remaining until the wreckers destroyed the houses next door. Despite promises that the original residents would be rehoused in the new development, only three or four families eventually moved back into Dover Square, the rest scattering throughout the city. The few non-white residents were hit particularly hard, since equivalent housing at such low rents was virtually impossible to find in the city.

Funds for the construction of Dover Square were provided by a federal housing program, section 221d3 of the National Housing Act, under which the federal government guaranteed the mortgage, provided mortgage insurance, heavily subsidized the interest, and provided the cleared land at minimal cost in order to attract private developers to high-risk, inner-city projects. Dover Square is owned by one of the largest private real estate developers in the city. He has little interest in either residential properties or slum neighborhoods, and privately confesses that the project, which he took on in the flush of enthusiasm for urban renewal in the early 1960s, has become a burden he would rather escape. Seventeen thousand units were constructed under the 221d3 program and its sequel, section 236, but both programs were financially unsound from the outset. According to the owners, the low, HUD-regulated rents were insufficient to cover operating expenses and mortgage payments. And recent increases in energy and maintenance costs are forcing foreclosure and sale of such developments throughout the city. Under these conditions, when tenants complain about high rents and inadequate maintenance, the owner's threat to abandon Dover Square and invest in a shopping center in the South is not an empty one.

The development has two sections: a row of seven-story high-rise buildings with 200 one- and two-bedroom apartments, and a section of four-story, low-rise buildings with 308 two-, three-, and four-bedroom units. The two parts are physically and socially isolated. The high-rise contains elderly people, students, and young couples, while the low-rise houses families predominantly. My research focused entirely on the low-rise. Since I wanted to compare perceptions of danger and strategies of managing danger of those who know people engaged in crime and those who do not, I studied the section of the project where most of the young people active in crime live. Those who live in the high-rise tend to be much more frightened of crime, however, and often view the entire low-rise section as a dangerous place full of thugs and criminals.

The population of Dover Square is extremely heterogeneous. According to statistics on family size and composition compiled from application forms submitted to the office at the time a family moves in, the population is 55 percent Chinese, 26 percent black, 9 percent white, 9 percent Hispanic, and 1 percent other.* The whites have smaller families than the Chinese or Hispanic residents, and many fewer white families have young or teenage children living with them. Most of the white families are older couples without children in residence, while most black and Hispanic families have young children or teenagers in the household. About half the Chinese families have young or teenage children in the household (see Figure 1).

Most tenants believe that the ethnic composition of the population was originally 30 percent white, 30 percent black, 30 percent Chinese, and 10 percent Hispanic. One

---

* Although there are some inaccuracies in the application forms as a source of information, I was able to correct errors and bring the information up to date for families I knew personally. This includes almost all the black and white families and over half the Chinese families. The ethnic breakdown of the population was gathered through interviewing and, as a last resort, knocking on doors.

Figure 1

Population Characteristics

Characteristic	Chinese	Black	White	Hispanic
Residence patterns				
Population	641	304	110	105
Percentage of total population	55%	14%	9%	9%
Number of households	161	82	37	19
Percentage of total households	52%	27%	12%	6%
Percentage in leased housing*	6%	26%	35%	79%
Number of households resident since 1966	67	62	28	13
Percentage of households resident since 1966	47%	75%	75%	68%
Average length of residence	7.2 yrs.	8.9 yrs.	8.9 yrs.	7.9 yrs.
Household characteristics				
Average family size	4.6	3.9	2.9	5.3
Percentage with children	54%	77%	33%	100%
Percentage with male wage earner only, 1976	37%	47%	40%	85%

Characteristic	Chinese	Black	White	Hispanic
Percentage with female wage earner only, 1976	3%	28%	24%	15%
Percentage with two wage earners, 1976	60%	25%	35%	0%
Occupation of head of household				
Number of heads of household surveyed	134	77	38	19
Percentage white collar, professional, managerial	8%	12%	5%	11%
Percentage skilled manual and technical	4%	26%	21%	11%
Percentage unskilled manual	11%	12%	11%	21%
Percentage maintenance, custodial, domestic	1%	18%	8%	11%
Percentage semi-skilled and unskilled food service	75%	8%	32%	5%
Percentage on welfare or relief	1%	25%	24%	42%

*Housing leased from project management by the local public housing authority.
Source: Office records of Dover Square project management.

study in 1967 did contain these statistics. The population has gradually shifted in composition, however. The proportion of Chinese families is increasing. Of the families who have moved in since Dover Square was first rented, two-thirds are Chinese, while only 15 percent are black, 7 percent white, and 8 percent Hispanic.

Although heterogeneous, the population is remarkably stable for a housing project. Sixty percent have lived in the project since it opened ten years ago. The blacks and whites are more stable than the other ethnic groups: three-quarters of both groups have lived in the development for ten years, in comparison to 68 percent of the Hispanic families and 47 percent of the Chinese families. The average length of residence is eight years, ranging from an average of 8.9 for blacks and whites to 7.9 for Hispanic and 7.2 for Chinese families (see Figure 1). Although the average length of residence of the Chinese population is substantially lower than that of the other ethnic groups, there is a core of Chinese families as large as the core of black families—sixty to seventy—who have lived in the project since it opened. Turnover is low; in the year 1975–1976, 5 percent of the apartments changed hands, and, based on statistics concerning the number of families who have moved out since the project opened, turnover has varied between 3.5 percent and 5 percent every year. Although many residents do not enjoy the social climate of the project, they stay because they have good housing at a low rent. They would like to move out, but cannot find comparable housing at the same price in this area of the city.

Each ethnic group is evenly scattered throughout the development. Tenants claim that the management tried to alternate ethnic groups from one apartment to the next when they first rented the project. The great demand for apartments and the management's unwillingness to allow substantial internal movement has impeded the formation of any ethnic enclaves, but the project is integrated by administrative fiat, not by choice.

Although all four ethnic groups are relatively recent immigrants to the city, almost none settled in Dover Square when they first arrived. Rather, the move to Dover Square was a step up into more expensive, desirable housing made after the first years of adjustment. When they first moved in, in 1967, almost all tenants paid more rent to live in Dover Square than they had paid in their previous apartments. Of the residents of Dover Square in 1976, 97 percent moved into the project from another location in the city. Most recent arrivals to the city settle in James Hill, hoping to move to Dover Square or Chinatown or to an ethnic community farther away from the city. More recent Syrian-Lebanese immigrants and black migrants also settle first in the cheaper, poorer housing in James Hill and adjacent neighborhoods, and only later move into Dover Square.

Because of regulations concerning income ceilings, the income of all project residents is approximately the same, according to information provided on the application forms. (This may be a biased source since applicants are aware of the income ceilings. But, the income figures are certified periodically.) The average annual family income in 1966 was $5,719 for black families, $5,294 for white families, and $5,337 for Hispanic families. Most Chinese families earn a substantial portion of their income in restaurant work, so that the figures on their incomes are unreliable. They do not usually include tips. These figures are not much below the median U.S. family income for 1965 (U.S. Bureau of the Census 1967: 333). Moreover, the average income of black and Hispanic families in Dover Square in 1966 was substantially above the U.S. median family income for non-whites in 1965 and well above the poverty line established in the same year (Orshansky 1965: 10). The per capita income of white families in 1966 was substantially higher than that of black families ($1,530 vs. $1,310), while that of Hispanic families, which tend to be larger, was much lower ($901). Since poverty line per capita incomes ranged from $1,580 for one-person families to $689 for six-person families in that year, it appears that most of the original Dover Square families were not among the very poor.

Ten percent of the original families were eligible for public housing and moved into apartments leased by the local housing authority, which paid the difference between what the tenant could afford and the rent of the apartment. Within a few years, other tenants already living in Dover

Square were also being subsidized, and by 1976 one-fifth of the apartments were being leased by the housing authority. Twenty-six percent of the blacks, 35 percent of the whites, 79 percent of the Hispanic families, and 6 percent of the Chinese families were in leased housing (see Figure 1).

To fight low wages and poverty, both parents in many families must work. Chinese families in particular rely on two incomes: in 60 percent of the Chinese families living in Dover Square in 1976, both men and women worked, and in just 3 percent was there only a female wage earner (see Figure 1). In contrast, of sixty black families, only 25 percent had two wage earners when they moved in, and 28 percent had only a single woman working. Of the twenty-eight white families resident in the project for ten years, 35 percent had two wage earners and 24 percent had only a female wage earner. However, only 15 percent of the Hispanic families were supported by women only, while none were supported by both men and women. In this regard, black and white families are more similar to each other than either group is to the Chinese.

Occupationally, the blacks constitute the Dover Square elite (see Figure 1). Whites and Chinese are concentrated in semi-skilled and unskilled occupations with minimal job security and low pay. White semi-professional and skilled workers have moved out of the project in significant numbers since it opened. One of the two remaining white-collar white families moved out in the summer of 1976. A higher proportion of black families is engaged in some kind of white-collar or semi-professional activity than in any other ethnic group: roughly 12 percent in comparison to 11 percent of the Hispanic residents, 8 percent of the Chinese, and 5 percent of the whites. Blacks are also disproportionately engaged in skilled manual and technical work. Twenty-six percent are employed in this kind of work, in comparison to 21 percent of the whites, 11 percent of the Hispanic families, and 4 percent of the Chinese. On the other hand, more whites and Chinese are engaged in unskilled and semi-skilled manual, domestic, and service work than blacks or Hispanics. Eighty-seven percent of the Chinese heads of house, 51 percent of the whites, 38 percent of the blacks, and 37 percent of the

Hispanics do this kind of work. Whites cluster in occupations dealing with food service. Thirty-two percent work as cooks, waiters, or bartenders, in comparison to 8 percent of the blacks and 5 percent of the Hispanic families. The Chinese are even more intensively concentrated in food service occupations. Seventy-five percent work as cooks and waiters in Chinese restaurants, and another 5 percent are managers or owners of Chinese restaurants.

About one-fourth of both black and white households receive welfare or some other form of relief in comparison to 42 percent of the Hispanic families and 1 percent of the Chinese. In their reliance on welfare, as in the proportion having two wage earners, black families and white families are more similar to each other than either group is to the Chinese.

THE PROJECT ENVIRONMENT

The exterior of the project immediately gives the visitor an impression of dirt, disorder, and decay, but the outside conceals the care and effort lavished on the interiors of apartments, which almost invariably are clean, attractive, and well-kept. The project consists of blocks of square brick buildings nestled around quiet, traffic-free courtyards and community play areas, punctuated by small shade trees and a few ragged plots of grass. The area is not a mass of sterile concrete or brick with the dismal, institutional monotony of conventional public housing. Each apartment has a private backyard, balcony, or roof terrace. Physical changes attest to a widespread concern about crime. Most of the windows on the first and second floors are protected by bars and even some of the spacious sliding doors onto the third floor balconies are covered with an elaborate grillwork costing at least four hundred to six hundred dollars. Several trees have been stripped of branches by people who worry that burglars will shinny along the branch to their window. Others have trimmed the trees so that they will not cast dark shadows at night. The play areas are overrun by large guard dogs, such as Doberman pinschers and German shepherds. Residents who might otherwise come to relax and let their children play are afraid to use these spaces.

The apartments in the project are modern, although not spacious. Each has a small kitchen which opens onto a combination dining area and living room. Floors are linoleum, but most apartments are carpeted by the tenants. I visited at least half of the 308 apartments in the development, and found almost all well furnished and clean, some with elegant furniture, heavy drapes, thick carpets, and massive color TV consoles. Most apartments are spotlessly clean, even those of families with small children. One woman, interviewed in her spotless pink-and-white kitchen, interrupted herself in mid-sentence to remove a single speck from her sparkling cabinet.

The decor and furnishings of apartments indicate the wide variety of life styles among the ethnic groups. Chinese homes are less likely to have the rich furniture and thick carpets found in black, Hispanic, and white homes, but are still clean and well furnished. In many, a commercial sewing machine sits beside the TV set, and a one-hundred pound sack of rice occupies a corner of the kitchen. Calendars from Chinese grocery stores and Chinese art adorn the walls. Some black families fill their homes with bric-a-brac and portraits of family members, others favor ornate lamps and large statues. A large color TV console is often present and usually on. Whites furnish their apartments similarly, occasionally featuring collections of bottles, antiques, plaster figurines, or hanging plants. Hispanic families have simpler furnishings with overstuffed chairs sheathed in protective plastic. Although the investment in furnishings varies, the vast majority of apartments reveal care and pride in their decoration and upkeep.

Outside the apartments, sidewalks are littered with paper, cans, and other small bits of garbage. Many fences are broken and curbs are covered with leftover garbage and broken glass. Abandoned stolen cars sit in the courts, gradually rusting and falling apart. A Volkswagen sat in one court for months while children played in it, then began to strip it, break the windows, and tear apart the upholstery. The street sweeper makes its rounds twice a week, but the parking lots are usually crammed with the cars of downtown commuters and students. It circles vainly in the center of each court and departs, leaving heaps of broken glass, banana peels, beer cans, and paper in the gutters. Many tenants complain that they keep the space in front of their houses clean but become discouraged by the mess on the sidewalks and in the street.

Graffiti adorns the concrete walls of the playground and names, phrases, and artistic renderings of naked women are inked onto the walls of stairwells and favorite hangouts. Names of members of the group that hangs out in the central playground are inscribed in white, black, yellow, and red spray paint, layer upon layer, signaling their occupation of this territory. A play area with swings and a slide is covered with broken glass, rendering it hazardous for small children. Children are innovative in finding new play objects. One summer they discovered grocery carts, and gleefully wheeled their friends all over the project. Rusting bodies of abandoned carts soon cluttered the remote corners of the project.

Each block of apartments consists of a series of two-story townhouses, one above the other. Every pair of apartments on the same level is serviced by a common porch or stairwell. The upper pair of apartments, occupying the third and fourth floors, are entered via an external stairwell in front of the building. This structure is both visually unattractive and dangerous. It is a massive appendage of concrete and glass on the front of the square brick buildings. Each stairwell consists of a series of short flights and landings, with several turns before the upper door is reached. The outer wall is made of translucent glass so it is impossible to see who is in the stairwell before beginning the ascent. Since the first flight of stairs faces the recessed porch of the two downstairs apartments, it has become a private place for teenagers to sit and visit, invisible to anyone walking through the courts. The stairwell itself sits in front of the doors to the downstairs apartments, so that a person standing in front of his door is somewhat hidden from passersby in the court. Many people dislike the semi-enclosed design of the front door and prefer the back door, which opens from a straight wall. Robberies frequently occur in the recessed areas of the front porch or in the stairwells. The victimization survey I conducted indicated that 30 percent of the robberies whose locations were known occurred here.

At the top of the stairwell, a short hall provides access to the upper two apartments. This hall is not visible from the street and therefore provides an ideal location for a drunk to sleep or a burglar to break down the door. Since most people cover their living room windows with curtains for privacy, they exercise no surveillance from that side of the house. Kitchen windows, on the other side of the house, are generally left uncurtained, but the view out these windows is significantly obstructed by the stairwell and a high fence around the garbage can. Consequently, the fact that all apartments face onto shared open space does not guarantee effective surveillance of these spaces because visibility from inside the apartments is significantly obstructed.

Surveillance is also inhibited by the fact that the apartments cluster around interior parking spaces rather than facing onto a street (see Figure 2). Residents rarely sit at their windows and watch the parking area in front of their apartments. Yet it was the constant surveillance of the street by regular window watchers that Jane Jacobs argued contributed so significantly to the order and lack of crime in the North End of Boston (1961). People in the North End watch the street because it provides an entertaining and changing scene. In Dover Square, however, there is little to watch. Children occasionally play baseball or soccer in the parking area, but there are few pedestrians and little traffic. The scene is neither varied nor interesting. Nor is there much sidewalk sociability. A few adults put chairs on their front steps and sit outside, saying hello to people who drive by, or stand for a time talking to friends who walk by, but mostly there is no one sitting in front of his house. Only one group of families regularly socializes in front of their apartments; they also live in the only block of apartments that faces outward onto a normal street. This lack of sidewalk sociability and window observation is particularly surprising since almost half the white and black families originally lived in the adjacent neighborhood of James Hill, where stoop-sitting is a traditional form of visiting and people do watch out their windows.

Although the layout of the project provides interior play and parking areas protected from dangerous street traffic, it also sacrifices the order and regularity of city streets for a bewildering maze of courts, paths, and row after row of identical buildings. Several people confessed that, when they visited it for the first time, they found the development very confusing and, although the project occupies an area no larger than four city blocks, had difficulty finding their way from one part of the development to another. They reported that this uncertainty and confusion made them feel uneasy. Some Dover Square residents said that they felt safer living in their previous apartments in James Hill, even with its higher crime rates, because that neighborhood had a regular grid of streets and the apartments had traditional front doors. Eight years after Dover Square was completed, the management finally painted numbers on the apartments and signs on the walls to indicate which court was which. For the first eight years, residents complained that it was virtually impossible for a stranger to find a particular apartment without asking a local resident for directions. Even long-term residents still find the project confusing. The repetition of building style in different spatial configurations renders difficult any comprehensive overview of the organization of the project. I asked more than fifteen residents of eight years or longer to draw a map of Dover Square, but none was able to accurately portray the relationship of courts, buildings, and play areas.

The complicated, confusing design of the project probably contributes to residents' sense that it is dangerous. Lynch, for example, argues that cities differ in their imageability: in the clarity of their paths, nodes, and edges (1960). Where these are unambiguous and easy to conceptualize, people are able to find their way more easily, and they find the areas attractive and pleasant. Where the images are restricted, ambiguous, or unclear, however, an unusual route is considered awkward or dangerous. Thus, parts of a city that are undifferentiated, where it is easy to get lost, and where all streets are the same, are places people find unpleasant and

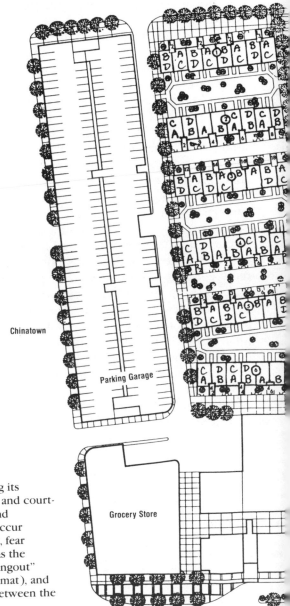

Chinatown

Parking Garage

Grocery Store

Figure 2

Map of Dover Square showing its
complex, mazelike walkways and courtyards, play areas, and dead-end
streets. Although robberies occur
throughout the development, fear
focuses on a few areas such as the
garage, the street youths' "hangout"
(the playground and laundromat), and
the narrow, dark walkways between the
buildings.

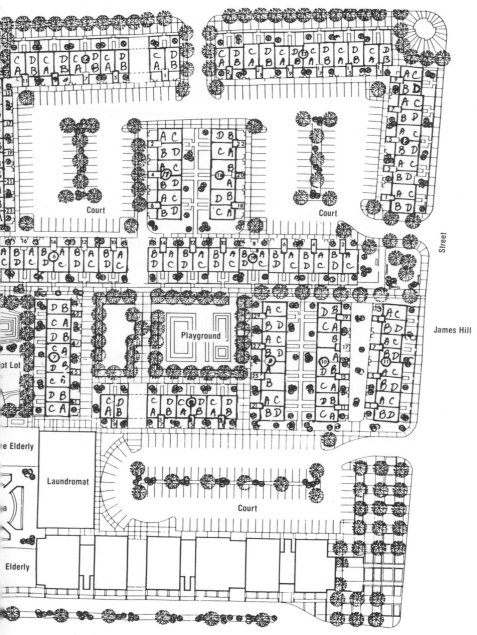

dangerous. Dover Square appears this way to outsiders and perhaps even to those residents who are still unable to grasp its organization. Robbers are quite aware of the advantages of the project's design, and frequently "vanish" into its maze after committing a robbery on its borders. The thieves believe that it is easy to lose the police in the project since there are so many corners to turn and alternative routes of escape.

Dover Square is served by a few small stores and shops, but none is a gathering place or social center the way small businesses are in the Italian community Suttles describes (1968) or in the black city neighborhoods portrayed by Liebow (1967) and Hannerz (1969). Nor do any shopkeepers take an active role in passing on gossip, settling disputes, performing small services for people, or maintaining order on the streets—all roles which urban ethnographies have repeatedly documented. The lack of local entrepreneurs and social centers is caused partly by economic constraints: the rents for the commercial space in the development are so high, by law, that they are prohibitive for a small variety store or lunch stand. Much of the commercial space stands empty or is used by social service agencies. One side of the development has a liquor store, an interior decoration shop, an infant center, a day care center, a hardware store, a day-labor exchange, a youth activities center, a window glass shop, and a multilingual library. None of the proprietors of these shops takes any leadership role in community affairs, and all are socially peripheral to Dover Square. A youth activities worker is active in the project, but he has had little success in converting his center into a community gathering place. A short-lived youth center was closed when boisterous teenagers broke the windows, and the sponoring agency withdrew its support. The liquor store installed three pinball machines and for a brief time was an important gathering place for the black young people, indicating a substantial demand for such a social center. However, the vice squad soon discovered that the machines were operating without a license and closed them down. The library is often empty or used by a few Chinese students seeking a quiet place to study.

A supermarket and a laundromat in Dover Square are both more important as social centers to the residents. The supermarket offers a kaleidoscope of shoppers and ethnic foods, but it is not a personal place where strangers get acquainted, nor is there a proprietor to introduce them. Many local residents do work as cashiers and stock boys in the store, and, as a result, they tend to know more residents from other ethnic groups than do other tenants. All ethnic groups are represented on the supermarket staff. Thus, the supermarket provides one of the few settings in which individuals of different ethnic groups regularly interact socially.

Interactions between shoppers do not necessarily break down ethnic barriers, however, and may simply reinforce feelings of separateness. For example, a black woman standing in line felt a cart run over her foot from behind her. She turned around to find a Chinese woman waiting in line and, assuming that the woman was being pushy, as she believed all Chinese women are, punched her. The Chinese woman, who had probably only bumped the other woman inadvertently, quickly retreated. On another occasion, a Chinese woman watched silently and in horror as an older white man in a ragged coat stuffed roasts and steaks into his pockets and inside his capacious coat, and then waddled out of the store. Such encounters between strangers do not create understanding and sympathy, but reinforce social distance.

The supermarket reflects the nature of social life in the development in that individuals of different ethnic groups occupy the same spaces, yet participate in entirely different social worlds. Young black boys sit along a window at the end of the store, watching the customers and hoping to help someone home with her bags for a tip. Old Chinese men sit along the same window, watching the customers and visiting with their Chinese friends, ignoring the presence of the boys, as the boys ignore the elderly men. The store is not dominated by any ethnic group, but is used by all.

The laundromat inside Dover Square comes closer to serving as a community center than any other location in the project. It is in the nature of doing laundry that one tends to stay for one or two hours while the clothes wash. People of all ethnic groups come to do their laundry, a few older people come to visit their friends, and the young black teenagers come to visit, play cards, and use the soft drink machine. The owner is afraid that their presence will drive away customers and is continually asking them to leave, but they have come to feel at home here. In spite of using the same space, however, the patrons of the laundromat do not socialize with strangers who are members of other ethnic groups. Members of different ethnic groups insulate themselves from one another by pretending that the others are not present. They use strategies such as avoiding eye contact, appearing to be occupied, and maintaining physical distance from others in sitting or folding clothes, all of which Lofland describes as characteristic of people using urban public spaces (1973). There is no segregation of the laundromat space into the preserve of one or another ethnic group, but individuals still keep space between themselves and strangers. Blacks and whites are more likely to interact with each other than are the Chinese to interact with them. Since many Chinese women do not speak English, their conversations in Chinese are inevitably private and insulated from other occupants of the space.

Similar mechanisms are employed in encounters on the courts and walkways of the project. Chinese and non-Chinese people are likely to pass one another without acknowledging that the other exists. Only those few individuals who are friends say hello or nod. Commonly, pedestrians observe one another carefully, but act as if they have not noticed one another. Most Chinese passersby try not to attract the attention of the blacks, hoping to be ignored and not harassed, while the blacks and whites regard the Chinese as strangers who are socially nonexistent. Many whites come from the adjacent neighborhood, where neighborly sociability is valued, and they find this strategy of the Chinese arrogant, unfriendly, and even hostile. To the Chinese, their own behavior is motivated simply by fear.

Two open spaces in Dover Square serve as important social centers. The playground, a large concrete crater equipped with a basketball net, is a favorite hangout for young people, mostly black youths. It offers curbs shaded by trees, and a court for interminable games of basketball, which persist until three or four in the morning, much to the distress of the residents living around the playground. During the summer, ten to twenty young people gather here regularly, often accompanied by their babies and dogs. It is very close to the laundromat, so that summer and winter hangouts are in roughly the same place. Because of its central location, however, it is hard to avoid the playground when walking through the project.

A second social center is the square: an open place, also equipped with a basketball net, that faces onto a street. The Chinese teenagers almost never use the basketball court in the playground, and the black teenagers almost never use the basketball court in the square. Benches around the square are often occupied by elderly Chinese ladies visiting with their friends. Younger children use the basketball court, but groups are either Chinese, or a mix of Chinese and blacks from the adjacent apartments.

The ebb and flow of activity during the course of a normal day illustrates the different ways each ethnic group uses the same public spaces. Because of differences in life styles, they even use the spaces at different times.

Early in the morning the working people appear, walking quickly through the project toward a nearby bus stop and subway station. Few wear a suit and tie or carry a briefcase. A few young Chinese men and women leave in their cars or walk to their white-collar jobs downtown. The middle-aged Chinese women leave at seven or eight in the morning for their jobs as stitchers in the garment factories of Chinatown and downtown, generally wearing conservative American clothes such as slacks and a sleeved print blouse. A few young black mothers walk with their children to a nearby nursery school. Some women go to the laundromat early to escape the gang of black youths.

Young black men and white men looking for their friends appear between nine and ten. They often plan the day's hustling to get money for marijuana. Several are accompanied by large German shepherds or other guard dogs that occasionally fight with one another. In winter the pattern is similar, except that they have to search out warm crannies in the project. Young black women pass by with their children, but will not stop to visit until later in the day when they have finished their shopping and laundry. The teenagers constantly drift in and out of the area, coalescing for a brief period for a conversation or event, drifting apart again as members leave to conduct individual business. One young man stops by to borrow some money from a friend; a woman passes by on her way to visit her boyfriend in jail. Groups form temporarily around a card game or other interesting activity, with the smaller boys creating an appreciative ring around the outside, or boys retreat to a more private stairwell to enjoy a "poke of reefer" (marijuana). Smaller children play in the playground oblivious to the teenagers. Older teenage girls whirl by on their bikes, circling the central gathering place, apparently less to see than to be seen. There is little permanent structure to these social groups. Each contains pairs of friends who are very "tight" with one another and many others linked through looser ties of friendship.

These groups gather on the hoods of cars parked in front of the laundromat, under a nearby underpass, or on a curb in the playground. Adults who are unaware of these predictable social patterns are continually aggravated by the teenagers sitting on their cars in front of the laundromat and will inveigh against the irresponsibility of youth rather than simply move their cars to another area of the parking lot. The laundromat entrance offers no other places to sit, yet is an ideal social center because people frequently pass it on their way to the laundromat, the grocery store, or the bus stop.

Later in the morning, a few elderly people venture out of the adjacent high-rise buildings to sit by their doors. They carry a few chairs out and hope to enjoy the activity of the sidewalk before the teenagers return home from school. Most stay close to the security guard provided by the housing authority, and many retreat to the safety of a roof terrace, which is open only to tenants of the high-rises. Several people I talked to said that they would prefer to sit along the sidewalk, but feared robbers and muggers. By protecting themselves, however, they are further isolating themselves from the rest of the neighborhood.

In the late morning, young Chinese mothers appear, heading for the grocery store, towing two or perhaps three toddlers and young children with them. Unlike boisterous and active black or white children, the Chinese children are usually quiet and obedient, following close behind their mothers but wide eyed with curiosity. Elderly Chinese ladies dressed in traditional dark grey or black loose blouses and short, loose pants, and wearing straight, chin-length bobs, also walk resolutely to the supermarket or to a fruit stand in the closest part of James Hill, trailing a few small children. A few older Chinese women sit and visit in the square. Meanwhile, the first black youths are beginning to bounce a basketball in the playground. In the late afternoon, as many as fifteen boys will gather for a serious basketball game, occasionally supervised by the local youth worker. Almost all the boys who use this area to play basketball are black, but they are joined by a few Hispanic boys. Occasionally a Chinese boy will take a shot at the net, but if a group of black boys appears, he will leave.

Between noon and two, adult Chinese men leave for work. A few appear in the late morning accompanying their wives and children to the store, but most have few free hours since they work until two or three every night and sleep late in the mornings. As the afternoon progresses, women return to the supermarket for a second trip, either for an item they have forgotten or in hopes of encountering a friend.

Late in the afternoon, the other working people return. Chinese women straggle home between four and six, singly or in pairs, carrying bags of food for dinner. They generally come from the subway station, filtering through one of the three openings on that side of the project. At this point, they are desirable purse-snatch victims since they may be carrying their weekly pay. Many women persist in carrying purses in spite of the obvious risks of doing so. Some Chinese children now emerge from apartments where they have been restricted all day under the care of a cautious grandmother. They start baseball games and games of catch in the parking lots directly in front of the house, where their parents can watch them, rather than going farther away to a place more suitable for such games.

Early in the evening, fragrances of cooking emanate from the various apartments, providing olfactory evidence of the diversity of the inhabitants. The garlic and ginger fragrance of Chinese cooking mixes with the smell of steaming rice, sweet potatoes and greens, middle-eastern spices, spaghetti, and hamburgers. As evening approaches, some small children play outside, often until late at night, but most are in. The black teenagers sit outside until late, and the basketball game continues. The old Chinese ladies and young mothers are gone; by dark the only people outside are the young black men and women. Few people sit on the stoops and visit in the evening. There is little activity to watch and most people are afraid to be out after dark. Later, the area seems quite deserted. In the winter, as soon as people are home from work they retreat inside, and the courts are empty early. A few people go to the store after dark, but rarely alone. It is said by some residents that prostitutes bring their customers to the parking lot and the courts late at night to transact business, although I have never observed it. Very late at night the Chinese restaurant workers return home. If they are fortunate enough to have a considerate driver, he will drop them at their door and wait until they are safely inside, but if they do not live next to the street or the driver is not so considerate, the worker will be left far from his door and faces a long and frightening walk from the nearest street past concrete columns, dark doorways, and narrow passages that could conceal muggers. Since the restaurant workers bring home their earnings in cash, they are occasionally robbed on their way home. Thus, although Dover Square residents pursue their distinct life styles in close proximity, their lives rarely intersect.

CHAPTER 3

Portraits
of
Dover
Square
Families

In order to convey the range of differences in culture and life style in Dover Square, this chapter will describe the personal histories, life styles, and cultural assumptions of four Dover Square families typical of the Chinese, black, and white communities. Each has distinct attitudes toward the problems of crime and danger in the project. I have spent considerable time in the homes of each family and have had long talks with several members, from which a picture of their attitudes and family life has emerged. All names and personal characteristics have been changed to preserve privacy.

THE WONG FAMILY

The Wongs are typical of Chinese families from rural peasant backgrounds in China. They have been somewhat more successful than other Dover Square families in achieving social mobility in America. Nevertheless, they face the same stresses and difficulties faced by other immigrant families coping with completely new cultural and social surroundings. Their attitudes toward the socially and ethnically heterogeneous environment that surrounds them is characteristic of many Chinese families in the project. As have many other Chinese families, they have lived in the project for ten years and have no intention of moving out.

The Wong apartment is crowded and full. Flowered sofas encircle a red carpet; shelves for all the family's possessions line the walls, which are adorned by Chinese calendars from local Chinatown stores. A large color TV set dominates the living area. Stereo sets, records, hockey sticks, and tennis shoes testify to the teenage children's Americanized interests, while a small cluster of shoes at the door bespeaks loyalty to the Chinese custom of wearing slippers, rather than street shoes, inside the house. Neon lights along the ceiling, and an air conditioner, allow the curtains and shades to be continually closed for privacy against the prying gaze of burglars. The dining area sports a formica table and folding metal chairs and serves as a center of family life. Food is a major topic of conversation; pride in Chinese cuisine and distaste for flat, dry American food is generally assumed, and evening meals are an event for which all family members are expected to appear. Rice is considered far healthier than any other food.

In the small kitchen are two refrigerators full of frozen chickens and ducks, a one-hundred-pound bag of rice, a large chopping block, an electric rice cooker, a wok, and attractive flowered curtains at the windows. A jar of special tea made from tea leaves sent from the father's village in China always sits on the counter and a large bag of oranges is readily available for guests and family. Chinese newspapers from New York's Chinatown are scattered through the house for Mr. Wong to read. The house, although small and full, is always neat, the dishes carefully washed, and the floors clean. The three bedrooms upstairs, for the two daughters, one son, and two parents, are similarly full but tidy. Behind the house, in a garden plot only four feet by four feet, the father grows his favorite Chinese vegetables. On summer evenings, he sits on his stoop and makes some effort to converse in his halting English with his black neighbor.

Mr. and Mrs. Wong are in their mid-forties and live in this apartment with a daughter, Wendy, twenty-four, another daughter, Susan, twenty, and a son Fred, sixteen. Mr. Wong's mother lives in another apartment in the project with her other son, although he is gone much of each week, working in a neighboring city where he owns a Chinese restaurant. The grandmother is a frequent visitor to the house, and once a week Mr. Wong's brother arrives with his wife and children to have dinner. Mr. Wong worked as a cook in a small Chinese restaurant for seven years, staying loyally at the same workplace despite offers to go elsewhere. When he broke his leg, however, he was laid off without pay or any guarantee of future employment. After completing a program in English-language training, he got a job in a stockroom. His English is adequate for simple conversations and he is eager to learn, but cannot carry out complex discussions. Mrs. Wong has worked as a stitcher in a garment factory for many years. Her eyesight is slowly deteriorating from the work, however. Since she does not speak English, she is restricted to working in Chinatown, where English is unnecessary. The two daughters both graduated from college, and the son plans to go to college as well. He will go to an elite, Ivy League college, as did his older sister.

Unlike many other Chinese families in Dover Square, the Wongs come from a relatively educated, land-owning family in China. Mr. Wong's grandfather came from China alone, hoping to bring his sons when they grew old enough. His family were landlords and although he was fair to his tenants, his wife, who stayed in China, was tyrannical, gambled away all the family money, and always told the children there was no money for food. Mr. Wong's father also came to the United States, where he set up a business with a partner. In the 1950s, when his wife heard that he was ill, she came to the United States to join him, but by the time she had forged her way through immigration barriers, he had died. The partner subsequently swindled the family out of their share of the business, and the Chinatown merchants supported the partner. At that time, the wife had no recourse outside Chinatown.

Despite these difficulties, however, the family managed to reassemble. The wife arranged for her daughter to immigrate, through marriage to an uneducated man who was nevertheless a citizen, and their family now lives in a nearby town. Soon after the triumph of the Chinese Communists, Mr. Wong's family fled to Hong Kong. Because their father was a citizen, both sons were able to move to the United States. At the age of thirty-one, Mr. Wong came to the U.S., and five years later, brought his wife and family. He is unusually educated for Dover Square. In China, Mr. Wong was a teacher in his village, having gone to Canton City to get an education. He worked in Hong Kong as a schoolteacher, then decided to come to the United States because rampant inflation and a low salary made life hard. He hoped for better opportunities for his children. Once in this country, however, he had no choice but restaurant work because of his inability to speak English. The family originally settled on the outskirts of Chinatown, but when the area was destroyed by urban renewal, moved into the project in the mid-1960s. Although they like their apartment, the family does not like the neighborhood.

The oldest daughter grew up in China and Hong Kong, speaks fluent Chinese, and retains traditional morals and world views. She still thinks in Chinese. The second daughter arrived when she was ten and is more Americanized, speaks English without an accent, and has more American ideas of morality. The son, who was very small when they arrived in the United States, speaks very little Chinese and is very American in body language, expression, and attitudes. When the two sisters converse, it is not unusual for the older to speak Chinese while the younger responds in English. The older sister thinks of herself as Chinese, the younger sister and brother think of themselves as Chinese-Americans. The younger two are aware of the marginal, economically depressed position of Chinese in American society and resent the way whites as well as wealthy Chinese exploit Chinese workers.

As a restaurant worker, Mr. Wong regularly worked twelve hours a day, six days a week, leaving home around noon and often returning after two in the morning. The hourly wage is low, but tips may make the pay good or poor depending on the quality of the restaurant and the number of other waiters. Workers have no contracts and no unemployment, retirement, or disability benefits, however. Women employed as stitchers, as Mrs. Wong is, typically work from early in the morning until five or six, so that husbands and wives rarely see one another, and children are left without parental care for most of the afternoon. Parents sacrifice themselves for their children's future in the hope that the children will be able to find better jobs and have an easier life. The oldest daughter, Wendy, works as a nurse, the second is training for a career in business management, and the son plans to make his future in science or engineering. Thus, this family displays patterns of upward social and economic mobility characteristic of many Chinese families in Dover Square.

Also typically, they maintain close ties to the father's family and to families who come from the same village in China as the father or the mother. Mrs. Wong's own kinsmen are in China, but two families from her village live in Dover Square, and she has a quasi-kinship relationship with them. Women generally keep up the kin ties with the husband's kinsmen and co-villagers as well as their own.

A major event for the family was the marriage of the oldest daughter to the son of a powerful family, also living in the project. The prospective father-in-law, blessed with seven sons, retired after concluding that none of his sons would be interested in helping him run a restaurant if he were to invest in one. He now lives on income provided by his sons from their highly paid jobs as engineers. Wendy's husband is a college graduate with a degree in engineering from a prestigious local college. Although both are children of poor restaurant workers and stitchers, they spent about fifteen thousand dollars on a wedding that included a thirteen-course banquet for five hundred people in a Chinatown restaurant; the money came from the paychecks of the bride and the groom. At the banquet, the bride was adorned with the appropriate chains and bracelets of heavy gold jewelry that are an important form of investment and security for many Chinese families, as well as symbols of wealth and prestige. The newlyweds moved into a renovated, expensive apartment in Chinatown, but after a few months of paying this high rent, chose to move into their own apartment in Dover Square.

Wendy, in accordance with traditional Chinese ideals of womanly modesty, virtue, and duty, expects to spend her life raising children for her husband, and has no thought of using birth control. She is considered a very virtuous woman according to Chinese ideals: she is calm, placid, and capable. She was regarded as a desirable marriage partner because she has a good job as a nurse and earns a tidy salary. Yet she also believes in being submissive and coquettish to men, as Chinese women traditionally have been expected to be, and assumes it is her role to do all the housework while the man does none. In her parents' family, Mrs. Wong rises at six, leaves for work at 6:30, returns at five in the afternoon, cooks until eight, and cleans the house until eleven or twelve, while Mr. Wong does a little cooking but no housework. Susan, the younger daughter, who has more American values, expects to have a different kind of relationship with her husband and does not plan to be so submissive and servile. In China, girls were considered far less desirable than boys and might be killed if the family were too poor to raise a girl and provide an adequate dowry for her. Although female infanticide is not practiced in the United States, the notion of dowry persists in the form of gold jewelry given to a bride at the wedding, and girls are still undervalued.

Other traditional notions also persist. According to Mrs. Wong, the good person is not the one who is isolated and does not talk to his neighbors, but one who is friendly and looks out for his neighbors. This, however, does not allow one to ask a neighbor to watch your house while you are away, since that constitutes a favor, an imposition on your neighbor's time, which one might ask of a relative but not of a friend. Ties with relatives generally imply greater expectations of aid and support than ties with friends or neighbors, and many Chinese residents are loath to ask their neighbors for favors of any kind. The virtuous person is industrious and clever, always working hard and competently. He or she always offers to help his relatives whenever they need it. At the time of the wedding, the Wongs found that some relatives energetically assisted in cooking and preparing, while others failed to appear at all or came only after the major work was completed. Mr. Wong's mother, for example, who spends most of her time playing mah-jongg, a game involving gambling, arrived for a family party but did nothing except play mah-jongg with her friends. She plays constantly with her neighbors in the project, and not only is she considered not virtuous but she also has acquired a nickname: "the mah-jongg lady."

Confrontations are to be avoided at all costs, even when someone else is clearly in the wrong. For example, the man living in the upstairs apartment dumped water on the Wong's garden, and Susan, the Americanized daughter, yelled at him to stop. Her mother was horrified and told her that this was a bad thing to do and that it would be far better to say nothing or to quietly go to his house and ask him not to continue. He was an older Chinese man, and it would be far better to show him respect. On the other hand, as Susan pointed out, he never dumped water on their garden again. In another incident, a Chinese neighbor infuriated Mrs. Wong by bringing two workmen into the Wong house to look at their neon lights, without a word of explanation or even a knock at the door. In accordance with her notions of conflict management, however, she said nothing to the neighbor. A third example shows how these situations are handled. When a neighbor failed to pay Mr. Wong's mother for tea cakes she bought in Chinatown at the neighbor's request, she said nothing to the woman herself, but told everyone else. Such indirect conflict resolution and gossip are far preferred to directly confronting someone with his offense.

Although the Wongs have never been burglarized and have experienced only one attempted purse snatch in the ten years they have lived in Dover Square, they are cautious about crime. They do not think the project is extremely dangerous as a place to live, but do consider their black and Puerto Rican neighbors dangerous. Mr. Wong refuses to go to James Hill, even to visit friends, because there are so many blacks there. When Susan was little, her parents told her never to talk back to a black child or it would kill her. She is now discouraged from marrying a white man and firmly prohibited from marrying a black one. To some extent, their attitudes about race are a residue from their experience in Hong Kong, where race prejudice is widespread and abusive policemen are often Pakistanis, who have darker skin. Even within the Hong Kong Chinese community, skin color is equated to social status and prestige.

However, experiences in the United States often reinforce these attitudes. For example, the Wongs live across the street from a black family that disliked them immediately just because they are Chinese. The small children threw rocks and eggs at the door, once hitting Mrs. Wong as she walked into the house, and drank the milk that the Wongs had delivered to their doorstep. This was a large family in which the parents fought with each other all the time. When Susan once took one of the small children to its mother to complain about what the child was doing, the mother said nothing to the child but promptly began beating it hard, a reaction that Susan thought did not help the child. Another black family nearby was always fighting, and the police continually came to the Wong's door by mistake. Down the sidewalk is the home of a third black family where the boy plays his stereo at full volume at two in the morning, but, as is the custom of the Chinese, the Wongs have never complained. Nor have they found out to which family the boy belongs. Farther down the sidewalk lives a large Puerto Rican family with a small pen full of loud dogs that bark at and frighten the Wongs as they walk past. The children constantly ask the Wongs for food.

On the other hand, another black neighbor is a middle-aged woman who is not afraid of the obstreperous children across the street and chases them away, preventing them from stealing the Wongs' milk. The Wongs feel much safer because this woman looks out for them and is not afraid of the black family that harasses and frightens them. Susan, in particular, thought that the black teenagers in the project were generally dangerous, but, intriguingly, after meeting several of the leaders of the youth group through me, changed her mind. She found them suddenly much less threatening and frightening. She presumed that they would not attack her since they now knew who she was and she knew who they were and could identify them. In her words, "They wouldn't rob me if they knew I knew who they were—they just wouldn't be so stupid. They will only pick on people who look afraid and as if they can't speak English. But, since I know who they are, they won't do anything to me, just for their own protection." She felt safer both because she could recognize them and because I, a friend of hers, knew them fairly well.

Susan finds other experiences as dangerous as the threat of crime. She is fearful of small children who harass her and mock Chinese tonal speech, and of adult men who make lecherous, flirtatious comments. It is primarily whites and Puerto Ricans who are guilty of these verbal sexual assaults.

Whites are dangerous because they have the impression that they can push Chinese people around with impunity, an attitude resented by many Chinese people. When Susan attended a predominantly white high school, for example, it was assumed that she would not take on any position of leadership or authority, in accordance with the prevailing white notion that they run affairs and that the Chinese should remain peripheral. In the past, it was commonly known among whites that one could eat in Chinatown and walk out without paying and the Chinese restaurant owner would say nothing. Blacks, according to Susan, do not take advantage of Chinese feelings of marginality and helplessness this way. She also is frightened by drunks and bums, particularly crowds around bars and in a local subway station frequented by drunks. Most of the drunks she encounters are white. Thus, the Wongs feel that they inhabit an environment rife with dangers of crime, insult, and harassment by their black, white, and Puerto Rican neighbors. They do not, however, live in constant fear.

THE JOHNSON FAMILY

The Johnsons are typical of the "respectable" blacks who live in Dover Square. The father, mother, and three children live in an attractive, carefully decorated apartment which they have inhabited for ten years. A flowered love seat and sofa match the green wall-to-wall carpeting and harmonize with the large color TV set that is always on. All the tables and chairs are adorned by expensive-looking lamps, china figurines made by Mrs. Johnson, and framed pictures of family members. The table for family meals is in the kitchen, so that the small living room seems more capacious. Although all surfaces, including a wooden coffee table, are decorated with pictures and figurines, the apartment does not seem cluttered. No books, magazines, or newspapers are in evidence. In all my visits, the house was always spotless, tidy, and showed no signs of the presence of three children in the home.

Mr. Johnson works at a nearby university as a painter, a job he has held for many years. In his spare time, he pursues his interest in photography and occasionally takes pictures at weddings and family gatherings. He is now in his mid-forties. Mrs. Johnson stays home all day cleaning, caring for the house, and occasionally going to Salvation Army classes for figurine painting. She is an avid watcher of soap operas, which she follows every day from 11:30 to 3:00 without fail. Her husband bemoans the ideas she gets about the perfidy of men and women from these shows. Their oldest daughter is fourteen, the son is about twelve, and the youngest daughter ten. Although they live in a mixed neighborhood, their children are being bused to predominantly white schools to help the city achieve racial balance.

Mr. and Mrs. Johnson both came from a rural area of Virginia, but Mr. Johnson left many years ago and grew up in Philadelphia, where he remembers there was gang warfare in the 1940s and 1950s. They have lived in this city for at least fifteen years, first in a rooming house in James Hill and later in Dover Square, where they moved to escape the rats and get a better apartment. Mr. Johnson's brother and sister both live nearby. He married Mrs. Johnson when she was just out of high school and brought her directly to the city from her family's farm in Virginia. She has found the adjustment to city living difficult, and longs to return to her family in the country. She is now thirty-four, but is still shy, soft-spoken with a Southern drawl, and quiet. She is much less worldly than he, spending most of her days in the house. She has a cousin in a neighboring town, whom she visits occasionally, but she considers her husband's siblings phony and avoids them. Nor is she friends with her neighbors in the project, although she knows several well enough to say hello to. She looks forward to annual visits to her relatives in Virginia, where she was raised in a strongly patriarchal, religious family. She fondly remembers singing in her church choir and reciting poems in church as a child.

Mr. Johnson, however, aspires to a better position in life, and is very interested in making contact with people of higher educational and social status. Although his wife feels uncomfortable with such people, he energetically pursues these contacts and plays down his ties with his Dover Square neighbors of lower social position. He claims that his closest friends are in the suburbs, and although he is friendly to many of his neighbors, he is not intimate with them. The Johnsons' acquaintances are all among the respectable blacks in Dover Square, families that similarly value stability, work, and church and condemn criminality. They participate in meetings of a white and black Catholic fellowship group, and in the past, Mr. Johnson was active in the tenants' association. Some blacks named him a leader in the project. He recently dropped out, however, because he felt he was doing too much work for free and feared making enemies. His withdrawal from the group coincided with the departure from the project of many of the middle-class liberal white leaders of the tenants' association. Although he knows the local street youth by name and knows where they live, he is not friendly with them and does not say hello when he sees them. The youths regard him as a person who is not a good street fighter and unable to protect himself. Mrs. Johnson also knows who the youths are, but carefully minds her own business when she sees them.

The Johnsons place a high value on a strong and cohesive family life in which parents watch carefully over their children. They condemn other black families in the project in which the parents don't care what their children do, do not pay any attention to them, and don't feed them. They also emphasize the value of work and school, and are anxious that their children get as good an education as possible. Family meals are an important event, and Mrs. Johnson typically spends the evening cooking. The Johnson children have difficulty with the other children in the project, however, particularly the street youths. Last winter, the boy had his bike stolen by youths who approached him with a wrench and knife and said that they wanted his bike. Both the Johnson boy and the friend with him surrendered their bikes, which the family never recovered. The youngest daughter, who is plump, is frequently teased and called a "fat pig" by some of her Dover Square neighbors at school. She sometimes needs to be rescued by her oldest sister from the youths who hit her and tease her. The older daughter believes that it is important to show such people that you are ready and able to fight and then they will leave you alone. Talking to a child's mother is of little avail since such children rarely listen to their mothers, and even if they are beaten, they are better only for a little while and then return to the same way of acting.

Although Mrs. Johnson is reserved and quiet, she also believes in confrontations when she feels that she or her children have been wronged. Once, when she was told by her son that his grade-school teacher had hit him simply for leaning over to pick up something, she marched into the school and demanded to talk to the teacher. Although the teacher denied it, a small Chinese boy confirmed the story. Later, the assistant principle called her to apologize. When her son had a paper route, one of the customers complained that the paper was late one morning. Since the fault lay in the newspaper itself, which delivered the copies late, she called the customer and they "exchanged words." When she suspected that another woman was attempting to seduce her husband, she similarly confronted her and demanded that she desist. Otherwise, however, Mrs. Johnson firmly believes in minding her own business and not getting involved in other people's affairs. As she walks through the project, she looks at the ground and does not talk to anyone.

The family is very concerned about burglary and careful never to leave the house unoccupied for any length of time. They are sure that the street youths who often congregate in the playground in front of their house watch Mrs. Johnson come and go and plan to break in as soon as they see her leaving. She never leaves the house until Mr. Johnson or the children come home, even though this places great restrictions on her movements. She prefers to do the laundry very early in the morning before the street youths have assumed their accustomed places in the laundromat. The family has never been burglarized, in contrast to many of their friends and neighbors among the respectable families, who are less cautious.

Yet, the Johnsons do not think Dover Square is more dangerous than anyplace else. The oldest daughter used to think it was dangerous, but now points out that it is much less so than nearby public housing projects in James Hill, where some of her friends live. The places in Dover Square that are dangerous change as the hangouts of the street youths change, since it is here that the particular hazards lie.

Mrs. Johnson feels the project is safe if you mind your own business and don't bother people, although she is conscious of the frequency of burglaries and robberies. She knows the street youths by name and tries to be friendly and say hello to them, but feels uneasy when she walks past them. Although she is quiet and doesn't say much, she hopes that they will assume she is tough and someone who should be left alone. Drunks, people who smoke marijuana, and maniacs are dangerous. One can never tell even about people who appear normal, however, since they may always turn on you and attack you.

Mr. Johnson is emphatic when he states that the project is not that dangerous: only eight or nine young people belong to the group that is active in crime, while at least two hundred to three hundred other young people who have nothing to do with crime live in the project. Furthermore, he believes that many of the youths who "hang out" conspicuously in the playground and commit crimes do not come from the project but from James Hill and James Hill housing projects. He is aware of their family problems and believes the root cause is a decline in family values: single mothers who are on welfare and take in any man who comes along and gives them a few dollars, and parents who let their children smoke or do whatever else they want to harm their health. These children feel neglected at home, so turn to the street where they find a group to which they can belong. They resent the fact that some people have money and things while they have none and turn to stealing to survive. Mr. Johnson's daughter pointed out that anyone who has better clothes or more money will be the subject of jealousy and gossip. Mr. Johnson feels it is understandable that youths without money should want to steal from those who have more.

Another cause of the problem is the inadequacy of the law and order system. Mr. Johnson thinks there should be more emphasis on punishment, that people have to learn that they cannot get away with things, and that the pimps and numbers men, the people whom the youths see have the money and prestige, should be controlled. Like almost all Dover Square residents, the Johnsons view the police as ineffective and the courts as too lenient. They know which project residents commit crimes in the project and the problems in their families that propelled them into crime, but feel that there is little that the police have done about the situation. Mr. Johnson pointed out that one of these youths was arrested but was back out on the street in three hours. Mr. Johnson never calls the police, feeling that it does no good, and Mrs. Johnson has called only once when she saw some youths climbing around on the roof and was afraid that they would hurt themselves. It took an hour for the police to come.

The Johnsons's attitudes toward the other ethnic groups in the project are typical of many of their black and white neighbors. They believe that the Chinese live in large groups, crowded together into small apartments with wall-to-wall mattresses and separate living quarters created by a curtain in the living room. Mr. Johnson observed that Chinese families will only open the door a crack and never let you in. Once when he witnessed a white boy being attacked by Chinese youths, he assumed that the boy had robbed them and was being punished and pointed out that it was dangerous to get involved with the Chinese. Although the Johnsons are friendly with their white and Hispanic neighbors as well as the respectable black families nearby, they have no friends among the Chinese residents.

The Johnsons are aware that they live in an environment with dangers both to the safety of their house and to the moral upbringing of their children and respond by being cautious and minimizing their social ties in the neighborhood, but they do not feel that their environment is unusually dangerous.

THE MALOOF FAMILY

The Maloofs are a Syrian-Lebanese family from the James Hill area who have lived in Dover Square for ten years. Their apartment is one of the most elegant and elaborately decorated in the project—a statement based on my own observations and on the fact that it was used as a model apartment by the project management and was included in the James Hill house tour one year. A walnut sofa and coffee table face a large walnut sideboard with enclosed TV set, the balcony window is graced with hanging plants, and the ceiling has dark beams, a feature of only a few of the apartments. Even the stairwell outside the apartment is immaculate, with fresh paint over the concrete blocks, a small rug at the door, and a birch log with a flower arrangement just outside. The interior stairs have carpet that matches the living room wall-to-wall rug and the walls have been repainted a soft yellow. An elegant wine rack decorates one wall, although Mr. Maloof does not drink and it holds no bottles. When I visited the family, the apartment always was spotless and immaculate and no books, magazines, or newspapers lay on the tables. The Maloofs are very proud of their home, but despite ten years of residence in Dover Square, are seriously planning to move out and have placed their names on the waiting list for another project in a suburban area. They have recently taken trips to Puerto Rico and Hawaii.

Mr. Maloof is in his late fifties and his wife is in her early fifties. They have three grown children: two daughters who are married and live in other sections of the city, and a son who was recently tragically murdered. Mr. Maloof has lived near Dover Square all his life, first in a Syrian community that was slowly taken over by the Chinese, then in James Hill. During World War II he fought in Europe, where he met and married his wife, who subsequently learned to speak English fluently although she still has a slight accent. She has now lived in the James Hill area for almost thirty years. For years Mr. Maloof worked as a painter, and for a few of those years he was a self-employed contractor with six or seven men working for him; then he spent several years employed by the project as a painter. Recently he had to have an eye operation, and as he approaches retirement age, he does not know whether he will be able to go back to work. His wife is employed by the police department as a meter maid.

Mr. Maloof feels very familiar with this neighborhood and cultural milieu, and he has several relatives who live in the area. His sister, made a widow by the violent death of her husband, lives in another apartment in the project, and a cousin lives in another apartment. Another sister lives in James Hill, as did his mother until she died ten years ago.

When he was younger, he was a competent street fighter, and he still keeps a gun in his house, which he was tempted to use when his son was murdered. One of his daughters married an Italian boy and now lives in an Italian neighborhood with their first child. The son had several black girlfriends and finally married a black girl who, according to one of the son's friends, was from a respectable family. His friends charge that his family refused to accept her because she was black, so the couple and their children settled in a nearby housing project. When the son served in Vietnam he became addicted to heroin and, on his return to the United States, became involved with a white gang of heroin dealers. The police once caught him in his apartment with heroin, but promised to let him off if he became an informer. After his information lead to several busts, rumors began to circulate that he would be killed. His friends think the murder—six bullets in the back of the head in a remote park, with his hands tied—was a punishment.

The Maloofs are very concerned about what they see as the deterioration in the quality of the project since they moved in, blaming management indifference, failure to make repairs quickly and efficiently, and failure to carefully screen and monitor prospective tenants. They feel, as many other white families do, that they moved into an exciting, multicultural environment with attractive new apartments, but that it has gone steadily downhill. They are much more worried about maintenance and management failures than they are about security. They feel the social status of the project declining around them. Neither they nor any other white family has settled any of their children in other apartments in the project, in comparison to both black and Chinese families, where this practice is common.

The Maloofs have been active members of the tenants' council for ten years, and have had many dealings with the project managers and owners. They are aware, in a way that few black or Chinese families are, of the extent to which the project's problems are caused by management policies and indifference. They argue that the maintenance men are poorly paid and do not work hard, and they are certain that many families pay bribes to move into the project. They see that no white families have moved in for at least two years, while the number of black, Chinese, and Hispanic families has steadily increased. They attribute this to corrupt managers who allow squatting and accept bribes from Chinese families for priority in rentals. Mrs. Maloof says she wants to leave because she is tired of being the only person who cleans the stairs and paths, who calls the management to complain, or who makes an effort to improve conditions. Mr. and Mrs. Maloof both emphasize the fact that when they moved into the project, it was 30 percent white, 30 percent black, 30 percent Chinese, and 10 percent Hispanic, but believe (erroneously) that it is now 60–70 percent Chinese and probably over 30 percent black. They complain that the management never evicts undesirable tenants and accuse the management of being afraid to throw out the local black youths who are leaders of the street group.

Their spleen is also directed against the growing number of Chinese families, who, they argue, are living in overcrowded, illegal conditions, have filthy apartments, hang chickens and ducks in their windows and living rooms, and never complain to the management about anything. Mr. Maloof is particularly irate about a Chinese family across the courtyard from him who, he believes, lives in a single apartment with twenty-two people and, once a month, brings out their drawers crawling with cockroaches. He is incensed that Chinese people come to the United States and fail to learn English, while his wife, facing the same situation, became fluent. He believes that they make a great deal of money as waiters, and with several wage earners in a family, are very rich. Yet, they do nothing when houses are robbed, never call the police, do not come to tenants' association meetings except when the discussion concerns rent increases, and, to his mind, take no responsibility for the local community. The older Chinese do not speak English, and the younger ones do not care.

Although their relations with respectable black families and other white families are generally cordial, the Maloofs resent one family of black neighbors who they think are hostile, filthy, and responsible for the cockroaches that plague them. Squabbles frequently erupt over use of the trash cans, which are shared and insufficient, and cleaning the common stairwell. One day, for example, Mrs. Maloof was cleaning the stairwell with a hose and moved the black neighbor's rug so that she could clean without getting it wet, and the neighbor yelled that she had better stop messing with her things and leave her to clean her own place. The black woman never puts her trash in the pail, but beside it, so that the dogs are constantly getting into it and Mrs. Maloof must clean up the mess.

I spent a fair amount of time visiting this black family, however, and their apartment was generally neat and clean. Cockroaches, once entrenched in a building, are virtually impossible to eradicate. The black woman is loud and aggressive, but is neither slovenly nor particularly hostile to whites. Furthermore, in visiting the Chinese family with the alleged twenty-two members and the cockroaches, I found that it actually consisted of a hard-working widowed woman with six children. I found no hanging chickens, wall-to-wall mattresses, or excessive filth. In this multicultural living environment, it appears that the normal stresses of dense urban living—the trash, noise, dogs, and differing standards of cleanliness—serve to exacerbate ethnic hostilities.

The Maloofs do not feel that the project is dangerous, nor are they particularly concerned about crime, although they do adopt some precautions when leaving for extended trips, such as arranging to have their mail taken in by a trusted neighbor and carrying out their suitcases after dark. They have never been victimized. Mr. Maloof attributes this to the fact that he knows the street youths and was friendly to them when they were growing up. He gave them money and candy and was always nice to them and thinks that, as a result, they will not bother him. In fact, when his son-in-law's new car was stolen, one of the leaders of the street youths helped him locate it. He knows a great deal about their family situations, history of arrests and imprisonment, and reasons why they got involved in crime. Mr. and Mrs. Maloof both think it is best not to accuse the street youths of crimes, or call the police, because the youths will retaliate.

Insofar as the project is dangerous, Mrs. Maloof thinks the reason is that nobody knows anyone else, not even their neighbors, and many people slip in and out illegally. It would be safer if the management took more care about who was living in the apartments. Mr. Maloof argues that the project is not dangerous for him because he knows who the youths are and is well liked, but that it is dangerous for outsiders who know no one. The problems are caused, he thinks, by low-income black families and by mothers who tell their children to leave their apartments while they are entertaining men friends. One night, for example, he saw a small black child outside carrying around a baby at ten. He is aware, however, that there are only four or five problem families in the whole project, and that often the mothers are good women who simply cannot control their children and are very poor. The courts contribute to the problem by allowing youths out of jail the day after they are arrested. The youths can then laugh at the police. Mrs. Maloof argues that the Miranda decision further undermines the police because the accused person has to be informed who is accusing him, marking the accuser for retaliation.

The Maloofs feel relatively confident of their safety in Dover Square because they can rely on a personalistic form of protection, but they do feel abandoned by the criminal justice system. They also feel oppressed by the changing social conditions around them that are creating a different kind of danger: a danger to their social status and to their sense of belonging in the neighborhood.

THE WILLIAMS FAMILY

Recent emigrants from a small farm in the rural South, this black family has also lived in Dover Square for ten years. In the difficult process of adapting to urban life, members of this family have struggled to escape poverty and avoid family disintegration. Although some members have worked steadily at good jobs, others have been less successful in avoiding the slide into crime. The older brother, Albert, now thirty-four, arrived in Dover Square first. He lived in the project for seven years with his wife and two children. Then the marriage broke apart, and he moved to Winslow, my pseudonym for the neighboring black community, with his mother and children, while his brother George took over the family apartment. George, aged twenty-four, has lived there for three years, first alone and then with the project beauty, Renee, who is twenty, and their one-year-old daughter. George is a leader in the street youth group, many of whose members spend hours in his apartment listening to music and visiting. He vacillates between working as a community organizer, as a manager of fashion shows, or as a pimp, but ideally would like to find a way to live by his wits, his charm, and his conversation, on the largesse of rich women, rather than by working at a tedious and unrewarding regular job. He has unusual intellectual abilities and is more sensitive to the nuances of interpersonal relationships than many of his peers in the project. Through a look at his family, we will gain a glimpse into the life of the street youths in the project.

George's apartment reveals both his flair for the dramatic and his political orientation. In bold red, green, and black, it expresses his enthusiasm for black nationalism. The rug is red, the sofas black, including a large, plush recliner that holds two people. Behind an elaborate stereo set is a wall covered with mirrors. There is no TV set. Although there is a table in the kitchen, there is no food in the refrigerator nor any evidence that the inhabitants of the apartment regularly cook and eat there. The furnishings are expensive, but the apartment is not always clean and tidy. On warm days, the door stands ajar and tempting items such as bikes and strollers are generally left outside, but are not stolen.

In addition to George, Renee, and the baby, another core member of the youth group, Bill, uses the apartment as his home base, leaving his clothes there and giving the address to his probation officer, although George admits that Bill does not sleep there and admits he does not know where Bill sleeps. For several months after she was evicted from her previous residence, George's aged aunt, Anna, lived in the apartment. A sad, small figure hunched quietly in the background, Anna rarely said anything or took any part in the busy social life of the apartment.

On most days, a stream of youths flows through the apartment, visiting George and their other friends. George prides himself on his role as a youth leader, an influence against drugs and crime, since he provides these young people some place to gather besides the street corners. Here, his images of himself, as both a community worker and a hustler, merge. This leadership role, however, has also earned him a reputation as a criminal and a bad person in the neighborhood. In fact, he rarely burglarizes or robs anyone, and did so only sporadically when he was younger, but he did flirt with pimping for a time.

The Williams family came from rural Georgia, where they owned a small farm that Aunt Anna somehow signed away for nothing, although the details are unclear. The family was poor and life hard, although George has fond memories of his childhood. He remembers his friends daring him to jump across muddy drainage ditches when he was dressed in his best clothes, then laughing as his mother beat him with an extension cord for getting dirty. Both his mother and older brother, who had to assume responsibility and care for the family when the parents split up, beat the younger children, either in the middle of the street or by backing them into a corner of the house and forcing them to strip. George, the youngest boy, remembers having welts all over his legs. His father, Mr. Williams, was a rolling stone who sired probably twenty children and is now seventy-seven and still living in Georgia. George estimates that he has fourteen brothers, counting his half-brothers and step-brothers: those his father had before he married his mother, those his mother had before marrying his father, and those from his father's other wives.

To escape poverty, Albert came north at the age of twenty. He worked hard in order to bring his mother and brothers north later. He came in 1962, and by 1967 was able to send for his mother, George, and a third brother. By that time, he was married and living in Dover Square. He was working as a campus policeman at a local university (where he met Mr. Johnson) and by the time of my research had been in this job for thirteen years. When he made a young woman pregnant, he married her because he thought that was the honorable thing to do. Because of the instability of his family during his childhood, he wanted all his children to have the same name, and he desperately wanted to give them a stable, cohesive family life. But his wife was not as interested in family life as he was. After eight years of marriage, she left him; she now works as a prison correctional officer. He won custody of the children and now lives with his mother. Although he goes out with women, he does not want to get involved and is more skeptical about the prospects of finding a wife who will meet his expectations. He has been trained as an electrician and moonlights at this work, so that, between his earnings from moonlighting and his earnings from his regular job at the university, he makes a respectable income. He has purchased an elegant white Cadillac, much to the envy of his younger brother, who aspires to the same status symbol, but does not want to work so hard.

The second brother became involved in drugs and now is remote from the family. He works in a factory on an assembly line and rarely visits George except to ask for money. Mrs. Williams has worked for many years as a hospital technician, and frequently visits George. She had her first child when she was thirteen and hopes for a better life for her children, but both she and Albert agree that they spoiled the younger brothers, who now think that they can have an easy life without working. Mrs. Williams estimates that over the years she has given George alone between fifteen and twenty thousand dollars and has helped him to buy four cars.

George was only fourteen when he came north; he eagerly and thoroughly adopted the urban life style. He regards Albert as square, even though he envies him his car. He quickly learned to fight and defend himself. When one of the youths of Dover Square, later to become a leader in the street group, mocked George's funny way of talking, the fourteen-year-old slammed a board into the other boy's face, breaking his jaw and winning the undying hostility of the boy and his family. When he was a teenager, he did some stealing, but he feels that his life was really changed by a woman who taught him the ways of "the life"—the techniques of pimping.

After several years in Dover Square, George moved to a nearby, predominantly Chinese, housing project, where he became interested in Chinese martial arts and Chinese street culture. When he was evicted for non-payment of rent, he moved back to Dover Square. He worked sporadically as a community development worker in the flurry of poverty programs of the 1960s and early 1970s, but now finds these jobs drying up. His aspirations for a comfortable, elegant life of leisure and prestige remain, but the route now seems obscure. He dropped out of school in the eighth grade and, although able to write, is barely literate. He wants to read books and to go to college, and has even attended a local college on a special program for a semester, but he does not have the diligence and patience necessary to begin at a basic level to overcome his poor reading and writing skills. Now, an intelligent man of twenty-four, he finds himself unqualified for any work that will provide him the challenge, the status, and the elegant life style he craves, that is, any work except being a pimp.

Most black residents of Dover Square agree that Renee is the finest girl in the project. George felt he had to have her. When he first met her he was poor, wore an old army coat, a turban, and old pants, and she would have nothing to do with him. So he got a "fine ride" (an elegant car), clothes, a friend to drive him around, and several women giving him money, and she took notice of him. Although Renee's mother was not pleased, Renee soon moved into George's apartment, a block away from her own house. Renee's mother works for an airline and keeps a very attractive house with wall-to-wall carpets and dramatic blue and green designs on the walls. She spends a great deal of money on her appearance, getting facials, manicures, and expensive hair treatments and buying clothes, and is constantly buying cosmetics and clothes for Renee. Her parents came from the South, but Renee's mother grew up in the North. Renee's family used to live in another housing project, in Winslow, but after the husband failed to pay the rent, they were evicted and Renee's mother left him. For ten or fifteen years, she has had a relationship with a white boyfriend who works nearby. This man has a wife and family in the suburbs, and only comes to visit in the daytime. Renee's mother had another white boyfriend before that.

Renee's father lives nearby in James Hill. He has a drug habit and survives on a variety of illegal but profitable activities. According to Renee, he is still an attractive man. Renee has an older and a younger brother. Her older brother and the older brother of one of the youths active in crime in the project were best friends. After flunking out of school in tenth grade, he joined the Air Force and is now in college in the South. The younger boy, who is fourteen, attends a school elsewhere in the state because Renee's mother is anxious to separate him from the influences of other Dover Square youths, particularly from a blossoming friendship with one of the street youths who takes several Valium tablets every day and who regularly visits George.

Renee graduated from a local high school after several years of being bused to a suburban high school in a voluntary integration program. She has worked as a teller in a bank and as a toll taker, but thinks vaguely about enrolling in art school. Her mother is distraught that she is living with George, whom the mother dislikes intensely, and wants her to work at the airport, where she can earn more money. Renee, however, would rather not work regularly and live according to a schedule every day. She prefers a more comfortable, relaxed way of life and is interested neither in a demanding job nor in domesticity. Yet she will bemoan the fact that there is never enough to eat in George's house and that she has gotten thin. Her interest in George persists only as long as he is economically successful, and when his money-making schemes fail and he falls on hard times, she tends to desert him for her mother's house.

When she returns to her mother's house, she immediately gains weight. She dislikes the young people who stream through George's house; when she was working at the bank, they carefully stayed away until she left for work. And she does not appreciate George's efforts to become a pimp. She also complains that he beats her, that he even hit her in the stomach when she was pregnant. Privately, she admits that she never expected to settle down with a man like George. For his part, George can become extremely jealous, which Renee finds both flattering and confining. He has been involved in several violent fights in the last two years with another man whom she used to date in Dover Square. One fight put George in a hospital with his kneecap broken and an eye permanently damaged from being hit with a chain. In moments of jealous rage, George will claim that the baby is not his, but belongs to his rival or to other young men in the project. Toward the end of my research, George became involved in a major battle with Renee's family and friends that resulted in his rapid departure from Dover Square and its social life.

At the same time, George is loathe to sacrifice his friendships and his role as a neighborhood leader for Renee. One example clearly illustrates George's role among the youths in the project. I watched him attempting to resolve a quarrel between two fifteen-year-old boys—one black, one white—and two young people they were trying to pimp. The black fifteen-year-old was trying to pimp a fourteen-year-old transvestite black boy. This boy prefers to dress in women's clothes, but his brother beats him up when he walks through the project in "drag." As a compromise he wears ambiguously feminine clothes at home and dresses as a woman to turn tricks in the local red-light district. The white fifteen-year-old was trying to pimp his Chinese girlfriend. All four live in Dover Square, none attends school regularly, and it is not clear what will happen to them in the future.

The two "girls" were complaining that their "men" beat them more than a pimp should and were being mean to them. The other two argued that they were not getting any money from their women, that they had not seen a penny for four months. George advised the men to be nicer to their women, to stop beating them so much, and to apologize to them. He pointed out that he had recently seen the transvestite give the older boy some money, which the older boy acknowledged, but claimed was only a pittance. George stressed the older boys' responsibility to buy clothes for their women and to give them things. Moreover, he told them they should look after their own appearances. He lambasted them for spending the money they got to get high, rather than using it to buy clothes for themselves and clean themselves up or paint their rooms. The two "girls" were crying during much of the conversation and said that they just felt like getting drunk or taking a Valium. George warned the older boys that if they did not start giving more instead of only taking, they would lose their women. After this conversation, he admitted to me privately that one problem was that both the transvestite and the Chinese girl really wanted him. I asked them later if they found George irresistible, and they agreed heartily. The summer before, the transvestite youth had worked for George as a prostitute. This example illustrates George's important role in providing sensible guidance to teenagers attempting to adapt to the life of the street.

George's economic existence is precarious, alternating between periods of great affluence and days of complete destitution. His strategies for handling money differ from those of the other families I have discussed and produce a quite different, much richer-looking style of life. To him, money should not be saved in case of future disasters, but should be invested in solidifying social relationships and building networks of followers. Whenever he has money, he gives it away quickly to those who form his circle, and prides himself on his generosity. In exchange, he is treated with respect and admiration by those who benefit from his largesse. An example is the way he disbursed a windfall of thirty-five dollars which he had received. He gave fifteen dollars to Renee to buy a coat to wear in a fashion show and to purchase a pretty dress for their little girl to wear in a formal picture that his mother was having taken. He gave $1.50 to the Chinese prostitute, who told him she was hungry, he spent one dollar playing pinball and buying himself a tonic, and he argued with Renee about whether more of the money should go to buy her tennis lessons. A few other friends asked him for money for pinball and food, and he readily acquiesced. None of the money was used to buy groceries for the house. George argues that ghetto people are more generous than rich people, that they give freely of what they have when others need it, hoping that the others will help them out when they are in need, but not necessarily expecting anything back. He gave a friend two thousand dollars to buy a car, for example, without worrying about whether he would ever see it again. Those who have least, he argues, give the most. He freely asks his mother for money when he needs it, claiming that it is his right since he is the baby in the family and threatening her that he will go into pimping if she refuses. She acknowledges that she has been very generous with him.

Although George's economic strategy seems to resem-

ble the strategy Stack observed among black women on welfare (1974), there is an important difference. In the exchange
networks Stack described, there was a pattern of reciprocity.
George, however, is involved in non-reciprocal exchanges:
the party who contributes more wins prestige and power, but
faces the real possibility that he will not be repaid in the
future. For example, his exchanges with his mother and
brother are entirely one-sided. Further, he was treated with
respect as long as he provided money readily to his friends
and allies within the project, but when his fortunes fell, when
he suffered two major financial disasters—two fashion shows
that generated only debts—his social standing plummeted.
Those he had so generously helped showed no inclination to
help him in his time of need, despite his demands for assistance. George became very bitter, feeling betrayed by those
who had been his friends, but had now deserted him. Even
Renee left him when he faced poverty, returning briefly when
he regained the flush of financial success, but disappearing
again when the full dimensions of his financial disaster became clear. George rarely experienced the smooth friction-
less circulation of wealth Stack observed in the Flats. I also
observed several other situations of unequal exchange in
which individuals found that those to whom they had given
in the past failed to repay them, usually because they had no
money or had to make hard choices between the conflicting
demands of kin and friends.

As I have said, George's goal in life is to set up the kind
of unequal economic exchange that occurs between a pimp
and prostitute or a gigolo and a rich woman. George's notion
of gaining wealth focuses on ways to make a lot quickly, and
he disdains the slow, plodding strategy of working and saving
followed by his brother, the Johnsons, and many other low-
income blacks. He would like to set up a business or run fashion shows, but assumes that in order to do this, he must first
acquire the appropriate "front," the appearance of material
success. If he had a Cadillac and elegant clothes, he thinks he
could go to a bank and request a loan to begin one of these
ventures. Although this approach seems backwards at first, he
is clearly not entirely wrong. None of the youths who form

the social circle around George works, so that all acquire money through various forms of hustling—quasi-legal or illegal strategies—as well as through the generosity of parents.

George and his friends also tend to buy expensive goods on credit, aware that if they fail to make the payments their purchases will be repossessed, but in the meantime they have the use of an elegant car, expensive furnishings, and a glamorous life style. He knows that if he makes a down payment of one-third of the price of a Cadillac and makes monthly payments, he pays high interest rates and risks repossession and the loss of the down payment, but gains the status of owning a luxury car. One of George's good friends acquired a Cadillac this way, arguing that with such a car, one can easily attract girls. As a result of these economic strategies, some black families appear richer than they are, while Chinese families, who consume little, but invest in gold and jade jewelry which is hidden in houses or in bank vaults, appear poorer than they are. Money comes easily to street blacks such as George, but they are also aware that the margin between affluence and desperate poverty is narrow and that any day their fortunes may fall to nothing.

I taped several interviews with George, so he can speak in his own words about his notions of pimping and crime, including the crime situation in Dover Square:

> Everything is a habit in America: crime was a habit, so everybody picked it up. Prostitution was a habit, so everyone picked it up too. Everybody wants to be a whore now, whether they say so or not. All the girls in the ghetto, and most of the girls in the suburbs too, because some of them come to town and see the "mack," and they want to be with that black fellow who has all these girls who say he makes love so wonderful, who understands everything about them, and they can say anything, can walk around and say do, do, do, and he won't think they're nuts, because he understands them, just that much, so they all want to be a part of that too. And it's because we created it for them to want to be part of. It's an exciting life. . . .
>
> Prostitution is good and it's bad, because being down-

town, getting cut, stabbed, and things of that nature are bad. A lot of times guys go down there to buy some and they get robbed. I don't think they should get robbed, but they wouldn't get robbed if they weren't so cheap with their money. They would have a fit if their daughter gave up some for a hundred dollars, yet they're going down there trying to buy some from someone else's daughter and talking about they only want to give up fifteen. And sometimes they'll only want to give up ten. This broad is dying to give her man some money tonight, because her man is saying, "Hey, baby, you got to give me some money because we got to pay some bills or you got to leave cause I don't need no broad that ain't got no money." And she might take a couple of tens, that is how bad it is getting. Two fellows can go for twenty. Addicts will go as low as anything, lower than five dollars. If her 'dope jones' is kicking, she will do anything to get rid of it. It's like having a toothache in your whole body, and you just can't control it. . . .

The things in books about pimps are true, but nobody writes about the itty-bitty pimps, they only write about the big pimps that everybody sees. That pimp might not get hassled as much, but the pimp downtown who walks all day driving that one whore, and the broad just makes enough money to get a hotel room that night and a little food for the next morning, and she has to go back out the next day, and that's all they do, go round in circles—ain't no Cadillacs coming out of that. It's told a lot that everybody makes fifty thousand dollars a year, but only the best pimps make that kind of money. It's hard to deal with seven or eight women. . . .

The women on the street have to be tough; they have to have a lot of heart because any woman who will walk the streets all night, get in all these men's cars they never saw before, and go off all these different places with all these strange dudes, they ain't no chickens. They got heart. Why do women do it? Because they are poor, plus they enjoy it. It is exciting, they hang out where all the stars come to town, all the pimps hang out, drinking champagne, laying up in a hotel, riding

around in a Cadillac, that's the life. They got this from
the TV—the media has a lot to do with it, plus the
money. They can wear pretty dresses, a real diamond
ring, they like all that. So they are going to do whatever
they can to get it. Even if it's for a week, they want to be
able to say, "I've been there, I've been to that hotel."

Give a pimp a young girl, she lives in a real tacky
apartment somewhere, with four or five brothers and
sisters, and she's dying to get out. She's tired of doing
all these chores, cleaning this, cleaning that, trying to
work to keep the family up, and going nowhere, getting
nothing. They still got carpets with big holes in them.
Then the girl meets the pimp, and he's sitting there in
this big fine car, with the big fur mink hat on and a big
mink coat and a diamond ring, and he's playing this
sweet music, and he says, "Where are you going? You
want me to take you there?" And she wants to sit in this
big fine Cadillac so she can wave to her girlfriends and
they will say, "Hey, she made it!" So they go to this big
restaurant, and he makes sure she doesn't know what to
order, makes sure she has never been there before.
"How do you like it?" he asks, and she says, "Oh, I've
been places like this before." And the music's nice. And
if he knows how to speak a little French or something,
that'll freak her right off. If he orders in French, it'll kill
her. He orders something, and she likes it. And she may
see a dress she likes, and he says, "You like it?" And he
buys it for her. He may drop as much as two hundred
wrapping this chick up. He may take her out a couple
more times. I'm talking about real pimping, not like
those penny ante dudes downtown. He might spend
two hundred or three hundred on her. Her mother can't
have an impact now. She has a new dress, rides in a fine
Cadillac, spends the night in a hotel, drinks champagne.
She be telling her girlfriends, "I love this nigger." He got
her. He talks so sweet and kind, he talks to her as if she's
a queen, calls her a ruby, a pearl. He says, "I know you
want to get out of that rat trap you in. I know you don't
like it down there in the ghetto. I been there before.
Look where I'm at now, look at this fine hotel, look at

this carpet, feel how deep it is." And that is messing with her head. . . .

White men don't make as good pimps as black men. They are too proper and dry when it comes down to dealing with the truth about how things are. They want to believe that women are different from men. They want to believe that women are meant to clean house and make babies, goody-goody, and you have to beg them to pull up their dress, because they don't really like sex. That is what the white guy thinks, and a lot of black people think the same way now, but there are a few, from Georgia, Alabama, and Mississippi, that think, she is human, she is like me. To reach her climax, she must like to do it. So then they go and sit around with the players and hear about these broads and how they like to do it, and next thing they come up to some girl and say, "Hey, I know you like to do it, I know you like to make love, and I know you thought about making love with me. And a lot of guys don't understand that. And you be sitting around here acting real quiet, and you be telling them no, and you don't do it because you have to respect the woman's image. But the reason you like me is that while you're with me, you don't have to do that, you can ask me, and you know that I understand that you are human, and that all women like to do it, and all women are that way."

George also has strong opinions about crime and danger in Dover Square:

The thing about Dover Square robberies is that they are blamed on a segment of the kids, because the police don't really know who is doing it. Anybody who lives in Dover Square they blame. There are about seven kids who live in Dover Square, five of them are in jail. I'm talking about seven dudes about my age who sit around and talk to girls, go to parties, are normal. I'm not talking about kids who sit in the house and read the Bible all day long, ain't nothing wrong with that, but they are not normal kids. They are above normal, because there is so much in that religion. But about seven normal kids in the project, and they put all of them in jail. Before, they didn't used to do nothing, but the police bothered them so much that they used to get angry, and then . . . . They bother me too, but I ignore them. . . .

Now, most of the crime that is committed here is coming from outside, from Winslow. Dover Square has been a model, that is a sweet little place to go. They say, if you go down there and break in, they don't even look for nobody else but the people who live there. News travels, and a lot of people knows that. Just about any-where in the city, they know that if you break in around here there are four or five people that are going to be blamed for it, so they know they can go there and do it and get away. That's why they were taking off the super-market so many times. Because Dover Square kids go to a party with other kids, and they be talking about how they be blamed for everything that happens and they say "Oh, yeah?" And think, "I might as well go rip that place off, because blah-blah will be blamed." . . . Of crime committed by outsiders, 60–65 percent is by drug ad-dicts, and the rest can be broken up into those who are poor and need money, and those who just want to be big in a crowd by being a thief. But there's very few of those, which a lot of people don't know.

Of the kids around here, it depends on the age. Most of those around fifteen to sixteen who steal, they just want movie money—maybe 60–65 percent do it for that reason. And their mothers tell them, I just gave you some money last week, so they say, I'm just going to take it. And the others, they don't even get movie money, so they just have to steal. There isn't any food in their re-frigerators and the welfare man is giving them such little change that it is all going to the rent. The majority of crimes committed in winter last year were by older kids—eighteen, nineteen, twenty, twenty-one, kind of grown, but in the summer, a lot of crime is done by the little kids, thirteen, fourteen, fifteen, which the cops come looking for the older kids about. A lot of them wanted to beat someone up just to beat them up, to practice, because they don't have anything to do. If there was a place to go, constructive facilities, it would be totally different. Last summer, I would let them in to my house to listen to music. Because then I knew that everyone walking up and down the street was safe from them. But it was causing me many problems because neighbors didn't understand that I was protecting them. I didn't want them to spend their time breaking into houses, and I didn't want them to be bored. But the neighbors didn't understand that.

The people who are being affected by crime don't understand that they are the cause of crime. I think a lot of people around here don't want other people's houses to be safe. People are beginning to be coldhearted, not caring enough, because if people cared enough about other people, they would care about theirs. In order to protect your house, you have to protect your neighbor's. You can't be always in your house, and any lock can be broken if a criminal really wants to get it. . . . An alarm is better, but a lot of people don't check whether they have an alarm or not. Good criminals do, most criminals do, but sometimes someone needs some dope right now, and he sees you go out, and he knows you are usually there by yourself, and he will go around into the back and go in. And some will just look around, see what looks like a good house, and if they don't see anyone in there, will just go into the house. They don't really care if you are in there or not. They don't give a hell if they meet you in the house. They'll fight. They take a chance of getting shot. If you have a toothache or are hungry, you take a chance. But there are some who are nasty people who just break into your house because they want to be rich. I don't have much sympathy for them.

Dope fiends are the best because the dope makes them think. Dope fiends are likely to watch your house carefully first, but also may just break in, without knowing if you are gone. . . . They have to steal maybe seven thousand dollars a year, so somebody has got to take the weight. The reason people do this is the underworld, the Mafia, and it is a big circle: you and me, we play the numbers, and they take the money in return, and they turn it over into narcotics, and then they put it into the street, and then someone gets a dope habit, and that same person comes right back around to us and robs us. So do we in fact cause the problem? If we don't contribute to the Mafia, they can't contribute to the problem. Every person thinks, well, my quarter didn't do that, didn't cause me to be robbed, but if everybody didn't give them no quarters, then no one would be robbed. It is not just the Mafia, but any criminalistical organization. The Mafia sounds Italian, and I don't think they are the only ones. There is a little black Mafia, an Italian Mafia, an Irish Mafia, a Jewish Mafia. Everybody got their own little Mafia. . . .

How can you protect yourself? Being friendly helps a lot. It helps with a regular thief who just wants to steal because he wants to get some money. I don't think that no one would want to break into a person's house if he or she is a friendly type of person, because thieves are people and they like people too, and if a person is really nice and kind to them, it really bothers them about stealing things from them. Some people can't help it, they'll steal anyway. A drug addict might break into your house anyway, but a drug addict will steal from his mother. But a regular thief—your chances are better by being friendly. . . .

Even with a junkie, being friendly will give you a 75 percent chance. Because a lot of times junkies would rather go rob somebody else than someone he really cares about. Even if you just stop and say hello to them on the street a few times, people care about you because you speak to them. Even that kind of person makes them feel good. Somebody will say, "Hey, that's my friend. You remember the lady I been talking to every day?" And they really don't be talking to you, they just be saying hi. This gives them a feeling that you like them because you speak. And everybody don't speak to them. So they might try, in most cases, not to rob you. The feeling and the urge would have to be a sensational burning in order for them to do it. Unless they're just the type of person who don't care about nobody, whether you speak to them or not. Like they're a beat freak, they want to beat everyone, take everything from everyone, they just don't care, they have no more feeling left in them. But if they have any type of morals left, they would begin to want to protect you from the other robbers. "Hey, man, don't rob that house, I've got another crib, man." They really think like that. A lot of junkies used to say, "George got nice things in his house." A lot of people wanted to rob my house. But nobody would do it. And I leave my door open a lot of time. . . .

And another thing. A lot of times people say, don't let no dope fiends into your house. You shouldn't let any dope fiend into your house, that's right. But you have to make them feel that you trust them a little bit. . . . Even an old lady who lives alone, if she is friendly, she is still better off than if she is not. If you mind your own business, never talk to anyone—that is bad. You don't have to let the dope addicts into the house, just do something nice for them, like bake a cake or something. That will last for two years. But there are people who gossip about who is doing what, and the criminals will get after them. And they will get after the adults they don't like in general. Some even put people in jail, and there they sit, planning their revenge for when they get out.

George and his family all feel very safe in Dover Square. George says that he "knows everybody" and is sure that no one will bother him or any of his friends or family. He is certain that anyone who claims to be a friend of his or comes to visit him will be immune from harm. He, unlike other young blacks, also does not think the Chinese are dangerous, probably because he knows far more than his peers about their culture and martial arts and has several Chinese friends. He even speaks a few words of street Chinese. Clearly, he is intimately connected to the social world of the street and familiar with its cultural patterns. I do not know whether he is right that the majority of project crime is committed by outsiders rather than locals, since I did not focus on who was responsible for what crimes. It is likely, however, that both outsiders and locals commit crime in the project. George clearly has an interest in playing down the criminal activities of his friends and emphasizing the baselessness of the accusations made by the neighbors he dislikes so intensely.

CHAPTER 4

A
Neighborhood
of
Strangers

Dover Square is a neighborhood in which residents continually encounter strangers. People who do not live in the development often use the laundromat or supermarket, park their cars in the courtyards and walk to their jobs downtown, or simply pass through the area. They are passersby, appearing in the project only fleetingly but never participating in its social life. They are the kind of strangers who, in Simmel's classic formulation, come today and go tomorrow (1950: 402–408). They are people who appear only for a moment, and then disappear never to return again.

Another kind of stranger inhabits Dover Square as well. This is the person who has lived next door or down the street as a neighbor for five or ten years, but who is still not known as an individual with a name or personal history. These people share public spaces, walkways, stores, and the laundromat with one another, yet remain anonymous. They continue to view one another only as members of social categories. This is the second kind of stranger Simmel describes: the person who comes today and stays tomorrow, but never becomes part of a social system. These are the people who are in a social system, but not of it. They may stay for a long time, but are potential wanderers, people who never give up their freedom to leave. In general, members of one ethnic group in Dover Square view members of other ethnic groups as this kind of stranger. Although well over half the families have lived together for ten years, they inhabit separate social worlds. Within each ethnic group are clusters of friends and kinsmen and paths of freely flowing communication, but be-

tween the groups the boundaries are sharp and social contacts rare. Because the groups are evenly dispersed throughout the project, people who live next door to each other
remain strangers. They use the same stores and laundromat
and traverse the same walkways, but their paths cross without touching.

Dover Square is not a community, in the sense of a cohesive local social unit to which residents feel identification and
belonging. By referring to it as a neighborhood, I describe
only its physical shape, not its social structure. It is more appropriate to analyze the social system in terms of social networks: the sets of social relationships that link individuals to
others in their social worlds (see Barnes 1954; Bott 1957;
Epstein 1961; Mitchell 1969; Boissevain 1974). Each person is
the center of a group of friends and kinsmen, and can be con-
ceptualized as a point from which radiate a series of links to
other people. This constellation forms an ego-centric social
network. Members of this network also know others, some of
whom the first person does not. These are second-order
links, friends of friends. By extension, each second-order link
also has social contacts, so that one can imagine a network of
social relationships extending outward from any individual
to first, second, and further orders of contact. Since these networks of relationship are also potential communication channels, mapping their structure and boundaries provides important clues to the flow of gossip and information through a
social system. Boundaries to social networks are likely to
form barriers to communication.

Each individual possesses two kinds of first-order network. One is his "intimate" network, a small set of close
friends, kinsmen, and people known personally and well. Ego
carries on regular social interaction with these people at a
high level of intimacy and trust. Members of these networks
generally share similar values and life styles since such consensus is usually a precondition to creating an intimate tie.
They also form the set of persons from whom allies and supporters are mobilized in times of crisis and conflict. The second kind of network is the "extended" network: a larger set
of neighbors and acquaintances who are known by name and
face, with whom ego engages in casual social interaction, but

who are not emotionally close. These networks often cut across differences in values, class, and life style and their constituent relationships carry no equivalent obligations of assistance or support. Nevertheless, they provide the same smooth communication channels characteristic of intimate networks.

Epstein makes a similar distinction between "effective" and "extended" networks (1961: 111). Those parts of an ego-centric network that are somewhat connected, in that their constituent members know each other, are the effective network, and those that lack this interconnection are the extended network. Effective networks consist of social equals; extended ones may cut across status boundaries. Although his criterion—connectedness—differs from the criteria I use—level of intimacy and trust, the content of the relationship, and the obligations of assistance—a high degree of connectedness generally accompanies my criteria. In general, intimate networks tend to be highly interconnected, extended ones much less so.

In Dover Square, intimate networks are almost always restricted to a single ethnic group. Extended networks cross-cut ethnic lines at a few points, but generally are also composed of people of the same ethnicity. A few individuals have intimate networks consisting almost entirely of a different ethnic group, such as the white youths who regularly hang out with the street blacks. Since each ethnic group is scattered throughout the area, the social organization of the project consists of a series of discrete, overarching social networks. One can imagine several layers of fishnet strung over the same space with a few threads running between the layers.

Gossip flows freely through both kinds of networks, passing from an individual to his second-, third-, and further-order links and circulating among first-order members who know one another. Judgmental gossip, which concerns events and evaluations of those events, depends upon some consensus about moral and immoral behavior and so more commonly circulates within intimate networks. Informational gossip, describing personalities and events, but devoid of judgments or interpretations of the meaning of these events, flows through extended as well as intimate networks (see Hannerz 1967). Judgmental gossip within an intimate network may deter rule-breaking; gossip within an extended network has less impact. Gossip in another network is usually a matter of greatest indifference to and has virtually no impact on the subject. When some of the black youths heard that they had reputations as notorious criminals among some Americanized Chinese, they were intrigued but unconcerned and made no effort to alter their behavior.

The social boundaries between ethnic groups persist because each group is encapsulated within a network of social relationships and set of institutions linked to nearby black, white, Chinese, and Hispanic communities (see Mayer 1961). The majority of families in the project regularly visit kinsmen, friends, churches, and social organizations in their nearby ethnic community. Jobs, friends, marriage partners, social services, and recreational opportunities are all primarily available within these communities. Consequently, relations with co-ethnics carry an expectation of continuity that is not characteristic of relations with neighbors in Dover Square. Neighbors are only temporary associates, here today but gone whenever they move away, while people in the same ethnic group are connected by enduring ties. The denser mesh of personal ties and group affiliations within ethnic groups means that Dover Square residents are far more accountable to their fellow ethnics than they are to their neighbors of different ethnicity.

THE CHINESE COMMUNITY

The pattern of encapsulation is most extreme for the Chinese residents. Because well over half of the adults speak little or no English, they are dependent on connections to Chinatown for access to jobs that do not require the ability to speak English. Chinatown provides opportunities for Chinese-language social services, recreational activities, religious services, and familiar foods. But even the younger generation, those born in America who speak excellent English, maintain close ties to the Chinese community in Chinatown and in Dover Square.

Chinatowns are traditionally cohesive, insular ethnic communities, a pattern of isolation developed in response to the pressures of American society, the immigration situation, and the "sojourner" pattern of immigration. Discriminatory U.S. legislation impeded Chinese immigration, while the hostile reaction of American society created encapsulated communities. The mob violence in California during the 1870s and 1880s drove immigrants out of agricultural, labor, mining, and railroad work into ghettos in large cities where they could protect themselves, and legislation passed by some states restricted Chinese access to some jobs, marriage to white women, and full legal rights in court. For the immigrant, security lay in maintaining close ties with kinsmen in Chinatown and in China, not in absorption into American society (Lee 1960; Sung 1967; Nee 1974).

Until the victory of the Chinese Communist Party on the mainland of China, most immigrants were "sojourners," adult males who came only for a temporary sojourn to send money home to their families in China, but planned to return to a life as the head of a prosperous family in the village. The bulk of Chinese immigrants to the U.S. (60 percent) came from Toishan, a tiny, mountainous district in Kwangtung Province near Canton City and Hong Kong in South China (Sung 1967: 10). The land is barren, rocky, and overpopulated, and remittances from men working overseas permitted their families to survive, perhaps to eat better than their neighbors, and maybe even to buy land in the village. Most immigrants expected to return to China and saw their trip as a necessary sacrifice for the good of the family. Consequently, they had neither the opportunity nor the incentive to learn English or to assimilate American culture. Their isolation was intensified by their retreat to inner-city ghettos in the late nineteenth century. A few rural Chinese fled to the cities of the East in this period; the Chinatown in the eastern city in which Dover Square is located was founded in 1875.

Discriminatory legislation stemmed the flow of legal immigrants, but a large number of Chinese arrived as illegal immigrants. These immigrants always felt insecure about their position in the U.S. The Chinese Exclusion Act of 1882 barred all Chinese laborers and allowed only officials, teachers, students, merchants, and travelers into the country. Although the act was repealed in 1943, it was replaced by a quota system that permitted only 105 Chinese immigrants annually, defining Chinese by race rather than by national origin. Only in 1965 were immigration restrictions on Chinese relaxed. Before 1965, Chinese immigrants were admitted if they were the children of citizens, however, and if their father had lived in the United States. This loophole inspired the widespread use of the "slot" system, in which young men pretended to be the legitimate children of citizens in order to gain entry to the country. A United States citizen could declare the birth of children in China, who thereby became citizens and eligible for immigration. Many citizens used this provision to bring in other youths as their children, as their "paper sons." Every time a citizen returned to China, he could register the birth of a child. Daughters' births were recorded as sons. The citizen then returned to China several years later and brought his teenage "son" to the United States. U.S. immigration officials, aware of the system, grilled each immigrant intensely concerning his identity, which forced the paper sons to memorize minute details of their false identity and subjected them to a grueling and frightening interrogation process.

The slot system intensified the encapsulation and isolation of the Chinese community, since the paper son was never quite at ease in the United States, fearing always that he would be discovered and repatriated. Paper sons strove to avoid American police and courts and were reluctant to protest or make demands on American society. An exposé of the system in San Francisco's Chinatown in 1957 revealed that possibly half of the residents of Chinatown were paper sons (Lee 1960: 309). By the mid-1970s, however, the Chinese community in the U.S. was far less isolated than it had been thirty years before. The relaxation of immigration restrictions, particularly against women, after World War II, permitted normal family life for the first time and produced the first substantial population of American-born Chinese. Further, the victory of the Chinese Communist Party in 1949 made it impossible for many immigrants to think of returning home and forced them to consider the U.S. as their permanent home. The traditional Chinatown establishment has far less control over the American Chinese than it has over their China-born parents. American Chinese frequently move to the suburbs and take white-collar jobs that they can find without relying on the Chinatown leaders. For the older immigrants who speak little or no English, however, the situation is not so different from that of the early twentieth century. They are still dependent on the Chinatown establishment for jobs, social services, and, to some extent, housing, if they wish to settle in Chinatown.

The relaxation of immigration restrictions in 1965 resulted in a wave of immigration equal in size to that of the peak years of the 1870s. These immigrants inundated the local Chinatown, increasing its population by 51 percent between 1960 and 1970 according to a local study. Although one-third of these immigrants were trained professional and technical workers, usually able to speak English, the bulk of the immigrants had few skills and no English-language ability. Even those who were skilled workers in Hong Kong were restricted to jobs in Chinese restaurants or in garment factories. Those who had professional skills and the ability to speak English quickly moved to the suburbs and found good jobs, but those who lacked these advantages were again dependent on Chinatown. Many were very poor, lived in overcrowded, deteriorating housing in Chinatown and worked such long hours that they were unable to learn English. They were encapsulated not because they planned to return home, but because they knew no English. Some of the young people, desperate to escape a dismal future in low-paying, dead-end restaurant work, became involved in crime and street gangs.

The Chinatown in this city is the fourth largest in the country. It is politically dominated by a small group of merchants, immigrants from Toishan province in the early twentieth century, who now control the major restaurants, stores, and bakeries. They comprise the Chinatown Merchants' Association, which is the core of the Chinatown Consolidated Benevolent Association, officially an umbrella organization representing all the groups in Chinatown. The merchants also have close ties to the city government, since the local representative of city hall has to be approved by the Benevolent

Association. He delivers the Chinatown vote to the mayor in exchange for having city services channeled through him. The mayor recently appointed a member of a powerful merchant family to a high-paying city job, and was rewarded with a landslide victory in Chinatown in the latest election.

In most cases, however, the benefits of these contacts accrue to the merchants rather than to poor workers. The merchants are particularly eager to attract tourists to Chinatown, and it is rumored that they pay a private protection force to guard the security of their restaurants. Rumors also circulate that Benevolent Association elections are rigged and that, in the last one, one of the candidates paid three dollars to each person who voted for him. The other important organizations in Chinatown are the family associations, the Koumintang, whose membership overlaps that of the Merchants' Association, several Chinese Christian churches, and two martial arts–athletic clubs. The residential basis of Chinatown is being slowly but inexorably eroded by downtown development, however, and it is becoming only a social and economic center for Chinese families scattered throughout the city. None of the leaders of the Merchants' Association now lives in Chinatown. Recent immigrants desperate to live near Chinatown are forced into deteriorating apartments in James Hill while they try to wangle an apartment in Dover Square or Chinatown.

The economic dependence of Dover Square's Chinese population on connections to Chinatown is extreme. According to the information provided on applications for housing at the management office, 86 percent of all Chinese households are supported by someone working in a Chinese restaurant, grocery, or shop. Two or three Chinese families run laundries. The second generation of American-born Chinese usually earn college degrees and move into white-collar jobs such as accounting, drafting, or engineering. Consequently, they are far less dependent than their parents on connections to Chinatown for jobs. Most Chinese women who work are employed in the garment industry as stitchers. Of the 65 percent of Chinese wives who are employed, 89 percent work as stitchers, 5 percent in other manual occupations, and 6 percent in white-collar or professional activities, but even this 6 percent tend to work in Chinese-language schools, teach bilingual education in the Chinatown schools, or work in a Chinatown organization.

Both men and women receive low pay for long hours of work. Restaurant workers are paid very little in wages, but make a substantial amount of their incomes in tips. Although tips may be as high as fifty dollars on a weekend in a good restaurant, they are lower at other times. Regular pay is about one hundred dollars a week. Work as a waiter or cook often lasts nine or ten hours a day, six days a week. Restaurants generally provide no retirement benefits, disability insurance, or job security. Present salaries must provide for the years of retirement as well. One man continued at the same restaurant for seven years rather than changing every two or three years, the more common pattern, in hopes of earning some job security. However, after he broke his leg and was forced to leave the job for a prolonged period, he found that his employer was no longer willing to rehire him. He had to live off his savings and his wife's earnings. With the tremendous increase in migration from Hong Kong since the mid-1960s, the labor market has been flooded with people desperate for a job that does not require English. Their availability keeps down wages and makes it difficult for workers who have been in the U.S. longer to demand better working conditions or more job security. Poverty and a lack of job security mean that Chinese men must maintain close connections to Chinatown so that, in the event that they lose one job, they can quickly find another.

Those restaurant workers who are able to save try to invest in their own Chinese restaurant. Three or four partners usually pool their capital to open a restaurant, and rely on the labor of family members to run it. In short, close ties with friends and relatives in and near Chinatown provide the only real hope of financial success and escape from the long hours and low pay of work as a waiter or cook for an immigrant without a good American education.

Women working in the garment industry also earn little, and have no hope for advancement or increased income. Since they also speak little or no English, they have few alternatives. Most garment workers do piecework, receiving only one hundred dollars a week or less, depending on how fast they can sew and how much work is available in the factory. The work is uncertain, and a company may experience periods when they have little work for any of their employees. Some women bring work home to do on the home machine or to prepare for the next day. A few women are able to do piecework at home, but most go to the factory, leaving their children with an older relative, if possible. The woman who has neither a mother nor a mother-in-law living with her must stay home or leave her children alone all day.

Thus, Chinese men and women face restricted job opportunities because of their inability to speak English and their lack of marketable skills. Moreover, both men and women are dependent on proximity to Chinatown to get to their work. Few people in the older generation own cars or can drive. Although most of the restaurants are in the suburbs, the owners provide vans that drive their workers out to the restaurant and back every day. The employer picks up the workers in the center of Chinatown and delivers them late at night back to their doorsteps. The garment factories are all either in Chinatown or close by in the downtown area, easily accessible by subway from Chinatown. A move to the suburbs means that one must either learn to drive and buy a car, or spend more time and money commuting. Both time and money are in short supply.

The Chinese families in Dover Square are inevitably connected to Chinatown not only for economic needs, but also for medical and legal services, and for social, recreational, and religious activities. Men seeking better restaurant jobs spend their day off in Chinatown talking with friends and potential employers about job possibilities. Banks in Chinatown have Chinese-speaking tellers, and one of the family associations has formed a credit union for its members. Anyone who wishes to buy familiar Chinese foods and other products must shop in Chinatown. Someone with medical problems can visit a Chinese druggist or go to a Chinese community health clinic or Chinese doctor or dentist. A person with legal problems can consult a Chinese lawyer or the Chinese-speaking manager of the Chinatown branch of city hall. Every wedding is solemnized by a major banquet for as many as five hundred people in a downtown Chinatown restaurant if the family can afford it. These banquets are a major event in the social life of Chinatown. Family associations also have annual banquets and community groups sponsor outings. For those who enjoy gambling, there are several gambling dens tucked into the corners and basements of Chinatown shops and buildings. An old-age center caters to the needs of elderly Chinese. Those who wish to worship at a Catholic or a Protestant church find both in Chinatown. Parents who wish their children to learn Chinese send them to the Chinese school in Chinatown daily. Even English-speaking young people go to Chinatown to participate in the Boy's Club, the YMCA, summer youth programs, and the two martial arts clubs.

The Chinese population of Dover Square can be roughly divided into four different categories. The first are those families who are of Toishanese peasant ancestry who have been in the country for many years and have succeeded in business. They own restaurants or shops, and are fairly wealthy. These families sooner or later move to prestigious suburbs and buy expensive homes. At least ten, but probably more, families fit into this category.

A second group are those Toishanese immigrants, such as the Wongs, who are still working as waiters, cooks, and stitchers. Their children generally have college educations and white-collar jobs. Based on my own contacts and the evidence from office records, I estimate that well over half the Chinese population of Dover Square fits into this category. Most adults in these families speak little or no English, but their children speak native English. Among these families, those with the greatest respect and prestige are those who are leaders in Chinatown organizations, those who are successful in business, and those who are educated, either in China or in the United States. I knew at least four families in Dover Square whose male heads immigrated as paper sons.

The American-born children of these Toishanese restaurant workers are very Americanized. They speak little Chinese, a source of embarrassment to them and irritation to their parents. Since they grew up with parents who worked long hours in restaurants and garment factories, they socialized mainly with peer groups who spoke English. These children feel tremendous pressure from their parents to get a college education and a good, secure job. Their parents feel that they have sacrificed themselves so that their children can have a better life. The effect of American education and peer group social life is to pull the child away from his parents, however, so that he is culturally isolated and has difficulty communicating with them. The generation gap assumes awesome proportions. Parents are eager to have their children learn Chinese and try to send them to Chinese school in addition to regular school, but few succeed in keeping their children in Chinese school long enough for them to develop any real proficiency in Chinese. For children who are academically successful, the expectations are not overly oppressive, but for others, they can be overwhelming. One young man dropped out of college, but hid the fact from his parents for months, working every day in a warehouse, but telling them he was going to school. The great majority of the children of Toishanese parents who live in Dover Square do go to college, many to elite private colleges on scholarships. A few have advanced degrees, usually in science, medicine, or engineering. It is often difficult for a young American-born Chinese to explain to his parents that a college degree is not a guarantee of a secure, high-paying job.

The third category of Dover Square Chinese are the more recent immigrants from Hong Kong who have professional skills and speak English. Only two or three such families live in Dover Square.

Finally, there are poor immigrants from Hong Kong who have arrived in the last ten years, but lack these advantages. They often live crammed into apartments with relatives until they can find a place of their own. Their children may have difficulty adjusting in school. Because of their parents' long working hours, the children turn to their peers on the street for help and sociability. About one-third of the Dover Square Chinese residents are more recent, less-skilled Hong Kong emigrants.

These recent immigrants differ substantially from the established Chinatown population of Toishanese, who came from a peasant background and were able to maintain their rural values and modes of behavior in the small, isolated Chinatown. The new immigrants are from Hong Kong, an urbane, sophisticated city. Although some are originally Toishanese who fled to Hong Kong, they lived for many years in the city. They speak Cantonese rather than Toishanese, which is a village dialect of Cantonese. One Cantonese speaker described Toishanese as an "inferior, slummy, more primitive language, good for cursing at people." The dialects are not easily mutually intelligible. The Hong Kong emigrants find American Chinatowns very conservative, even more so than rural China today. An example is the case of a young man who went to Hong Kong to find a traditional Chinese wife because he found American Chinese women too independent. He wanted a wife who would accept living with his parents. When he returned to the U.S. with his "traditional" wife, however, he soon discovered that she was not accustomed to couples living with the husband's parents, and had no intention herself of living in this conservative fashion. They soon moved away from his family.

For all Chinese residents in Dover Square, kinship is the most important social relationship. A few kinship ties cut across the division between groups of Chinese. Established Toishanese families sometimes help their relatives who have lived for ten or twenty years in Hong Kong to move to the U.S. Occasionally, an American Chinese man returns to Hong Kong to find a bride. The woman then hopes to bring her own family over from Hong Kong once she is established in the U.S. One Toishanese descendant in Dover Square married a Hong Kong woman who then helped her mother, father, and five brothers and sisters immigrate to the United States. Otherwise, the Toishanese and Cantonese populations tend to remain separate.

At least one-third of Dover Square families are kinsmen to another family living in the project. I am aware of at least twenty families in which separate segments of the extended family live in two or even three different apartments in the project. In at least four cases, the child of a Dover Square family married and moved into his own apartment in the project.

Chinese families have achieved this density of kin links within the project in spite of a management policy of admitting new tenants on the basis of need and position on the waiting list. The list is long, and the wait for a two-bedroom apartment may be two years. The wait for a larger apartment is even longer. This management policy admits strangers rather than friends or kinsmen to the project. Nevertheless, residents of all ethnic groups have developed techniques for circumventing management policy and settling their friends and relatives in nearby apartments. One technique is squatting. When one family moves out, another moves in without informing the office. When confronted with a *fait accompli*, the management lets the new family stay. In the last year, two families successfully squatted and moved into a new apartment close to their relatives. One family was black, the other Hispanic.

The second technique is an extended version of squatting. One family gradually moves in with another, while the other moves out slowly, so that there is never a conspicuous shift of goods, furniture, or people. A third approach is to call the office the minute one learns that an apartment will become available and to use personal influence to persuade the manager to allow a friend or relative to move in ahead of his turn on the waiting list. A fourth approach is to bribe an employee in the office either to get an apartment or to have the application put higher on the waiting list. Although I know of only a few cases where I am sure this transaction took place, Chinese residents believe the practice is widespread, particularly in the past. The demand for housing near Chinatown is intense, so that those who have more wealth or better kinship connections to residents in the project take advantage of these assets.

Chinese family units in Dover Square are largely nuclear, according to the application forms. (This source of data, however, may exaggerate the number of nuclear households, since the government restricts the number of individuals who may occupy an apartment, based on the number of bedrooms available.) I was able to cross-check the data for the families I knew, and I found it to be essentially accurate, although severe overcrowding is more likely to occur among recent immigrants from Hong Kong than among established Toishanese families, who provided most of my contacts. Of-

fice records indicate that 73 percent of the families are nuclear and 22 percent are nuclear with additional agnatic or
uterine relatives. Of the families with additional relatives,
three-fourths are agnatic kinsmen and one-fourth uterine,
suggesting that the traditional patrilocal residence pattern
persists.* Eleven percent of the families have a husband's parent in the household and only 3 percent have a co-resident
parent of the wife. Only 1 percent of the families has a female
head, and most of these are widows. Two percent have single
male heads of house.

Another tie uniting Chinese residents is that between
residents of the same village in China. This binds only Toishanese peasant villagers. At least two families that I know
of in the project are related to one another through such a
tie and regularly attend each other's weddings and birthday
celebrations. Families with the same surname belong to the
same family association, and occasionally engage in common
social activities. Marriage within this group is still considered
incestuous.

Other important social relationships link together Chinese residents. A few families who were neighbors in Chinatown formed lasting friendships and moved to the project
together when their homes in Chinatown were destroyed.
One-third of the families moved in from Chinatown, one-
third from James Hill. Both men and women form friendships
with their neighbors at work. Women gossip and exchange
stories of crime over their sewing machines, while men talk
in the restaurants. Two women refused to move out of the
project despite their anxiety over crime because they had so
many friends there. At the wedding of the Wongs' daughter,
they found that their Dover Square friends were more helpful
than their relatives. Since many men and women play mah-

---

*Kinship ties between women may be assuming increasing importance,
however. Of those twelve cases of multiple family segments living in different apartments in the project, four are agnatically related and eight
are related through uterine ties. Although this data is hardly conclusive, it
suggests that patrilocal ideology influences co-residence decisions, while
uterine ties are important in decisions about where to find a separate
apartment.

jongg in different apartments in the project, they develop circles of mah-jongg friends. Young people make friends in school and in Chinese youth clubs.

Thus, the Chinese community is knitted together by several kinds of social relationships. Although different categories of Chinese live in the project, extended networks frequently cut across the divisions. Communication about reputations and identities flows freely through the extended social networks of the Chinese community. Further, all Chinese residents are connected to and more or less dependent upon the institutions of Chinatown for jobs, social services, and important social relationships. Relations with these institutions are enduring even if individuals move from one neighborhood to another. The result is that Chinese residents are encapsulated in Chinatown's social and institutional structure, which inhibits their freedom to flaunt public opinion or desert the community.

THE BLACK COMMUNITY

The black population of Dover Square can be roughly divided into three groups: the respectable families who work for a living and value a cohesive family life, marital stability, and steady work; the hustler families who are generally poorer and struggle to survive through legal and illegal means; and the street youths, young people who regularly socialize together and live by crime and hustling.

Those who like to think of themselves as respectable make up about three-fourths of all the black families. Generally, they are supported by a male head of house who works, and they condemn their neighbors who hustle rather than work. They strive to keep their children away from the street youths who lounge conspicuously in the playground, but are not always successful. For many of these families, the church is a central focus of social life. But, because they attend a wide variety of churches in James Hill and Winslow, the neighboring black community, rather than one local church, their common interest has not made them a cohesive social group. Smaller networks of friends make up subdivisions within the group, and there are about ten respectable families who are completely socially isolated.

The other families, which I have labeled hustlers because that is the term they use for the variety of quasi-legal and illegal strategies they adopt to make a living, constitute one-quarter of the black families. They are generally poorer than the respectable families. Some of the parents did illegal things in the past, while a few are currently engaged in gambling, prostitution, or fencing stolen goods. Those heads of household who work generally hold uncertain, unreliable, and low-paying jobs, often in custodial, food, or domestic services. Others earn a marginal existence through welfare payments supplemented by other forms of hustling, a pattern among very poor families also noted by Valentine (1978). Although they rarely form close friendships with the youths who hang out in the playground, the hustler families are, if not necessarily approving, at least friendly and sympathetic toward them. They tend to look the other way when their children commit crimes. Most of the street youths come from hustler families.

Both the respectable and hustler categories include families that live on welfare and are headed by women. Some women who raise their children on welfare are able to maintain a position in the respectable social circle and keep their children away from the street group. Others find themselves unable to counteract the attractions the street has for their children. The following incident clearly illustrates the pressures faced by poor parents:

> One youth began his career in crime at the age of thirteen when he was hanging with his fifteen-year-old friends on Christmas Eve. The meager welfare payments that supported his mother and his eight brothers and sisters had not provided any surplus for Christmas presents. His friends had attempted to rob a few drunks that evening, but without success; being unusually persistent, this youth decided to try a different pocket on a particularly inebriated man. To his glee, he found a roll of bills totaling three hundred dollars. His perspicacity

not only won him considerable prestige among his friends but also made it possible for his family to have a bountiful Christmas. His mother accepted his story that he had found the money, and he was able to give generous cash gifts to his mother and all of his siblings.

The street group, between twenty and thirty young blacks aged fourteen to twenty-five, are convinced that there are more pleasant and profitable ways of life than the drudgery of a steady job. They support themselves through a variety of activities such as pimping, prostitution, drug pushing, selling marijuana, gambling, burglary, purse snatching, pocket picking, and robbery. Occasionally, one of them will take a job, but only as an interim arrangement, not as a permanent commitment. The respectable families hope to achieve security through monotonous work, but these youths hope for quick wealth through a legitimate business, such as a night club, dry cleaning or clothing store, or through some form of illegal hustle. They consider themselves "down"; those who work are "straight" and not very clever. The respectable families call these youths the "fast crowd."

They constitute a dense, interconnected social network of individuals who have grown up together, have fallen in love with each other, sired one another's children, and become one another's mortal enemies. They spend many hours lounging together, in the playground in the summer, in the laundromat in the winter, and will help each other in times of crisis, particularly when help means participating in an exciting street fight. When they go to night clubs or parties, they generally go to James Hill or Winslow. Several members have relatives in James Hill or Winslow. The group's boundary is fuzzy: at the periphery are people who join and leave at different times. Residents of public housing projects in James Hill and Winslow residents occasionally join the Dover Square group. Not everyone in the group is black: two whites, two Chinese, and two Hispanics more or less regularly hang out with them.

Project crime is commonly blamed on the street group. Since I did not examine in detail who committed what crimes, in part because this kind of an investigation would

have awakened serious suspicions that I was working for the
police department, I do not know if it is true that these
youths are responsible for all the crime in the project. On the
one hand, it is clear that some of the local crime is committed
by outsiders who do not live in the project or socialize there.
On the other hand, some of these youths claim credit for several of the more famous crimes and acknowledge that they
have masterminded burglary rings in the project in the past.

In this neighborhood, street crime, prostitution, and
other forms of hustling are part of the cultural repertoire of
the black residents. Whites and Chinese also commit crimes,
but typically become involved in other activities such as car
theft, fraud, gambling, drug traffic, and the numbers racket.
Street crime and prostitution are demanding, complex activities and, like other occupational skills, the proper techniques and strategies are learned through social networks.
After committing a crime, a youth usually runs back to the
hangout and breathlessly recreates the experience for his
friends. They discuss the event and provide useful advice.
Friends exchange street lore about how to choose good robbery locations, how to pinpoint a victim, how to escape the
police, how to avoid a sentence, which crimes earn severe
sentences and which do not, how to handle partners who
steal from you, and which neighbors are likely to call the police. One young man, for example, decided that robbing elderly people was dangerous because they are so fragile that
they might fall down and injure themselves, increasing his
sentence for the robbery. He recommends trying to avoid hitting or kicking a victim since, he thinks, this changes the
charge from a misdemeanor to a felony.

It is important to recognize that the street group represents a relatively small proportion of the blacks in the project. At most, it contains no more than thirty or thirty-five individuals, but the core contains only about twenty males and
females. Of these, ten are sufficiently active in criminal activities to have been arrested and sentenced, while another
eleven are involved in prostitution or pimping. Although the
group is predominantly black, among those who actually
have been arrested or who claim to have committed street
crimes are seven blacks, two whites, and one Chinese; among

those active in prostitution are eight blacks, one Chinese, one white, and one Hispanic. Many of these youths take drugs, principally heroin, but also Valium and marijuana. The fifteen black youths come from eight different project families—in other words, from only 10 percent of the black families in the project. The whites come from two different families, as do the Chinese. Not all black families have children, but of those who do, only one-third have children who are in any way associated with the street group. In the vast majority of black families neither the parents nor the children are involved in hustling.

Further, for many youths, involvement in crime is only a passing, teenage phase. Of the nine black youths most active in crime a few years ago, one is now in the army, two are in school, and two are seeking some legitimate way to live a comfortable and easy life. Four are still committing crimes and are in and out of jail, but only one of these says that he plans to spend the rest of his life in crime. As they move into their mid-twenties, many of these youths abandon the hazardous and strenuous life of street crime.

Most of the youths currently involved in crime come from troubled families. In one family, for example, both parents were alcoholics and the father regularly beat his wife. The wife eventually left and is now a wandering drunk in another part of the city. The father works nights and does little to supervise his children. The older boy is a junkie and has been convicted for stealing, the younger is a transvestite prostitute whose "tricks" call him at home because his father is oblivious to his behavior and easily fooled. In another family, the father, a maintenance man and rent collector, regularly cheated his employer by accepting bribes to reserve apartments and putting his hand into the till on rent day. These activities, as well as a series of burglaries committed by his son, eventually got him fired. Still, the parents have had a relatively stable marriage. According to the neighbors, whenever their children got into trouble with the law, the mother always managed to get them out. Of the nine children, only one is committed to a life of crime. This boy believes that his father was abused and exploited by whites and views his criminal activity as a kind of retaliation for this humiliation.

He has been in jail off and on for the last three years and is firmly convinced that he will continue to survive by stealing. Another child was a criminal, but in his late twenties has decided to try a different way of life. A third family consists of a single woman striving to raise nine children alone on welfare. One daughter has become a prostitute, and a son has been a burglar, although he claims he now wants to stop; the other seven children are not involved in illegal activities. In a fourth family, the father lives in another town and the children were raised by the father's mother. While her three grandchildren were growing up, she was frequently away from home, working as a domestic servant for a wealthy, politically powerful family. Through the intervention of her employer, she was often able to extricate her grandson from numerous scrapes with the law. Many of her neighbors agree that this spoiled the boy, who learned that he could do wrong and get away with it. She gradually found that she could not control him. Similarly, in a fifth family, a woman whose mother was never home, because the mother was always gone from early morning until late at night working as a domestic for a white family, became a prostitute for a few wealthy men. Because she felt so deserted by a mother who left her breakfast and dinner, but was never there, she was determined to be home for her own children. Nevertheless, one of her daughters became a prostitute, a junkie, and, at the age of fourteen, a mother.

In a sixth family, another grandmother, also the father's mother, is raising a teenage boy on her own. She stays home on welfare, but despairs of being able to control him. When neighbors confront her with his misconduct, she denies that he ever does anything wrong and claims that he is innocent and maligned. At fifteen years old, he is beginning to explore the titillating world of drugs, prostitution, and crime. He knows that he can do what he wants with impunity.

In the white family with two boys active in crime, the mother never adapted to the move, forced on her by urban renewal, from her old neighborhood in James Hill. After several years of illness and grief in Dover Square, she died, leaving her husband to deal with the problems of two teenage boys. His alcoholism exacerbated the situation. Another

white family, in which a daughter became a prostitute, consists of a deaf husband and a deaf and dumb wife who are unable to protect their daughter from the influences of the
street life around them. She worked for a black pimp who
lived in the project and beat her mercilessly, until she committed suicide at the age of twenty by jumping off a building.

This survey of the family situations of most of the youths
active in local crime reveals recurring patterns of alcoholism,
parental illegal activities, overindulgence, and extreme poverty. But we deceive ourselves if we view these families as
typical "low-income black families." In fact, they represent
the kind of social failure that occurs in every class and ethnic
group, exacerbated in Dover Square by the pressures of long
working hours, a shortage of money, and the ever-present
temptations of the street and the fast life. These families are
considered atypical and troubled even by their black neighbors in this community.

Although the respectable families, the hustlers, and the
street youths each pursue a distinct style of life and create
separate social networks, they are aware of the identities
of members of other groups. Intimate networks are restricted
to these subgroups, but extended networks frequently cut
across the divisions, allowing information about reputations
and identities to flow easily between the subgroups. When
one of the leaders of the street group was released from jail,
for example, Mr. Johnson, a respectable black, said hello to
him, but then went home and warned his family to take additional precautions against burglary. All of the other respectable black adults I talked to could recognize and identify
members of the street group and knew something of their
reputations and family situations. The street youths, in turn,
know half to two-thirds of the respectable adults and almost
all of the hustler adults. A few kin ties even cut across the
boundary between respectable families and street youths.
One woman in the respectable group has raised three children who socialize exclusively with the street youths. In
three other families, only one child out of many has deserted
the respectable social world to hang with the playground
group. Most of the children who do not belong to the street
group know these youths and feel a mixture of admiration,

envy, and disdain towards them. The street youths are prominent and highly visible personalities on the local social scene,
lounging in public areas such as the playground and laundromat and displaying both wealth and self-assurance. George
Williams is typical of this group and one of its leading
members.

The black population of Dover Square is knitted together by a web of kin ties and friendships formed before
they moved into the project. At least one-fifth of the families
have kin living elsewhere in the project. According to office
records, 44 percent of the families have both a husband
and wife co-resident; half are headed by a mother or several
women who are related to each other and who cooperate in
childraising. In two families, the mother's brother is an active
participant; in one case, he actually lives in another apartment in Dover Square. Most of the hustler families have single parents, but not all single-parent families are hustlers nor
are all their children members of the street group. Six children, five of them daughters and one a son, have settled their
families in other apartments in Dover Square. At least nine
families brought with them friendships formed when they
were neighbors in James Hill. Altogether, 45 percent of the
black families in Dover Square came from James Hill and another 48 percent from Winslow, so that many more than I
have documented may have known one another before they
moved in.

Thus, black families in Dover Square belong to social
networks that extend to James Hill and to Winslow, and they
participate in the institutions of these two communities. But
Dover Square's blacks are less dependent on institutions in
neighboring communities than the project's Chinese residents are dependent on Chinatown. Dover Square's black
population can be divided into three subgroups according to
their social characteristics, but kinship ties, previous acquaintance, and familiarity from being former neighbors cross-cut
these divisions. Members of each subgroup know the identities and reputations of at least some of the members of other
subgroups, and through their extended networks have access
to information about all the black families living in the
project.

THE WHITE COMMUNITY

The white population is more diverse and less interrelated than either the blacks or the Chinese. About fifteen families, more than one-third of the white families in the project, are Syrian-Lebanese who have moved from James Hill. They maintain close ties with their friends and kinsmen in James Hill. For example, one woman visits her parents and ten brothers and sisters every day, another regrets that she ever left the James Hill street where she grew up and where all her friends and family still live, and a third youth called on his James Hill friends as allies when he was attacked by a group of Dover Square black youths. The Maloofs are typical of those who retain strong loyalties to their old ethnic neighborhood in James Hill. These families return to the Syrian-Lebanese community to visit, shop, and attend church and social clubs. Most are second- and third-generation descendants of immigrants who arrived at the turn of the century and settled in an area that is now part of either Chinatown or Dover Square. The rest of the families are a potpourri of white ethnics: eight Irish, three Italian, one Greek, one Jewish, one Australian, and ten other families. When it first opened, the project attracted a group of more educated, middle-class whites who were active in community organizing efforts, but with the waning of the inner-city esprit de corps of the 1960s, all have moved out.

The white families are a shrinking minority. Since the project opened, over half the white families have moved out and the proportion of whites has fallen from 30 percent to 12 percent. In 1975–1976, five white families and two black-white families moved away while three black, eleven Chinese, and no white families moved in. Only five white families moved in during the 1970s. Several of the remaining white families talk about leaving, but many cannot afford to. Those who are left feel that they are living in an increasingly alien environment. Those contemplating departure tend to withdraw from participation in local affairs and abandon their efforts to grapple with the project's intractable social and economic problems, which seriously weakens the already frail structure of community organization. The families most satisfied with the project are the Syrian-Lebanese residents who have lived in James Hill all of their lives and have friends and kinsmen nearby. They realize that Dover Square provides good housing at lower prices than James Hill, yet located near enough to participate in James Hill's social world.

Unlike the blacks and the Chinese, few kinship ties unite the white families, nor do their grown children settle in the project. An aged mother moved in to be close to her daughter, but no other parent-child pair lives in Dover Square. An aunt and a niece occupy nearby apartments, and two cousins live in separate apartments, but all of these are Syrian-Lebanese families from James Hill. The failure to settle adult children in the project underscores whites' intentions not to remain, as well as the greater availability of good housing for whites elsewhere in the city. Many of the whites are older couples or single individuals living alone. Two-thirds have no children in the house, in contrast to 46 percent of Chinese families, 33 percent of the black families, and none of the Hispanic families. Forty-four percent of the white families have both a husband and wife at home, 42 percent are headed by women, and 12 percent are headed by men alone. These proportions are roughly the same as those of black families, and, as is true of blacks, between 10 percent and 20 percent of the female-headed households are the result of the husband's death. The few white youths in the project socialize either with the street group or with friends outside the project. Many of the whites who moved in from James Hill, about half of the white families, maintain pre-existing social ties from that neighborhood and return for its recreational and social activities, but the other half are from neighborhoods all over the city and suburbs. They brought no kin or friends with them and now retain connections with a wide variety of neighborhoods all over the city. Many have children living in the suburbs or in other cities.

Thus, the white community is less interconnected than either the Chinese or the black community. Most whites feel they are a beleaguered and isolated minority. For the Syrian-Lebanese there is a nearby ethnic community, James Hill, with which they maintain enduring relationships and intimate, non-localized social networks, but they and other whites have found little incentive to create or maintain close ties with their non-white or even white neighbors who are not fellow ethnics. They are here today, but expect to be gone tomorrow.

RELATIONS BETWEEN ETHNIC GROUPS

Social boundaries between the ethnic groups are sharp and persistent. No common institutional affiliations cross-cut these lines except for the Catholic Church, which draws together a few respectable black families and some whites, and the tenants' association, which similarly incorporates a few activist whites, blacks, and Chinese. Otherwise, friendships or shared group affiliations are rare. The major exception is the street group, which has a multi-ethnic composition and is characterized by intimate social ties. Even though two-thirds of the children in the project attended the same elementary school before the onset of school busing, they rarely formed lasting friendships there. Curriculum tracking further separated the groups. One Chinese woman, for example, was amazed to find that she had gone to the same school with a notorious leader of the street group whom she thought she had never met before. By high-school age, project children are scattered throughout the city: in elite schools that have entrance exams, in trade schools, in parochial schools, or in suburban schools that they can attend through a voluntary busing program. Different ethnic groups tend to go to different schools. Busing will probably accentuate this situation.

The only organization that united members of all ethnic groups was the original tenants' association, created soon after the project opened. Led by activist white liberals and respectable blacks, it drew in Chinese and Hispanic participants as well. Fifty or sixty people participated in committees that focused on tenant-management relations, or on recreation, or published a community newsletter in English, Spanish, and Chinese. Leaders organized block parties and led political struggles against the management about rent increases, poor maintenance, and the right to own washing machines and dogs. In 1971, one-fifth of the families participated in a battle against a rent increase.

During the mid-1970s, however, this association deteriorated. The original leaders moved out and the mood of optimism dissipated. Meetings rarely occurred and were attended by only ten to fifteen whites and blacks. In 1975, an effort to appoint representatives from each courtyard produced only white volunteers. The association appeared unable to enlist the joint participation of the Chinese residents, a fatal problem as the proportion of Chinese increased. One meeting in 1976, about a steep rent increase, did draw together whites, blacks, and Chinese and was conducted in both Chinese and English, but it ended up with a stormy confrontation between a large, domineering black woman and an aggressive young American-Chinese woman who took over the meeting. Some of the white and black leaders expressed resentment that the proceedings were translated into Chinese and felt uneasy that they could not understand what was being said. They soon withdrew from the group. At a second meeting a month later, two-thirds of those who attended were Chinese. Two whites and a scattering of blacks appeared, but none of the white or black leaders of the tenants' association came. They were not interested in a group in which the Chinese assumed a leading role and their own position was marginal. Their deep suspicion of the Chinese was revealed by a rumor circulating among whites and blacks that a small meeting organized to discuss security problems among Chinese residents was actually an effort to establish a separate tenants' association exclusively for Chinese. By the end of 1976, there were no more meetings, and the tenants' association appeared defunct. Even a sharp increase in the rent had failed to generate common activity to resist it, largely because of the enormous difficulty of political organization across a sharp language barrier and a deep gulf of suspicion and distrust bridged by few lines of communication or social contact.

No leaders have emerged who are recognized by all ethnic groups. When I asked people who the leaders in the community were, each person mentioned someone prominent in his own ethnic group, usually in his own subdivision of the ethnic group. Young blacks mentioned a prominent young black; older blacks and whites mentioned a well-known white woman. Local leaders have not emerged even from the representatives elected to speak for Dover Square on the James Hill urban renewal board. This organization has been in existence for about ten years. Although Chinese, blacks, and whites have been elected to the board, and although board membership is recognized as a leadership role by all residents, who expect these representatives to do something for the neighborhood, no one has turned it into an effective political position. The Chinese representatives, all of whom have been young American-born college-educated men and women, have all dropped out of the organization and of other community organizing efforts because of other demands on their time. Older Chinese people, who have more time, have been prevented from assuming leadership roles because of their lack of knowledge of English and of the workings of American institutions. Thus, even the tenants' association cannot act as an effective bridge between ethnic groups, a mechanism for one group to reach, learn about, and potentially control the behavior of other groups.

The management of the project has also failed to serve as a political center for all the ethnic groups or as a broker for settling disputes between individuals in different ethnic groups. Although the first manager was quite interested and involved in the community, he left after four years, and the subsequent managers have seen their role as a custodial one. There has been a rapid turnover of managers, with four different men holding the job in the last six years. All of the managers have been white males; none has been able to speak either Spanish or Chinese. None has lived in the area. One man continually warned me about walking around "down here" even in the daytime, implying that the project was a jungle unsafe for young women even in broad daylight. He cited his own training in the Green Berets, which he felt prepared him for dealing with the dangers of this environment. He also advocated carrying a gun.

The manager has too many other duties to become involved in settling disputes between residents or to serve as an effective broker between ethnic groups, even if he had the interest and ability. The manager focuses entirely on the maintenance of the buildings and collecting the rent. Managers in other projects of this kind, usually with a larger office staff, are active in community organization and in providing political leadership and mechanisms for settling disputes within the community. Not only do the Dover Square managers not intervene personally in disputes but they are also unable to evict a tenant whom all the neighbors agree is a detriment to the neighborhood. Building a case for eviction is difficult and expensive and requires more organization and money than the management is willing to provide. Those few tenants who are evicted are almost always guilty of rent arrears, rather than of creating a nuisance in the neighborhood. In a similar project in James Hill, the management took a leading role in evicting a family engaged in prostitution and drug sales, which greatly concerned their neighbors. This avenue for exercising control over one's neighbors, however, is absent in Dover Square.

Thus, because of the social structure of the neighborhood, individuals are encapsulated within networks of ongoing social relationships with members of their own ethnic and class groups, not with their neighbors. Shared membership in corporate groups, kin networks, job situations, and community organizations creates an expectation of future interaction within ethnic groups. Dover Square residents had contacts with others in their ethnic group before they moved in and will maintain many of these relationships after they move out, since they will continue to encounter one another in the context of the shared ethnic community. There is, however, no similar expectation of continuity in social relationships with neighbors of different ethnic groups. Even for families who have lived next door to one another for ten years, there is still no anticipation that after they move out, their relationship will continue. This expectation of termination discourages investment of time and energy in the creation of a relationship and reinforces boundaries between social networks. People are reluctant to initiate contacts with others who are culturally different and not connected to their social network in any enduring way. This reluctance prevents the creation of crosscutting ties and impedes the

flow of information about reputations, about those individuals who are trustworthy and those who are not. Thus, it increases the prevalence of relations between strangers within
the project.

CRIME AND SOCIAL BOUNDARIES

In many ways, the social structure of Dover Square itself contributes to the high crime rate. Crime occurs because of the
conjunction of two factors: poverty and anonymity. The former establishes the incentive to steal, the latter creates opportunities to steal successfully. Low income, unemployment, and racial discrimination drive individuals to crime as a
strategy for avoiding physical discomforts, hunger, and social
isolation that comes from not having the money for socializing with friends. It is poverty that drives people to weigh
their own survival and that of their family against the loss that
may be incurred by a stranger; it is poverty that pressures
people to choose family over loyalty to abstract norms of fair-
ness. Many poor people resent those who have more: those
who, for example, wear down-filled parkas on cold days,
while they shiver in thin coats. As one young black man put
it, "To me, street crime is a form of guerilla warfare, just like
Vietnam, but here in the streets." Children who learn early
that they must fend for themselves, that their survival depends upon skills exercised at the expense of strangers, often
adopt this pattern as a lifelong strategy. It is not so different
from the behavior of the exploitative businessman whose jus-
tification for paying his workers low wages is that his children need a college education. Poverty is one of the factors
that diverts the energies and creative imaginations of adoles-
cents from constructive exploration and thrill-seeking to the
excitement of vandalism, crime, street fighting, and the fast
life. Not everyone who commits crimes is driven by hunger,
but street crime is committed preponderantly by poor people. Street crime is an occupation that entails greater risks
than other kinds of work: the risk of physical harm from angry victims, the chance of arrest and conviction. It is not an
attractive option for people with better alternatives. In general, the high-risk, low-return forms of crime, principally

street crime and burglary, are performed by poor people, often racial minorities, for whom other opportunities are unavailable.

Anonymity, caused by the heterogeneous ethnic composition of the project, facilitates predation as a mode of survival by allowing criminals to rob their neighbors with minimal fear of apprehension. Many Dover Square residents observed that, in general, criminals prefer not to work close to home, where they can be too easily identified by their neighbors. But in Dover Square, where neighbors are often strangers, a resident can rob or burglarize families close to him without fear of identification. This means he can commit crimes in his home territory, one which to him is relatively safe, predictable, and familiar, while appearing to his victims as if he were a stranger from a distant area. He can rob the same people whose daily habits and material possessions are easily visible to him.

CHAPTER 5

The
Meaning
of
Danger

Danger has a variety of meanings for Dover Square residents. It means encounters with muggers on deserted streets, invasion by culturally alien neighbors, stumbling over disheveled drunks asleep on the sidewalk. But essentially danger is fear of the stranger, the person who is potentially harmful, but whose behavior seems unpredictable and beyond control. Those Dover Square residents who are the most convinced that their environment is dangerous tend to be not those most victimized, but those who lack any social connection to the street youths. Such people see themselves awash in a sea of dangerous strangers.

PERCEPTIONS OF DANGER

Perceptions of the Chinese Residents

The refrain repeated over and over by Chinese residents is that Dover Square is a dangerous place to live, that the threat of crime surrounds them, and that the dangerous people are the blacks who live in the project. Within these parameters, however, are important individual differences between young and old, male and female, and English speakers and Chinese speakers. I discussed the meaning of danger with one or more members of about eighty-five Chinese households, 60 percent of those in the project, selected more or less randomly. About half the interviews were conducted in English, half in Chinese. Clearly, determining the meaning of the same term in two languages poses translation problems. I discussed the proper word to use in Chinese with both my interpreter and educated Chinese adults, and concluded that the term we used, although not the exact English equivalent, was as close as possible. The Chinese word for danger means, roughly, taking a chance or doing something risky, such as venturing onto the ledge of a high building or walking home alone late at night. When asking about dangerous people, we used a word which translates as bad people, in terms of being morally bad or those who rob and steal and harass others. Although the Chinese terms include some things that do not fall under the English term and vice versa, this appeared to be the best translation. In fact, the general opinions of those interviewed in English and those in Chinese appeared to be very similar in content, although different in degree. The latter generally expressed more fear. I believe that this translation did not create serious distortions in the data.

The great majority of Chinese people believe that the project is dangerous because of the blacks and Hispanics who live there. Most believe that the blacks single out the Chinese as victims because they think that the Chinese are rich and have large amounts of cash hidden in their homes. My Chinese interviewees had rarely heard about crimes experienced by their white or black neighbors. The Chinese are angry at what they see as the disproportionate predation they experience from blacks and are incensed by the amount of crime suffered by the most vulnerable individuals: Chinese-speaking women, old people, and men returning late from their restaurant jobs. They are rarely able to distinguish the street youths from the respectable blacks, and many confess that all blacks look alike to them.

On the other hand, many blacks resent the Chinese for their meteoric economic rise. As George Williams put it, "They have just arrived and already own restaurants and businesses, while we have been here much longer and have only bubble gum stores." Blacks are also aware of the hostility and distrust most Chinese feel against them, which they find unjustified and insulting. A black youth worker described his frustration when he knocked on the doors of many Chinese families, inviting them to send their children to his program, only to find few willing even to open their doors to him.

When my Chinese research assistant and I interviewed some of these families a few days later, they described how frightened they had been when a black man recently came to their door. The widespread Chinese fear of black crime veils a deep hostility between the two groups.

The comments of several Chinese residents illustrate their feelings about the dangers of Dover Square. One old Chinese-speaking woman said that the dangerous people are the blacks who hang around. She doesn't know who the specific people are, but they are all over. It is impossible to catch them. They commit crimes when the police are not there, and by the time the police come, they are gone. Another woman confessed that she is afraid of all blacks, that they all look alike to her, and that if she sees a black person while she is walking through the project, she clutches her purse tightly. A third woman said that no place is safe, although the laundry is particularly dangerous because the black youths hang out there. She avoids using it as much as possible. She doesn't know any of the youths who cause the trouble, but is afraid of all the blacks, who all look alike to her. When I asked her if all whites looked alike as well, she agreed that they did. A middle-aged Chinese-speaking man said that the project is dangerous because almost every Chinese person he knows has had his apartment broken into or has been robbed. He does not know who is doing it, except that they are blacks. Chinatown is definitely safer because there are fewer robberies there. Several Chinese people felt that the black youths constantly watch them and their habits, making schedules of their comings and goings, to determine the safest time to rob their houses.

Danger does not end with the fear of crime, however. Many families feel harassed by groups of black and Hispanic children and young teenagers who sit on the steps and porches in front of their houses, smoke and visit, and throw eggs or rocks at the door and even at the inhabitants when they open the door to tell them to leave. Some actively harass the Chinese residents by ringing the doorbell, then laughing and running away when someone comes to the door. Others leave trash and urinate in the stairwell, and inscribe their names and obscene art work on its concrete walls. Even when the youths do nothing but sit on the steps, they often frighten Chinese housewives who believe the youths are just waiting for them to leave the house so they can burglarize it. In fact, most of these gatherings are not for the purpose of plotting robberies.

Chinese residents feel threatened by the black and Hispanic youths who call them "Chink" and mock their tonal language with singsong imitations. One young girl said that she didn't think such youths would hurt her, but they did make her feel uneasy when she walked by. Young Chinese women are frightened by men who make flirtatious, lecherous comments, such as, "Hey, beautiful!" that are not inherently insulting, but are felt to be demeaning, degrading, and threatening. Although many women mainly fear blacks, there are whites and Puerto Ricans who also behave this way. Blacks, whites, and Hispanics are physically larger than the Chinese and often seem loud, pushy, and, to some extent, frightening just because of that. Some Chinese also think neighborhood drunks, mostly whites and Indians, are dangerous because "you can never tell what they are likely to do." The local subway station is feared because it is a regular hangout for white drunks. According to a young American Chinese man, "you can't know what they are doing there; they are just hanging out all day and not working."

Many Chinese people say that Chinatown is much safer than Dover Square. They do not feel nearly so uneasy surrounded by Chinese people. On the other hand, a significant minority thinks that Chinatown is dangerous because of the gang fights between rival martial arts clubs and teenage toughs and because of a Mafia-type organization that, some claim, is connected to the Chinatown establishment and involved in smuggling drugs. Several Chinese people acknowledged that it is better not to get involved in Chinatown affairs of this kind since it is easy to get killed. They described cases of retaliatory murders, people shot through the wrists, and other forms of violent retribution visited on those who step out of line.

The Chinese fear whites both because they believe whites are likely to commit crimes and for a more subtle and fundamental reason: because whites control a society that has long assigned the Chinese a position of marginality. Through long years of bitter experience the Chinese have learned that whites are not to be trusted. Not surprisingly, this situation awakens feelings of deep resentment, particularly among American Chinese who, more thoroughly than their Chinese-speaking parents, understand their position in American society. One effect of this sense of marginality is an unwillingness to take responsibility for one's neighbors, even if they are Chinese, and a reluctance to become involved with the American police or court system. While the fear of blacks is an immediate, daily experience of living with people believed to be predatory and violent, the fear of whites is based on resentment at the tardy and grudging acceptance of Chinese people into American society. Chinese see whites as strange and incomprehensible, as "ghosts" and "barbarians," the literal translation of the term for white man (Kingston 1976).

The Chinese residents generally feel that they have been abandoned by the police. To be safe, all they can do is make sure they never leave the house unoccupied, never go outside after dark, and put barricades of locks on the doors and bars on the windows. Almost all residents I talked to said that the police were useless. They do not come when they are called, they arrive too late, and when they do arrive, they do nothing but write down a list of what was stolen. They never get the property back or catch the criminals. Some are convinced that the police pay more attention to white victims than to Chinese victims. In fact, the probability of catching a robber or burglar and convicting him is very low nationwide, with fewer than one burglar in fifty and one robber in twelve receiving some punishment (Clark 1970: 101). The police may well feel that there is little they can do about a routine robbery or burglary and may well communicate this to the victims, which the Chinese interpret as another indication of their marginality in the eyes of the whites.

In this city with a virtually all-white police force, encounters with police are often fraught with insult and humiliation. Police officers seem large and overbearing and commonly tell the Chinese families, "It is your fault; you people keep too much money in your houses." For the Chinese who speak no English, it is virtually impossible to call the police, but even those who can call rarely do so because they fear retaliation from criminals and think that a call to the police will mean frequent court appearances and lost days of work and wages. Some even distrust the police, arguing that if you tell the police how much money was stolen, the thieves will find out.

But significant individual differences can be found within this pattern of fear among the Chinese residents. Those most fearful are Chinese-speaking women, both housewives, who are restricted to the home all day, and stitchers, who spend their days gossiping over their sewing machines about crimes inflicted on their Chinese neighbors. These women feel particularly vulnerable since they cannot speak English, cannot call the police, and cannot understand what the black youths are saying. Many women feel that there is no safe place anywhere in the project. A woman living above a black family says that she thinks all blacks look alike, and since there are so many people who live there, she has no idea who belongs and who does not. There are always teenagers down there who are coming and going. She has three black families living in her building, and is very unhappy about it. She does not feel at all safe, and would like to move elsewhere. One woman said that she is very frightened of all the black people around her, particularly the youths, but is afraid to call the police about them because they will find out and retaliate. Since women generally are more recent arrivals in the United States than men and live much more sheltered lives, they have fewer opportunities for learning English and discovering the inner workings of American society. The great majority of adult women speak only Chinese. They hear little about who the black criminals are, even from their children, have virtually no personal contact with blacks, and feel surrounded by people they cannot understand. They generally see the project as a very dangerous world.

Adult Chinese men, in contrast, typically have lived in the United States longer, speak more English, and feel less vulnerable. Although Chinese men are also aware of the high rates of victimization of Chinese in the project, they are less preoccupied with its dangers, spend less time gossiping about crimes, and feel more able to deal with the threat of crime. They also spend less time at home. They are more likely to have speaking relationships with black neighbors and may have some links to black or white social networks that provide a little information about who is responsible for local crime. One man, for example, who has lived in the U.S. for twenty-five years and speaks English quite well, says that only 10 percent of the blacks and others are bad. He thinks that most of the crime is committed by people from outside the project. He also knows that some of his white and black neighbors have been victimized. He does not think Dover Square is any more dangerous than other areas, but believes that it always is important to be careful and not to walk around alone at night.

American-Chinese teenagers are typically less frightened than their parents. They speak fluent English and have a far more extensive understanding of American society, the culture of the street, and the role of the police, even though very few socialize with the street youth. Both young men and young women think that the project is dangerous because there are frequent crimes, but find it no worse than anyplace else. A few say they will not be victimized because the youths know who they are. Most have heard the names of some of the most notorious youths and know when they are in or out of jail. Generational and language barriers preclude communicating this information to parents, however. The American Chinese teenagers who have lived in Dover Square for a long time rarely say that all blacks look alike or lump them into a single category of dangerous people. Since they speak English and have a few social contacts within the black and white communities, they have access to somewhat better information about the identities and reputations of the local youths blamed for crime. This information allows them to make finer distinctions than their mothers can between those blacks who are dangerous and those who are not.

A few Chinese families feel very safe in Dover Square. These families have come to trust black neighbors who have offered to look out for them. One Chinese family has a black neighbor who told them that if they ever had any problems, they should simply knock on the wall and he would come, and that they should not bother to call the police. This family is delighted about the relationship and careful to give the neighbor presents in exchange. The relationship has developed even though the wife speaks almost no English. Another Chinese youth thinks the playground is a dangerous place because of the black youths who hang out there, but he has befriended a black neighbor who knows them. He feels safe when he walks past the black youths with this boy who says hello to them. He assumes that when the youths see he is a friend of the black boy, they will not bother him. Yet he feels nervous when he walks past these same youths by himself. Thus, the few Chinese residents who can take advantage of the personal ties of their black neighbors to the street youths feel much safer than those who much rely only on the shaky protection of the police or their Chinese neighbors.

In sum, Chinese residents are most frightened when they are unable to differentiate those few blacks who are likely to commit crimes from the great majority who are not. Any information about specific identities and reputations diminishes this generalized fear by focusing concern on a few particular, recognizable individuals. Apparently, it is more frightening to contend with a faceless, hostile, predatory social group than it is to confront a few specific individuals who are known to commit crimes. Those who feel most frightened are those who see all blacks as strangers.

Perceptions of the White Residents

I interviewed twenty-two white families, about half the number in the project. Most agreed that Dover Square is a dangerous place to live and that there is a great deal of crime. Many said, however, that the project is not dangerous for them since they know who the local youths committing crime are and say hello to them. Since the youths know them, these whites think they will not be bothered. Some were generous to these youths when they were growing up; others have threatened retaliation if the street youths bother them. The whites who feel safest are those who can rely on such personalized protection. They generally feel less abandoned by the police, but note sadly that even after the criminals are sent away, they are soon on the street again because the courts are too lenient.

Whites have connections to the management through the tenants' association, to the police through friends and relatives on the force, and to local political leaders through involvement in ward politics shared by none of the other ethnic groups. Consequently, whites have more resources outside the community to draw on to cope with crime, even if few of these resources are effective. Many whites expressed the view that the only way to improve the safety of Dover Square was to have better screening of the tenants and to evict those who are known troublemakers. The Syrian-Lebanese residents stress how much safer they feel in their community in James Hill, where neighbors will intervene to stop a crime and people are constantly watching out their windows.

As among the Chinese, there are important internal variations among whites. Single women with small children under ten and older couples with no children are most frightened. Both groups lack information about social contacts with the street youths that teenage children can provide, and both groups lack the means to retaliate for incidents of victimization. Their fear is related to their feelings of vulnerability and helplessness. These women feel safer when male neighbors, either white or black, offer to look out for them. One, for example, did not feel particularly afraid, but after her apartment was broken into four times while she was living alone with her small children, she became so frightened of blacks that she moved into a white neighborhood.

The whites who consider their environment least dangerous are those who know most about the street youths. One woman lives next door to one of the most notorious youths. She has always been friendly to him and finds that he actually protects her. Once, when someone tried to break into her house while she was away, he told the burglar to go elsewhere. In another woman's view, it is very important to know the names of the children in the project, because as soon as you call them by name, they know that they can be identified and will not do anything to you. Similarly, a woman said that she thinks she will not be bothered because she knows most of the youths who make trouble and always says hello and calls them by name when she sees them. They, in turn, are very friendly to her.

A white boy who regularly socializes with the street youths laughed at the idea that Dover Square might be dangerous. It is very safe for him because he knows all the people there and they all know him and would not bother him or rob him. Since he spends his social life with blacks, however, he thinks that white boys are somewhat more dangerous for him than blacks because they are likely to call him "nigger lover." Winslow, the local black neighborhood, is also dangerous since it is full of black teenagers who do not know who he is.

Thus, for whites as well as for Chinese, there is an awareness that Dover Square is an environment of crime and danger, yet personal ties to the street youths or to others who know them provide a form of protection and a sense of safety. Under these conditions, the threatening people are not a mass of strangers but a few individuals located in social space and attached to particular families.

Whites perceive Chinese residents as dangerous in a different way. Most say the Chinese are peaceful people and will not hurt them, but feel that they are invading and taking over the project. Whites frequently exaggerate the proportion of Chinese living in Dover Square, claiming that it is now at least 60 percent and probably 90 percent Chinese. The Chinese pose a danger not to individual safety and property, but to the continued existence of the community. Many complain that they feel as if they are living in Chinatown, surrounded by people who are very different from them. In a variety of ways, whites think that the Chinese do not make good neighbors. The leaders of the tenants' association bemoan the fact that Chinese tenants never complain to the management, do not get involved in tenant-management relations, never call the police, refuse to participate in local political organizations, and take no responsibility for the state of the neighborhood. In fact, Chinese residents are generally so convinced of their peripheral, outsider status in Dover Square that they rarely intervene in crimes or become involved in local politics.

They are generally shy and withdrawn when they walk through the project, hoping to escape notice and victimization. Many whites, used to more neighborly sociability, interpret their reserve as aloofness and arrogance. One woman complained that she does not really like blacks, but, unlike the Chinese, "at least they say hello to you."

White hostility against the Chinese focuses on differences in life style and culture that have come to symbolize the feeling that, as one woman put it, they are "just too different." She said that her children were quite used to playing with black children, but that the Chinese family that moved in next door was just too strange, eating strange foods and hanging up chickens on strings. Whites commonly complain that the Chinese have too many illegal occupants living in overcrowded apartments with wall-to-wall mattresses to accommodate the hordes. They also believe that all Chinese homes are filthy with garbage and overrun by cockroaches. One woman who was deeply offended by what she believed was the Chinese habit of hanging up chickens, even in closets, said that she had never actually been in a Chinese family's house, but thought that she would never go because she would be so disgusted. Other blacks and whites are hostile because they see the Chinese as "foreigners" who take their jobs. A few years ago a black and a white family joined together to sit on the steps and physically block a Chinese family from moving in. These attitudes are most intense among whites who have no Chinese friends and have very little contact with American Chinese. Those whites who do know American Chinese and, through them, other Chinese families regard the Chinese as peaceful, non-troublesome neighbors.

Apart from the blacks and the Chinese, other sources of danger in Dover Square mentioned by whites were the drunks who sleep in the hallways, the people who gossip about them all the time, and the police who conduct high-speed chases through the playgrounds and courtyards of the project. In general, the white population's sense of danger varies with their experience with street life, their personal connections to the street group, and their feelings that they have somewhere to turn if they are victimized. Those most isolated socially from the street youth and their cultural world are those most acutely aware of the danger around them.

Perceptions of the Black Residents

Blacks generally feel that Dover Square is a dangerous place in which crime is rife, but almost all agree that only a few of the people who are responsible for local crime come from the project. The majority are outsiders from James Hill and Winslow. These opinions were garnered from discussions with thirty-seven families, almost half the black families in the project. Most of the people I talked to said that the key to avoiding danger is knowing how to handle others. Safety springs from knowing which people are likely to be criminal and predatory and handling them delicately: avoiding close contact, but not communicating suspicion. One must constantly gauge who can be trusted and who cannot. Blacks uniformly attribute crime to social problems such as poverty, unemployment, and boredom among teenagers, as well as the stresses of particular family situations caused by personal instability, alcoholism, drugs, overindulgence, or overprotection.

Although both blacks and Chinese frequently gossip about crime, the content of their gossip differs radically. Through their extended networks blacks obtain information about who is committing crimes, as well as who their victims are, but the social networks of the Chinese describe only victims. In gossip among the Chinese, perpetrators are faceless blacks, rather than particular individuals with histories and reputations, and victims are exclusively Chinese. Thus, social networks channel and block the flow of information about crime and criminals, significantly influencing the way each group perceives the dangers of the project.

As with the whites and the Chinese, the blacks' notion of danger does not mean just the risk of crime. Some blacks expressed anxiety over winos who come into their hallways and sleep at night and when it is raining, urinating in the halls and blocking the doorways. One young woman who grew up in the city finds the countryside dangerous, particularly unlighted suburban streets darkened by shadows from trees all around. She constantly looks over her shoulder at the trees, expecting bad people everywhere, and only feels safe when she is back in the city with its well-lighted streets.

Another danger described by many black residents, but particularly by young males, is the police. George Williams, for example, says that the police are dangerous because they are always after someone, and anytime they need a suspect they will come into Dover Square looking for someone who is "short and dark" or "tall and dark." Other blacks also mention the propensity of the police to arrest anyone who matches even a vague description. George points out that any time a crime happens, the police always assume it is the work of one of a few individuals. In fact, a few victims described being shown pictures of "known troublemakers" in the police station when they were trying to identify who had robbed them. One of the street youths said that Dover Square is dangerous because the police pick on it; it could be made safer if they could take away the police. He pointed out that the police are often unpleasant to him, yell at him, and hold him responsible for everything that happens in Dover Square. I witnessed one incident in which a white police officer attempted to throw this youth out of the laundromat, which he regards as a home of sorts. The officer was indeed belligerent, abusive, and insulting. A young man who closely resembles his brother, who is a notorious burglar, described as the most dangerous experience of his life his encounter late one night, soon after his brother escaped from jail, with some police officers in a deserted alley. One policeman thrust a large gun in his stomach and told him they were taking him in, but fortunately he was able to produce some identification and was released. The police told him he was very lucky he was not his brother, which further rattled the young man.

In a somewhat different way, the blacks also view the Chinese as dangerous. It is commonly believed among blacks, as among whites, that the Chinese live in filthy, overcrowded apartments, full of illegal aliens, and that they take no responsibility for the neighborhood by cleaning their steps, confronting the management, or intervening in crimes. They attract cockroaches and produce vile smells by hanging up

chickens and fish to dry. A black maintenance man spread stories about Chinese families with large bags of rice full of mag-
gots as big as the grains of rice, and garbage piled high in the
sink. One man said the problem is that these families come
and work at the minimum wage, often running their sewing
machines at home until late at night as the daughters and sisters all take a turn at the piecework. Others claim that two,
three, and four families live in a single apartment, producing
too much dirt and trash for the trash cans. And each family
has five names so that they can use the first two or three in
one place and save the other ones for some other place. (This
observation probably reflects confusion caused by the Chinese custom of listing the surname first. In any case, most
blacks cannot tell which names are first names and which sur-
names.) Further, the names on the door often do not correspond to the people who live there. Many people believe that
if a Chinese family offers the management a big bribe, they
will be able to move in, regardless of who they are or how
many people plan to occupy the apartment.

At a more basic level, many blacks sense the hostility
and fear of Chinese residents and deeply resent these attitudes. As one youth put it, "Before they come over to this
country, they already all have an attitude. They must have a
training session in Hong Kong where they tell them that
black people are all bad and scary." He points out that these
fears persist even though blacks are not solely responsible for
local crime, and one of the more active burglars is Chinese. A
member of the respectable group also said that Chinese regard all blacks as sneaky, bad people to be avoided at all costs.
He ran a small business in Dover Square for a few years with a
Chinese girl as cashier. When Chinese customers came in,
they were amazed and shocked that she would work for a
black man.

Some of the street youths and the hustler families are familiar with the emerging street life of Chinatown, with its
teenage gang wars, crime, and drug traffic. For these people,
the Chinese are dangerous because of their violence. One
young woman said that a corner of Dover Square is dangerous because it is a lonely, quiet place with just Chinese
there, and "they will really go after you." Several of the street

youths believe that if any Chinese person observes them robbing someone who is Chinese, they will all gang up and retaliate. Although such a confrontation occurred once, in general, Chinese families bemoan the lack of this very unanimity, complaining that Chinese families never help each other out. A young black woman thinks the Chinese are all very dangerous. They all look alike to her, and she does not know which ones are violent and which are not. Another young woman said that Chinatown is dangerous and she would never go there alone, although she might go down with a friend. She did once visit a restaurant and was impressed with how polite the waiter was, but she still feels uneasy there. The street youths are in awe of skilled martial arts fighters and circulate stories of ruthless punishments meted out by the Chinatown underworld, such as shooting through the wrists or neck, designed to cripple rather than to kill. As in other misunderstandings between ethnic groups, they have some acquaintance with this slice of the Chinatown social world and assume, incorrectly, that these traits are characteristic of the entire population.

A sharp line separates the attitudes toward danger of respectable families and the street youths. The respectable families believe that their environment is dangerous and that they must always be cautious and distrustful of those around them to protect themselves from victimization. Many have been robbed or burglarized and are fully aware of how frequently this happens. Most assert, however, that Dover Square is no more dangerous than any place else. They adopt the personalistic styles of managing danger used by whites, befriending even those they distrust and making sure not to treat them with suspicion and hostility, at least overtly. Respectable families who have teenage children and access to information about the street youths feel less afraid than those who are elderly, living alone, or unconnected to local black social networks and therefore cut off from this vital protective information.

Respectable families generally believe that it is outsiders or people they do not know who are dangerous. They know that a few project youths commit crimes and almost always know who they are and where they live. But it is not these youths who are seen as particularly dangerous. One couple pointed out that most of the crime problem is caused by three or four people. They could describe in detail the family situations of these youths and the reasons they became involved in crime. A middle-aged woman said that the dangerous people are a gang of youths who live around the project and will beat you up, but that she knows a few and is friendly to them. She does not think these would bother her because she knows where they live and who their parents are. A man in his thirties does not think the project is dangerous because there are only a few youths involved and "everybody knows who they are and who is doing what." A middle-aged woman said that she feels safe in Dover Square because she knows the majority of people who live there and is not afraid of those she knows. She has watched most of these youths grow up from little children and does not find them frightening. It is only people she has never seen before whom she fears.

Yet, most respectable families are as cautious in trusting those around them as the Johnsons are. One woman, for example, has heard that most people are robbed by people who have been in their houses. She was unhappy when one of her daughters brought home a boyfriend with a friend who was a complete stranger fresh from Alabama, about whom she knew nothing. Her younger sons also bring home friends to play with who sometimes pick things up. Things like dolls, toys, and small amounts of change are always disappearing. It is hard to know whom to trust, but one cannot simply avoid everyone.

For respectable families, the environment contains a further danger: the risk that their children will be tempted into the fast life, with its easy money, glamor, and excitement. This means abandoning the ideals of work, family, church, and stability in favor of a more chaotic life of crime, hustling, and usually drugs. In Dover Square, the street youths play out this life style with "flash" and "front" on their very doorsteps. Some parents attempt to seclude their children from these influences by restricting them rigidly to the house, but such an approach often backfires as the children approach adolescence. When they finally escape parental strictures, they are often wilder and more enthusiastic about the street life than others who have grown up seeing more of the good and bad side of this life style, as the Johnson children have.

The hustler families, whose children are often members of the street group, are more convinced that the only dangers in the project are caused by outsiders, although some also rail against the "nosy" people who are always causing trouble for other people by failing to "mind their own business." They assert that it is the outsiders who do the robbing and snatch the purses, and that their children are unjustly accused. Most feel safe in the project because they "know everybody" and are "known." One of these women said that the project is quite dangerous for many of the people who live here, but not for her because she has a reputation for self-confidence and strength. When her daughter was thirteen she was seduced by one of the leaders of the youth group. This woman went up to him and yelled that she would call the police and, if that did not work, would have his legs broken and, if that failed, would have him killed. She did take him to court for statutory rape, but says she dropped the case because there were so many other charges against him. She is convinced that this incident persuaded the youths that she means business. She now walks around the project at two in the morning and never worries about being attacked. Nor does she fear the local street youths at all because she thinks they know her, respect her, and regard her as tough.

The attitudes of the street youths stand in marked contrast to those of the respectable families. Not only the few youths actually committing crimes, but their close friends, sisters, and brothers think the project is very safe. Some acknowledge that Dover Square is dangerous, but laugh at the notion that it is dangerous for them. One young woman complained that not only is Dover Square not dangerous, but it is very quiet and even a little dull. The young men are not afraid to walk through Dover Square alone at three in the morning and are convinced that no one will bother them. The young women feel a little uneasy about walking around alone in the middle of the night, but feel fairly confident that they will be

safe. The youths argue that they know everyone and everyone knows them, so that no one would dare to bother them
or anyone else in their families. Further, they are the people
committing most of the crimes anyway. The only dangerous
people are outsiders. Yet, both Chinatown and Winslow seem
dangerous because of the gang fighting and drug traffic there.

Within the project, there is one group the street youths
find dangerous: those who are "nosy," who gossip and exaggerate and fail to "mind their own business." Their greatest
invective is reserved for those who call the police and accuse
them of committing crimes of which they complain they are
innocent. Those who are robbed or burglarized are often
people who have "big mouths," who talk too much. One
young man asserted that most of the burglaries are directed
against people who have "bad attitudes" toward the youths
and deserve to be robbed. In fact, I estimate that about 40
percent of the twenty-one robberies and burglaries of black
families I heard about were retaliatory acts. The youths draw
a sharp line between those who yell out the window at a robber or burglar and tell him to stop and those who call the
police. The former are often respected as strong people,
while the latter are universally detested. Often, the hustler
families tell the youths to stop, while the respectable families
call the police.

Other teenagers who live in Dover Square and are
friendly with these youths, but not members of the street
group, similarly find the project a safe place to live. Two
young women pointed out that a nearby project in James Hill
is much more dangerous, with heavy drug traffic and so many
teenage mothers that they call it the "Mother Project." Dover
Square, in contrast, is dull. The young people never do anything but play basketball all the time. Excitement must be
found elsewhere. These youths agree that the project is not
dangerous for them, but think that it is dangerous for old
people and outsiders who come in and flash their money.
They also feel that the dangerous people are outsiders from
James Hill and Winslow. As one of these young black women
told me and my Chinese research assistant, who has lived in
Dover Square for ten years, "To you, the boys are all dan-

gerous because you can't tell them apart, but to me, they are George, Johnny, and Jamesy, and I know who to look out for and who will not bother me."

THE ANALYSIS OF DANGER

How can we explain these widely differing perceptions of danger among individuals and ethnic groups who inhabit the same environment? First, it is clear that danger refers to a wide range of harm and hazards and is not limited to the risk of assault or theft of property. Nor is it restricted to incidents of violence. It incorporates a whole range of injuries, insults, and intrusions on an individual's sense of self and his world. Further, notions of danger are interwoven with group conflicts and animosities. Incidents of predation, insult, or apparent disrespect are reinterpreted and redefined in the context of intergroup hostilities. For example, the Chinese view of blacks as dangerous and criminal is exacerbated by their belief that blacks prey exclusively on them, while the blacks' view of the Chinese as dangerous focuses on their hostile and suspicious attitudes, their reputed skill in the martial arts, and their implacable retaliation.

Crime contributes to these notions of danger, but its impact shifts with the nature of intergroup conflict. The risk of victimization, for example, has a different meaning for respectable blacks who know the local youth than it does for Chinese, to whom these youths are members of an undifferentiated group of hostile and ruthless strangers. It is not simply the risk of crime that Dover Square residents find dangerous, but the chance of random, vicious, unwarranted attack by a stranger who belongs to a hostile group.

Dangerous experiences include far more than crime. Insults, mockery, racial slurs, harassment, and flirtatious sexual comments that assault a person's sense of order, propriety, and self-respect awaken feelings of danger even when they contain no threat of actual physical violence. They are degrading and humiliating experiences, veiled attacks in an unspoken battle between hostile ethnic groups. Gossip, which assaults reputation, is another potent hazard. The deterioration of the moral order of a neighborhood, including the bad influences of street youths, the prevalence of drunks, parents who neglect their children, and people who live according to a very different moral code, evoke feelings that the neighborhood is dangerous. Some Dover Square residents see danger in the evidence of a downhill slide in the social status of the neighborhood: the trash, broken fences, graffiti, rusting cars, and general appearance of neglect and indifference that suggest that no one cares about the neighborhood. Such subtle signals may contribute to the inexplicable "loss of faith" in urban neighborhoods that often puzzles planners and politicians.

Another non-violent form of danger is the invasion of a culturally and racially distinct ethnic group that threatens to dominate the community. The white residents, and to a lesser extent the blacks, find this a potent source of concern. Differences in culture and life style come to symbolize the threat posed by the invading group. Such fears may be typical of situations of ethnic transition. In Dover Square, the increasing Chinese population is a threat to the white and black population's community as a cohesive, orderly, and predictable world where neighbors are sociable and assist one another in times of crisis. Finally, some Dover Square residents, primarily black residents, especially the street youths, fear the police and the "nosy" people who summon the police, which, as I said earlier, reflects the hostilities between the predominantly white police force and blacks in this city.

Danger and Cultural Distance

Cultural differences exacerbate feelings of danger. Encounters with culturally alien people are infused by anxiety and uncertainty, which inhibit social interaction and reinforce social boundaries. The greater the cultural difference, the more intense the feeling of danger and the sharper the social boundaries. In Dover Square, blacks and whites, significantly similar in culture and life style, feel relatively little animosity and suspicion toward one another, but Chinese residents are separated from both blacks and whites by a great cultural distance. A comparison of the values, patterns of work and consumption, success in social mobility, standards of respect and prestige, family organization, attitudes toward sex and aggressiveness, and styles of interpersonal interaction and conflict among the three ethnic groups suggests the formative role of cultural distance in constructing notions of danger and solidifying social boundaries.

In Dover Square, Chinese residents value privacy, control of emotional expression, and polite social interaction. Voices are subdued, emotions are under control, and social relationships, particularly outside the family, are formal. Although deep affection underlies family relationships, physical expressions of affection are rare. Chinese adults are typically neither verbally nor behaviorally aggressive in social situations. The older generation adapted to American society by "walking away from trouble," not by fighting the white power structure. Conflicts are managed by superficial politeness and indirect attacks through gossip and subtle retaliation.

Economic success, academic achievement, and social mobility are highly valued. Parents sacrifice so that their children can have a better life; children who do not succeed suffer great anguish. One young man pretended to attend college every day for months after he flunked out, secretly working at a warehouse instead. Educated people are highly respected, and parents are proud of the academic achievements of their children. Because their work usually offers no security or benefits, many families live in a way that suggests relative poverty: their lives are organized around the virtues of thrift and saving, as well as the need to prepare for sickness, retirement, and family expenses such as weddings. Most keep large quantities of cash or valuables, such as gold and jade jewelry, in their homes or in bank vaults. Only 1 percent of the families in the project are on welfare.

Females are expected to be shy, modest, and deferential to men. Teenage girls are protected by their families and prevented from having too much freedom or social contact with boys. Adult women are expected to behave with sexual modesty and reserve. Women dress conservatively, avoiding shorts, halters, and even sleeveless blouses. Young women wear fashionable clothes, but never sensuous or revealing styles. Most wear their hair long and straight and put on little or no makeup. Older women generally wear their hair in a short permanent wave, nicknamed a "carrot top," while elderly, more traditional women retain the shapeless black pants, and blouse and severe short bob chopped off at the chin, viewed as respectable in the China they came from.

Patterns of social interaction among blacks are very different. Most blacks are gregarious, boisterous, and occasionally aggressive. Shouting and fighting are common among friends and enemies, but these encounters are not necessarily hostile. I observed one mother and daughter arguing loudly but good-naturedly about where someone lived. The volume suggested a major confrontation, but there was no anger in the dispute; it was simply a conventional mode of hammering out a small difference of opinion. Blacks believe in the importance of confrontation and standing up for themselves in order to avoid being exploited, as Mrs. Johnson's behavior illustrates clearly. Many parents refuse to acknowledge their childrens' misbehavior and instead attack the complainer. The best way to protect oneself from crime is to gain a reputation as a tough person who will fight back.

Women are not protected and sheltered from sexual encounters in this black community. Young women dress attractively and often sensually. It is assumed that sexual attraction underlies most male-female encounters and that women as well as men are anxious for the adventure and excitement of a liaison with a desirable, attractive partner. The flirtatious comments of males are meant simply to find out which women are available, predicated on the assumption that most are interested. Sexual comments are intended to be invitations, not threats.

Respect in interpersonal relations comes through "front," the material trappings of success, and skill in conversation and managing others. Elegant clothes, luxury cars, and plush apartments convey an enviable impression of wealth and status. None of the blacks affect the studied ragged look of the blue-jean-clad middle class, preferring fashionable clothes and expensive cars. As George explains, "If I drive an old car, I just look like a poor nigger, but if a white person drives an old car, people figure he must be a rich person just driving an old car." Since blacks often buy "on time," using surplus income to make payments, and would rather risk repossession than save beforehand, they appear to be richer than Chinese families although their economic level is not very different.

Respect also comes from being clever, from the ability to talk others into doing what one wants them to, and from making a living by wit and guile rather than hard work and drudgery. These economic strategies do not produce the academic credentials or high-paying jobs of the Chinese, however, and Dover Square blacks have not experienced the social mobility of the Chinese. Their children do not attend elite colleges or enter professional jobs, both because of their value structure and the persisting barriers of racial discrimination.

Women gain respect through their role in their families, their jobs, or in the church or community. Women between the ages of forty and sixty are strong forces in both family and community, while men of this age appear to have a more peripheral role. Many women value their independence. Their lives are not bereft of men, but they refuse to relinquish power over themselves and their children to men. Stack also observed that women of this economic level value strength, resourcefulness, and self-assertiveness (1974). Several young women felt that, if necessary, they could handle themselves in a street fight.

White patterns of social interaction, family organization, conflict management, and economics are similar to those of the blacks. Aggressiveness is admired, and people who are tough, able to defend themselves, and clever in talking themselves out of tight situations are respected. Differences of opinion are often expressed in loud voices. There is a similar emphasis on "front," on material success. These whites have also failed to achieve social mobility. Most are the remnants of more successful families who have moved out into the suburbs. Few of their children have achieved the educational or professional successes of the Chinese children. They generally perform the same low-skilled, low-paying jobs of most blacks. One-quarter of both black and white families are supported by welfare. White families also have fluid structures, with about the same proportion of woman-headed house-holds, where boyfriends drift in and out, as among black families.

Whites from James Hill bring with them a great emphasis on sociability between neighbors. Most parts of James Hill have active neighborhood associations, and in the past, before the ethnic communities were diluted by gentrifying elites, stoop-sitting and visiting on the sidewalks were the essence of social life. One Dover Square resident described her old James Hill neighborhood in glowing terms, saying that all her neighbors knew each other and watched out for each other. It might take a housewife an hour to walk down the block, visiting all her friends on the way. In James Hill, children formed youth groups organized by block and were closely supervised by the families on the street. Although they started having children at an early age, the young people retained close ties to their parents. Toughness, the ability to drink, and an interest in sexual adventures permeated the culture of the young people. Many were familiar with street life and dabbled in crime, hustling, and drugs. White emigrants from James Hill are particularly conscious of the loss of community and neighborly sociability that they have suffered and continually feel frustrated by the lack of friendship and assistance between neighbors in Dover Square.

The language barrier sharpens the distrust that these cultural differences inspire between the Chinese and the English-speaking segments of the population. Chinese people who speak no English constantly feel helpless in dealing with American society and often have to rely on young children to translate for them in banks and courthouses. Since they cannot understand what whites are saying, the presence of any white person can signal danger. Once, without an interpreter, I knocked on the door of a Chinese family, knowing that some members of the family spoke English. No one answered the door, but a Chinese neighbor came out to see what was happening. Since he spoke no English, and I no Chinese, I could not explain my purpose to him. He saw only a white person at his neighbor's door and assumed that they were in trouble. A smile of fear covered his face as he searched frantically for a child who could speak English. The ten year old who finally appeared could not translate the words for research, interview, or questionnaire into Chinese, and I left with the frustrated feeling that I had awakened fears that I could not quiet until evening, when I would return with my research assistant to explain in Chinese the purpose of my visit. Such encounters leave Chinese residents frightened and uncertain and non-Chinese frustrated and, perhaps, angry.

On the other hand, English-speaking people in Dover Square often resent the Chinese for their continued use of a strange, incomprehensible language, their failure to learn English, and, underlying this, their apparent unwillingness to assimilate. Several people I spoke to felt that the Chinese should adjust as other immigrant groups have adjusted before them. Many whites perceive the Chinese as aloof, clannish, and arrogant because they do not say hello on the sidewalks and do not visit on door steps, although this separation is enforced by the language barrier.

Because of cultural differences and the lack of communication across ethnic lines, residents often interpret the apparently inexplicable behavior of their neighbors through the lens of their own culture, leading to further misunderstanding. For example, when whites and blacks observe large families of Chinese living in the same household, they think the residents are taking in boarders and friends, not living as large, extended families. The Chinese view black and white families as shifting populations of friends and visitors which makes no sense in terms of their images of a nuclear family. When a black maintenance man discovered locks on each bedroom door of a Chinese family's apartment, he assumed that this was because the separate families inhabiting the same apartment did not trust one another. In fact, they were designed to increase the family's security in the event of a burglarly. Significantly, those whites and blacks who have friends and social contacts within the Chinese community are much less likely to make such assumptions since they have access to better information about why people behave as they do.

Thus, the ethnic groups in Dover Square have sharply different values about family, work, thrift and consumption, aggressiveness, assertiveness, sexual display and modesty, neighborly obligations, and strategies of managing social conflict. These differences lead to misinterpretations of the behavior of other ethnic groups. Apparently strange behavior is viewed in terms of one's own cultural frame of reference, devoid of the insights that could be obtained if accurate information flowed through social networks. The cultural distance between the English-speaking and Chinese-speaking residents of the project exacerbates mutual feelings of danger and distrust and inhibits residents from initiating social interaction across this boundary.

Danger and Crime

Clearly, ethnic groups differ significantly in their perceptions of the danger of crime in the project. Intriguingly, these differences do not parallel rates of victimization. A survey of the victimization experiences since moving in of two-thirds of all households in the project reveals very similar patterns for blacks and Chinese. I interviewed 244 individuals, representing 201 households: 51 percent of the black households, 62 percent of the white households, 68 percent of Chinese households, and 68 percent of Hispanic households. Fifty-three percent of the black families interviewed said that they had experienced a robbery, burglary, or assault, while 46 percent of Chinese had the same experience. About one-third of the families in each group have experienced no crimes, while 14 percent of each have been robbed, burglarized, or assaulted more than once. Whites have been victimized at the highest rate: 63 percent were robbed, burglarized, or assaulted, 30 percent more than once, and only 20 percent have been totally spared.

The results of a formal, closed-ended questionnaire confirms my more impressionistic account of ethnic variations in perceptions of danger. One hundred and one residents, representing all four ethnic groups, both sexes, three age categories, and three lengths of residence in the project were asked, "Is Dover Square a dangerous place to live?" They had five possible responses: extremely, very, fairly, not very, and not at all. Chinese respondents were most concerned about danger and blacks least: 31 percent of the Chinese said Dover Square was dangerous and only 18 percent said that it was not at all dangerous, while only 13 percent of blacks said it was dangerous and 65 percent said it was not at all dangerous. Despite their high rate of victimization, whites appear curiously divided: 44 percent said the project was dangerous, but 33 percent said it was not at all dangerous (see Table 1).

It appears that notions of danger are related to whom one knows and whom one does not know: they are a function of the shape and boundaries of social networks. Those who know the street youths personally or have channels of information about them through their extended networks find their environment less dangerous than those who lack these connections. Blacks and many of the whites know these youths as individuals with names, addresses, and reputations, while most Chinese see them as strangers they cannot distinguish from all the other blacks in the project. The Chinese do not confront a few known troublemakers, but a faceless mass of strangers all of whom are out to get them. It is encounters with strangers who are criminal and hostile that inspires a sense of danger, not simply the risk of crime. Perceived vulnerability intensifies these feelings, but as we will see in the next chapter, vulnerability depends to some extent on knowledge of social identities as well.

The questionnaire findings support the hypothesis that danger is inspired by strangers. Eighty-seven percent of the blacks, 61 percent of the whites, and 43 percent of the Chinese said they know the teenagers by name or know where they live and who their parents are, although most of the Chinese know the street youths only in a very superficial way. These differences in knowledge parallel ethnic variations in perceptions of danger. Further, when the entire sample of 101 is pooled, without regard for ethnic differences, those who know the street youths find the project less dangerous than those who do not, at a statistically significant level (see Table 2). Half of the respondents who know the street youths say the project is not at all dangerous, while less than a quarter of those to whom they are strangers feel the same way. Moreover, this relationship holds almost regardless of whether the respondent has been a victim. The correlation between knowing the identities of the youths and perceiving less danger in the project is statistically significant for members of households that have been victimized never, once, or twice. However, for those individuals whose families have suffered three or more cases of victimization, the project is considered dangerous even if they know the identities of the youths. It appears that above a certain level of predation, even knowing the hazardous people does not inspire feelings of safety (see Table 3).

The internal variations in perceptions of danger of each group correspond to this pattern. American Chinese teenagers who know more about the street youths are less concerned about danger than their parents, to whom the youths are strangers. Similarly, the Syrian-Lebanese whites from James Hill and the hustler and street blacks are relatively unconcerned, while more isolated whites and blacks feel surrounded by danger. Both knowledge of identities and familiarity with the cultural milieu of street life diminish feelings of danger.

The questionnaire results suggest that a sense of danger is not correlated with age, sex, number of times victimized, number of friends who live in the project, or the expectation of staying for a long time in Dover Square, but is related to ethnicity, number of years of residence in the project, expectation of help from neighbors, and whether or not the respondent considers himself a good street fighter. The highest correlations occur between perception of danger and familiarity with the street youths, expectation of victimization, ethnicity, fear of walking alone at night, ability as a street fighter, and number of precautions taken (see Table 4). Dover Square is considered safer by people who come from environments they thought were more frightening, such as crime-ridden public housing projects, than it is by people who moved there from lower-crime areas, such as the suburbs. Of those who thought their former neighborhood was safer than Dover Square, 42 percent found the project dangerous, while of those who thought their former neighborhood was equally or more dangerous, only 7 percent found Dover Square to be dangerous (see Table 5). Thus, evaluations of danger are relative and reflect past experience. It appears that people become accustomed to a certain level of crime and that increases in that level spark their sense of danger.

Dangerous Places

Another way to understand the meaning of danger is to examine how Dover Square residents distinguish between safe and dangerous places. Ninety residents of Dover Square indicated on a printed map of the project the places they considered safe and those they considered dangerous and why. Almost all the Chinese respondents and about one-third of the blacks, whites, and Hispanics left substantial portions of their maps blank, claiming that the blank portions were areas they did not know or neutral, neither safe nor dangerous. The maps were then compared to the actual distribution of robberies gleaned from the victimization survey.

The maps reveal that places considered dangerous are not necessarily those where crime is most frequent, nor are places thought to be safe actually free from crime. In fact, it appears that other factors, such as architectural design, the social identities of the habitual users of a location, and familiarity are as important as the incidence of crime. Everyone initially responded by defining dangerous places as those where crimes occur, but other criteria soon crept in. Narrow, enclosed pathways appear dangerous, while open areas with good visibility seem safe. Robbers agree that narrow, enclosed places are ideal for their activities, particularly if they are dark and shadowy, since the victim will have more difficulty identifying the assailant. But, although these areas are widely feared, only one-quarter of all the robberies I recorded took place in them (see Table 6).

Familiar areas also are considered safer than unfamiliar ones. Most people said that their side of the project is safe, while the other side is dangerous. Those who live in the center said the peripheries are dangerous, while those who live on the borders said they are afraid to venture into the center of the development. Yet the victimization survey showed no difference in crime rates between the various sections of the project. The area in front of one's house was considered the safest place in the project: a higher proportion of respondents singled out this area than any other area. Yet almost two-thirds of all robberies occur here, either in the stairwell or immediately in front of the house. Robbers like to follow a victim home, then attack in the semi-enclosed porch or stairwell area while the victim fumbles in his or her pockets for a key. Here, the sense of safety created by familiarity seems unwarranted.

The kind of people who habitually use a space also influences its reputation as safe or dangerous. The hangouts of the street youths are regarded as some of the most dangerous places in the project, although very few crimes happen there. A four-story parking garage and the playground have both been commandeered as gathering spots by these youths and are seen as dangerous by a higher proportion of respondents than any other locations. Those who are friends of the street youths or members of the group find the playground a very safe place, however. It is an open and easily visible area, and not only are crimes there infrequent, but the youths agree that it is a poor place to commit a robbery. They do fight with each other there and decorate the walls with graffitti, but neither of these activities threatens passersby. Thus, the area is considered dangerous, not because of what happens there, but because of the reputations of the people who regularly use it.

Intriguingly, if the entire population of map-drawers is divided up according to their relationship to the street youths, it becomes clear that perceptions of the danger of the playground are directly related to whether or not these youths are strangers to them. To those who know the street youths as friends, their hangouts—the playground, the laundromat, and the front of the laundromat—all appear safe. Those who are acquainted with the street youths, but not friends of theirs, are divided, with two-thirds considering the locations dangerous. Those who do not know them, however, universally label all three areas as dangerous (see Table 7). Yet, all three groups agree about the danger of other parts of the project, such as the supermarket and another open square. The street youths view the playground as one of the safest places in the project, while they regard the border-ing streets as more dangerous. On the other hand, residents who do not know the street youths have the opposite opin-ion, viewing the playground as more dangerous than the sur-rounding streets. Again, it appears that places habitually occupied by friends are considered safer than areas occu-pied by strangers, especially areas occupied by threatening strangers.

Finally, map-drawers felt that areas dominated by their own ethnic group were safer than those dominated by other groups. More blacks than Chinese see the playground as safe, while the square, an area normally used by Chinese ladies to sit and visit, is seen as safe by a higher proportion of Chinese than blacks (see Table 6). About thirty residents drew free-hand maps of the city indicating safe and dangerous neigh-borhoods, and again, most indicated that the territories of their own ethnic group were safe and those of other groups were not. A few differentiated a portion of their ethnic com-munity as dangerous because of the fights that occur there, but all indicated that areas occupied by hostile ethnic groups were dangerous for them.

Thus, notions of safe and dangerous places take into ac-count territory, ethnic hostilities and conflicts, the presence of hostile strangers, familiarity, the availability of friends, and the design of spaces, as well as the incidence of crime. In-triguingly, respondents generally make explicit reference only to the incidence of crime; the other criteria emerge unconsciously.

CRIME RATES AND THE MEANING OF CRIME

Not only are Dover Square's residents' notions of danger seemingly independent of crime rates but their perceptions of what constitutes a serious crime also differ from the defini-tions put forward by the police and the FBI. Unlike the po-lice, residents take the social context of a crime into account in evaluating whether or not it is serious. The level of risk that residents perceive is thus not adequately measured by police statistics on calls for assistance or to report crimes. Scholars have repeatedly emphasized the inaccuracy of reported crime statistics as a measure of the volume of crime; this study suggests that statistics also fail to measure the impact of crime on the average citizen (see Wilson 1966; Biderman and Reiss 1967; Wolfgang 1967; Pepinsky 1980).

According to the police and the FBI, serious crimes are homicide, rape, robbery (theft of property by force or threat of force), assault, burglary (unlawful entry of a building with intent to steal), larceny (theft of property without use of force or fraud), and auto theft. These constitute the seven "index" crimes that are generally aggregated in discussions of crime rates and trends. Arson, receiving stolen property, vandalism, fraud, prostitution, family squabbles, drunkenness, and passing worthless checks constitute a second category of less serious crimes. Yet a comparison of the results of my victimization survey with police statistics for the same area and time period reveals that Dover Square residents differ in the way they define crimes they consider serious. Each of 244 residents was asked, "Have you ever been the victim of a crime?" This allowed the respondent to define for himself the meaning of crime.

Two significant differences appear between the police statistics and the survey data for the project. First, theft not accompanied by a personal confrontation—larcenies—are frequently not reported by victims, although they are classified as serious crimes by the police. I recorded only half as many larcenies per thousand residents during the four-year period between 1972 and 1976 as were reported to the police in the same period (see Table 8). Although residents may call the police for assistance at the time of the theft in the hope of regaining the stolen property, such incidents are of minor significance to the victim and are quickly forgotten, a pattern that occurs nationwide as well (McIntyre 1967: 37). Yet larcenies represent a high proportion of crimes reported to the police. In Dover Square, one-third of the crimes recorded by the police between 1972 and 1976 were larcenies, and in 1975, according to the Uniform Crime Report, 53 percent of all index crimes nationwide were larcenies. Thus, aggregate measures of serious crime that lump larceny with personal crimes of violence exaggerate the frequency with which victims experience crimes they view as serious.

On the other hand, victims perceive crimes of violence committed by strangers as serious, even if they are unsuccessful attempts or if little property is stolen. Robberies, burglaries, and purse snatches, each implying the potential for violence and typically committed by strangers, are reported in the victimization survey more often than they are to the police. In the victimization survey, I found an average annual burglary rate six times higher than that recorded by the police (see Table 8). Attempted burglaries account for part of this discrepancy. An attempted burglary, even if nothing is stolen, still implies that the house is not an invulnerable, safe place and proves that there are people trying to invade it. Dover Square residents who return home to find a window pried loose or crowbar marks on the door, or who interrupt a burglar and send him scurrying out a window without his spoils, consider these incidents serious crimes and recall them when asked about experiences with victimization. Most residents, however, hesitate to call when there has been little or no property stolen and feel that calling is futile in any case. Nationwide, in 1975 only 7 percent of reported burglaries were attempts (Uniform Crime Reports 1975: 28). Attempted robberies and purse snatches also rarely precipitated a call to the police. And many residents failed to report even successful robberies, believing that there was very little the police could do, or else that they would face retaliation. I recorded an average annual robbery and attempted robbery rate of sixteen per thousand residents in comparison with police statistics of thirteen per thousand.

On the other hand, some forms of violence defined as crimes by the police are not perceived as crimes by the victims. The key determinant is the relationship between assailant and victim. An assault, a physical attack by one person on another, is defined as a crime by the police regardless of the relationship between assailant and victim, but Dover Square residents regard assaults as crimes only if they are committed by strangers. The same attack committed by a friend or an acquaintance is not seen as a crime. In the victimization survey, several residents, whom I was aware from previous conversations recently had been assaulted by people they knew, both friends and enemies, failed to mention these incidents to me when queried about their experiences with victimization. Yet these same persons did report assaults committed by strangers. For example, one young man angered his girlfriend's brothers, who accused him of making her a drug addict. They attacked the boy and beat him. In another altercation, two acquaintances fought, using chains and dogs, to win the attentions of a girl. Another boy had his bike stolen at knife point by a neighbor he knew and recognized. In two families, a family member was killed by his associates in gangland activities. Yet none of these violent incidents was mentioned when I asked about victimization. These individuals, however, did report a variety of other violent incidents as cases of victimization. One man was robbed while selling drugs to a customer in a public housing project ten blocks from Dover Square. Another was robbed and assaulted in a hallway of the project while buying drugs from someone he barely knew. A third was assaulted by strangers as he walked into the project in the middle of the afternoon. A fourth, walking on the street alone at three in the morning, was jumped and beaten by three strangers who tried to steal his diamond jewelry. It appears that residents perceive as crime unprovoked violence by strangers, but not fights to settle disputes or avenge insults between people who know one another.

An extended case study illustrates how the meaning of an assault changes as the relationship between the assailant and his victim shifts. In this case, which involved George and Renee, the meaning of assault shifted as the relationship became more distant.

> Renee and George fought frequently during their years together, both of them threatening and striking one another in the course of their quarrels. The relationship gradually deteriorated, and Renee moved back to her mother's house in another part of Dover Square. Renee and George continued to see one another off and on, but George, Renee, and their friends considered the relationship over.
>
> One day soon after the split, George spotted Renee riding with their baby in a car with James, his worst en-

emy, also a Dover Square resident. George claimed that Renee was taking too big a risk with their baby to put her in James' car, since she knew how much James hated George. (Thus, he justified his complaint about Renee riding with James not in terms of his claims over Renee, but in terms of his claims over his daughter. This emphasis indicated that he also accepted a downward shift in their relationship.) In addition to accusing her, he also slapped her, in public, in front of several of their friends.

Renee's mother was interviewed twice about her experiences with victimization, both before and after this incident. Before, while George and Renee were living together, she made no comments about the fact that her daughter occasionally was hit by her boyfriend. She probably knew about it since mother and daughter were close and lived nearby. After the incident, she told the interviewer that her daughter had been the victim of a crime: she had been assaulted. This incident was defined as a crime, where previous beatings had not been viewed that way. The only change was in the nature of the relationship. When George played the role of husband, he had the right to beat her, but after the split, he did not. His beating was viewed as crime.

A second incident illustrates the same point. Immediately after this fracas, George moved out of Dover Square, leaving his apartment in the care of a friend. Renee then returned to the apartment, taking the stereo, TV set, and other items that George claimed were his. In response to a question about victimization, he said that Renee had robbed him, but failed to mention her threats and assaults of previous years. His new relationship to Renee now made her removal of the stereo and TV set a crime.

Thus, both the meaning of crime and the meaning of danger are complex, multi-faceted, and contextually relative. Neighborhood crime rates are clearly a poor guide to perceptions of danger. Many separate strands intertwine to create the fear of crime in Dover Square.

A THEORY OF DANGER

Insights drawn from the experience of one neighborhood that has unique problems and a resident group of criminals make it possible to construct a theory about the social conditions under which danger becomes a salient issue. The theory may not be applicable elsewhere, but it offers an hypothesis worth testing in other neighborhoods: The sense of danger is rooted in feelings of uncertainty, helplessness, and vulnerability triggered by encounters with strangers who belong to unfamiliar, hostile, and potentially harmful groups. The dangerous group generally differs in ethnic background, but suspicion may also arise due to differences in class and life style. Knowledge of the identities of potentially hostile people, and familiarity with their ways of life tend to diminish feelings of danger.

A stranger is not perceived as a unique individual having a personal history, reputation, and location in social space. Instead, visible and obvious cues, such as age, sex, dress, demeanor, ethnicity, location, and mode of speaking, are used to place a stranger in a social category associated with certain expected behaviors. Mitchell states that categorical relationships "arise in situations where, by the nature of things, contacts must be superficial and perfunctory" (1966: 52). He argues that categories codify and order social interaction in otherwise uncertain, unstructured urban situations (1956). Sociology of the stranger has identified two types of stranger: the newcomer and the marginal man. The newcomer is a temporarily unidentified person; the marginal man is someone who remains a stranger because he never truly belongs to any group. Unlike the newcomer, however, he is perceived as an individual (see Park 1952; Wood 1934; Schuetz 1944; Greifer 1945; Siu 1952; McLemore 1970; Levine 1979).

Categories emerge from experience and from shared cultural expectations. Each category is a compromise with reality. Categories inevitably ignore individual variations and may even lump very different individuals together. Because accurate and finely honed social categories develop through cultural familiarity and social contact, socially distant and unfamiliar strangers will be assigned to grosser and less refined categories than those who inhabit more familiar social worlds. The less contact an individual has with members of other groups, the less accurately will he categorize these groups. Thus entire ethnic or age groups may be inaccurately categorized as dangerous, immoral, or threatening.

Furthermore, predictions of behavior based on categories, even with accurate categories, are far less certain than predictions based on knowledge of the particular habits and propensities of an individual. The stranger's behavior is likely to appear unexpected and unprovoked, leaving the observer with the feeling that there is little he can do to avoid attack. Psychological studies show that fear comes from the experience of helplessness in the face of harm, the sense that there is no place or time of safety nor any course of action which will guarantee safety (Seligman 1975).

Strangers thus are feared and considered dangerous because they are particularly difficult to predict or control.

In Dover Square, Chinese residents know little about the black residents and are unable to distinguish the few youths who are likely to rob or attack them from the vast majority who have no such intention. Because social networks are circumscribed by ethnic boundaries, the Chinese are excluded from the flow of information among blacks, and to a lesser extent among whites, about particular youths and their reputations. They categorize all blacks as dangerous people. They feel surrounded by threatening individuals. Syrian-Lebanese whites, in contrast, can distinguish a few individuals known to commit crimes and are familiar with street life and its cues for identifying potential criminals. They are more sophisticated in drawing distinctions between black strangers. Blacks are even more skilled at perceiving these differences.

On the other hand, blacks are unsophisticated in distinguishing among Chinese residents. They believe all Chinese are rich, which ignores differences between restaurant owners and workers, and between established Toishanese families whose children have professional jobs and recent, poverty-stricken Hong Kong immigrants. Some street youths think all Chinese are skilled in the martial arts and involved in the Chinatown underworld or gang fighting, again assuming that the few recent immigrants and failed scholars who have turned to the street life represent the entire population. Whites who complain about illegal aliens, overcrowded apartments, and strange dietary habits similarly fail to distinguish between recent immigrants from Hong Kong—who are forced to live with relatives in crowded apartments, as they had to in Hong Kong, and are used to spartan food habits—and families who have been in the United States much longer and have moved into their own apartments and acquired many characteristics of American culture. Finally, both blacks and Chinese assume that the whites are closely linked to the white power structure and have disproportionate control over what happens in the project. The reality is that, although they do have more ties to the police and the management than blacks or Chinese, in the context of American society, Dover Square's whites are at the bottom of the status hierarchy and have very little economic or political clout.

As we have seen, the sharpest social cleavage in the project is between the Chinese and the English-speaking segments of the population. This is reflected in the construction of categorical identities. Blacks and whites are more sophisticated in drawing internal distinctions between strangers in each other's group than either is about the Chinese or the Chinese are about blacks and whites.

The process of recognizing individuals and drawing internal distinctions becomes more difficult when groups are racially different. People learn which variations in physical characteristics are emic, or meaningful, in differentiating individuals in their own racial group. But, these may not be meaningful in other races. Whites, for example, rely on hair color and eye color to differentiate individuals, but for blacks and Chinese, these features are invariant. Blacks stress skin shade, and Chinese emphasize face and eye shape, while whites tend to ignore these features. The tendency to miss important cues because they are not emic to the observer accounts for the commonly expressed sentiments, "All blacks look alike," "All Chinese look alike," and "All whites look alike." Blacks often observe that whites are poor at telling them apart or at recognizing family resemblances. One enterprising robber realized that this was an advantage for him when robbing whites, since they had difficulty identifying him again. As an example of this process, even though I am a brown-eyed brunette, I was once confused with a blue-eyed blond by a black woman who apparently noticed only that I was white.

Symbolic Meanings of Danger in Small-Scale Societies

Notions of danger in small-scale societies studied by anthropologists reveal intriguing similarities to the conceptions of Dover Square residents. Every society imposes symbolic meanings on events and objects. Symbolic anthropologists attempt to understand the processes by which these cultural meanings are constructed and become systems and how they are related to features of social structure. Further, they seek cross-cultural regularities in the construction of symbolic systems and their relationship to social patterns.

Douglas and Turner, two leading symbolic anthropologists, have linked conceptions of danger to features of social organization. In her analysis of purity and pollution, Douglas argues that danger is something out of place (1966). What is unclear and contradictory in society tends to be considered polluting, unclean, and dangerous. Persons who occupy transitional or ambiguous statuses, such as the unborn child or the boy undergoing a rite of passage, are thought to have the power to harm and to be particularly vulnerable to harm (1966: 114–126). Individuals who occupy ambiguous or weakly defined roles, or operate in inarticulate parts of the social system, are accused of possessing involuntary spiritual powers such as witchcraft. Those who occupy interstitial positions, operating in a social subsystem in which they are not full members but appear as intruders, are also thought to wield dangerous powers. Such people have a clearly defined status in one subsystem and an ambiguous one in another, for example, the father in the Trobriand or Ashanti matrilineage or the mother's brother in the Tikopia or Tallensi patrilineage.

Douglas argues that outsiders appear dangerous in Western, secular society as well as in simple, ritually oriented social systems. She cites the reluctance to accept back into society those who have been outside society in mental hospitals or prisons. These people remain marginal and are considered unreliable and possessed of negative social attributes: the taint of being outsiders remains. The rest of society feels it must protect itself from these dangerous individuals (1966: 117–118).*

Turner develops this argument further in his discussion of the ritual state of liminality, the stage of transition between one state and another during which the individual does not occupy any status that is part of the hierarchical structure of society (1967: 93). This ritual state represents non-structure, and consequently appears dangerous and anarchical to those concerned with maintaining the structure of society. Those in liminal states are often regarded as possessing dangerous, polluting, and inauspicious magico-religious powers (1969: 109). Turner distinguishes between two polluting, dangerous states: those that are caused by ambiguously or contradictorily defined statuses and those that derive from ritualized transitional states (1967: 97). The first are states defectively defined and ordered; the second are those that cannot be structured, such as liminal states.

Thus, in small-scale societies, according to Douglas and Turner, those who do not fit into the ordered hierarchy, those

---

*Needham takes issue with Douglas's definition of danger, arguing that there is nothing intrinsically dangerous about a boundary (1979: 43–47). Hazards may befall someone who fails to follow the proper course of ritual, but, as long as he behaves properly, he will not be in danger. Needham, however, misinterprets Douglas by emphasizing the role of boundaries rather than the role of ambiguous and marginal social positions. It is the uncertainty and strangeness of these social positions, not their association with boundaries, that renders them dangerous. My analysis supports Douglas's notion that danger adheres to people in ambiguous and marginal social positions. In both urban and small-scale societies, it appears that the difficulty of predicting and controlling such people, not the simple threat of retribution, generates a sense of danger. By defining danger too narrowly, as the risk of physical harm, Needham ignores the range of non-violent psychic and moral harms incorporated in notions of danger in the society I studied, and perhaps also in those Douglas has examined.

who are beyond the society's power to order and control behavior, are often viewed as a threat by those seeking reasons for their misfortunes. The residents of a high-crime neighborhood use the same principles to pinpoint the source of the hazards they face. They similarly perceive dangerous persons as those who are unfamiliar and unknown, those who are outside their predictable social world.

Clearly, there are vast differences between simple and complex societies in their organization and in the kinds of hazards their members encounter. The resident of a small-scale society is afraid of accidents, wasting disease, political and economic defeat, and death; the urbanite particularly fears violent attacks and neighborhood change. The causes of misfortune are also perceived differently. A person in a small-scale society believes that many of his misfortunes are caused by the action of supernatural forces propelled by another's illwill: the urbanite sees his misfortunes as the undeserved consequences of random hostile acts committed by others. Yet in both kinds of society those who suffer misfortune do not know where the final responsibility lies. They do not know exactly whom to blame, nor is there any obvious connection between perpetrator and misfortune (Sansom 1972: 198–199). Consequently, they locate the source of the danger they face in persons who are not full members of their social and cultural world. As strangers, such persons always have the potential for appearing dangerous; in a climate of concern about violent crime or supernatural ills, it is these strangers who will be blamed.

CHAPTER 6

Managing Danger

In this Hobbesian world, individuals deserted by the state and abandoned by their neighbors are forced to manage danger on their own. Strategies for coping fall into three basic patterns. The first, a commonly used approach, is cognitive mapping: the construction of cognitive categories that delineate places, times, and persons that are dangerous and safe. The second includes a variety of offensive strategies based on the management of interpersonal relationships and the skillful handling of potentially harmful persons. A reputation for being tough, hard to push around, and willing to retaliate provides a kind of armor against attack and against feelings of danger. Yet to be known implies that one also knows others; these strategies function only within the context of personalized relationships. A third pattern of coping is defensive withdrawal: retreat into homes fortified by locks, bars, and dogs, from which one ventures only in the glare of daylight, armed with guns and accompanied by allies. Yet security achieved in this fashion can be shattered as easily as the shell of protection can be cracked: by a crowbar mark on the door, by a window pried loose, by a burglar discovered in the house. And, despite these defenses, one must still venture outside.

STRATEGIES OF CRIME

Robbers and burglars in Dover Square adopt sophisticated strategies to identify good victims—to maximize their incomes—and to avoid detection and punishment—to minimize their risks. A successful robber must know how to pick a victim: he tries to predict who is likely to scream and who will not, who will fight back and who will not, who will call the police or testify in court and who will not. Robbers construct social categories of their own to make these decisions. People who speak Chinese, for example, are ideal victims because they cannot call the police or testify in court. One young man said that he could identify those Chinese who do not speak English: they smile by opening and closing their mouths and bowing their heads a little bit. Chinese women are particularly good victims since they are frightened and rarely resist or call out. Chinese women returning from garment factories, and restaurant workers walking home late at night, are both likely to carry cash earned at work. Other favorite victims are outsiders, especially white men who work in nearby office buildings and park their cars in the project. Their briefcases, suits, and expensive cars are red flags to robbers.

If someone has money, he may intimate this by putting his hands in his pockets if he sees someone likely to rob him. Similarly, a woman who looks afraid and clutches her purse broadcasts that she is a good victim. Robbers look for people who appear scared, who cross the street to avoid them, who walk fast and nervously, and who are not friendly. If someone passes by giving off these signals, he may inspire a robber who was not even thinking about stealing just then.

On the other hand, some social categories define poor victims. The local robbers believe that Irish are bad victims because they are known to be bold and stand up to thieves; Jews love their money and will kill over a penny; Italians are gangsters. Many Chinese are tough and know kung fu, but old women rarely do. Although whites have no particular image of toughness, they have all the guns and control things. It is better to rob a business rather than to take a poor person's money, since the poor person will fight harder for it. Several of the black youths who commit robberies said that they would not rob a black person, particularly a woman or someone who is young and strong. One young man claimed that he avoids black victims because he believes that blacks are likely to be poor and suffer more hardship from a theft than whites, while another said it is because they are more likely to know him or know someone else who knows him. However, despite this ideal, where alternative victims are lacking, blacks do rob other blacks. Further, some blacks are robbed or burglarized because they "gossip too much," talking about who has done what when they are not really sure. As George put it, "If these people didn't talk to their friends all the time and blame people unfairly for committing crimes, it would cut down on robberies."

To rob successfully, robbers must also discover who has money and where it is hidden. One approach is to station oneself near the check-cashing window at the supermarket and "scope"—watch who cashes a check and where he or she puts the money. Another strategy is to approach a stranger and ask for change for a twenty-dollar bill, examining the contents and location of his wallet when he pulls it out to help. Well-dressed people are tempting. Sometimes a robber regularly observes a potential victim's daily habits to determine when he comes home with his paycheck. One man was robbed regularly every week as he came home from work until his friends suggested that he adopt a different technique for bringing home his pay. Robbery of welfare checks arriving on the same day every month became so frequent that the welfare department began to send out checks on staggered days. One young man stressed the importance of watching people very carefully and getting to know their habits, being prepared sometimes to wait even two or three weeks before robbing or burglarizing them.

Burglaries require extensive knowledge of the victim's possessions and daily habits. The burglar observes when a new TV set or stereo is delivered to the house and watches the residents come and go. He may hear the stereo at night or see movers carry the possessions into the house. Of particular interest are people who look as if they have money: who have nice cars, clothes, and jewelry. People who live regular, patterned lives and leave the house at the same time every day make better victims than those who are more erratic or who are home all day. As one burglar said, "It takes heart to go into a house, and you want to know that it is empty and that there is something worth taking."

Ethnic and personal animosities often determine the choice of victim. The most active burglars among the project youths hate the Chinese, particularly their tendency to retaliate for crimes by sending youth gangs after them, or by putting out a "contract" on them. They resent the wealth of the Chinese, their rapid ascension into the middle class, and their unfriendly demeanor. Several of the black youths cited the hostility and bad attitude of the Chinese as reason for attacking them. One young man pointed out that the Chinese are foreigners, do not belong here, and make too much money. Whites, on the other hand, are resented because they control society and deny access to minorities. And individuals who are "nosy" and who call the police are attacked by those they accuse. Between one-third and one-half of the burglaries of black families I recorded were justified by local youths as acts of retaliation. People who are friendly to the street youths and who do not report them to the police are spared.

Robbers and burglars are highly skilled at avoiding detection. Robberies happen very fast: the robber quickly takes the purse or wallet and escapes. Ideal locations for robberies are those with multiple escape routes, those where a few turns allow the youth to vanish. Robbers also avoid places within eyesight of people known to be "nosy," preferring spots that are not visible at all, or visible only to people who are certain not to intervene. Dark, poorly lighted locations and nighttime are both preferred because these conditions make it difficult for the victim to see the assailant, much less identify him later, and fewer people look out their windows at night. Robbers also prefer to attack from behind so that they cannot be seen. They believe that victims rarely look at faces anyway, only at clothes. After a successful robbery, they often go home and change clothes before returning to the playground to discuss the exploit with friends. For some time, a multi-ethnic burglary ring operated in Dover Square, exploiting the lack of contact between ethnic groups. Two blacks, two Chinese, and one white cooperated, with each group tipping off the others about potential victims in his own group. The Chinese youths, for example, knew the regular habits and working times of the Chinese families and told the blacks, who did the stealing. When a wedding banquet occurred in Chinatown, drawing many Chinese families out of their homes, the Chinese youths informed the blacks and whites, who carried out the burglary and gave part of the take to the Chinese waiting around the corner. Similarly, the Chinese carried out the burglary when a black youth told them that a black acquaintance had just purchased an expensive TV set or camera.

The youths committing crimes are also sophisticated about the police and court system. One young man never used a weapon in robberies because, if he got caught, the charge would no longer be larceny, a misdemeanor, but assault and battery, a felony. Another said he avoids female victims, since judges are likely to be harder on an accused person when the offense is against a woman and are less likely to believe his story. The street youths know the names and reputations of many of the detectives in the local district police station and have some acquaintance with local judges and probation officers. They think in terms of what kinds of stories judges will believe. For example, one morning I met one of the street youths dressed in an immaculate suit, a very unusual garb for him, who said that he was going to court that day and wanted to show that he was an upstanding citizen. He was going to claim that he was in school. Another young man robbed an acquaintance in broad daylight, arguing that no judge would believe that someone would actually do that.

The most notorious local burglar, a young man in and out of jail for the three years preceding my study of Dover Square, who claims that he plans to spend the rest of his life in crime, expressed his views about crime and himself during a brief period when he was back out on the street:

> Crime is a form of guerilla warfare. I really hate the Chinese, so that I think they are good victims. Burglars do not all get caught sooner or later; it depends on their skill and their luck. But even if I get caught and spend six months in jail, if I make $30,000 before that, that isn't bad, it isn't really being caught at all. I can make between $100 and $150 a day stealing, and there is always the chance of a windfall, of making much more. It is exciting and it takes heart to be a burglar. Burglary is

much harder than robbery. Robbing you have to guess how people are going to react, but you can usually tell: you can make a guess, an estimate. But it is important to be fast.

If anybody comes to attack me, I will fight back and break two legs, two arms, or whatever is necessary. I don't mess around. One thing jail does is make you bitter, make you so that you don't care, which is why people beat someone over the head when they are being robbed. They don't care if they hurt them. I don't like to use violence, but if someone uses it against me, I will do it right back. If someone takes out a gun, I will shoot him, because I don't want to get shot myself. Women should carry an ice pick and be prepared to stab someone if they attack them. I don't know when I learned this, learned to fight, but I was quite young.

STRATEGIES OF PROTECTION

Cognitive Mapping

One way residents of Dover Square cope with the hazardous environment is to develop cognitive models or maps of places, persons, and times that they view as safe and dangerous. These maps are subjective representations imposed on the physical realities of space and time, distortions of reality that reflect the individual's past experience and knowledge. They guide movements through the project and behavior toward strangers.

The notion of a cognitive map as a spatial representation developed in psychology, geography, and planning (e.g., Lynch 1960; Downs and Stea 1973; Gould and White 1974; Proshansky, Ittelson, and Rivlin 1976) is a particularly useful tool for anthropologists interested in the ways individuals perceive and conceptualize their worlds. Suttles' notion of the "defended neighborhood" is a kind of cognitive map (1972). He argues that urbanites divide the continuous physical structure of the city into a series of discrete neighborhoods, "creative impositions" on the continuity of actual city form. The defended neighborhood is a mental abstraction of an area that is perceived as safe. These maps serve to guide and channel the urbanite's movements through the city, inducing him to restrict his activities to his own neighborhood. The defended neighborhood "restricts the range of association and decreases anonymity; it thrusts people together into a common network of social relations that overlap rather than diverge from one another" (1972: 32). Suttles, however, confuses the idea of a "defended neighborhood" with the real physical space defended by gangs. Both are kinds of "defended neighborhood," but of a very different order.

The process of constructing cognitive maps involves drawing distinctions and making generalizations. Maps of areas that are well known are more finely differentiated; maps of unfamiliar areas are broken into larger, less detailed sections. The process parallels the construction of categorical identities. If a person hears about a crime in a familiar area, he may decide that the corner, block, or immediate neighborhood is dangerous, but will not extend this attitude to the entire neighborhood. Hearing of a similar incident in an unfamiliar area, one of the blank spaces on his cognitive map, he is likely to generalize his sense of danger to the entire section since he cannot pinpoint a particular streetcorner or street he should avoid. Through this process of generalization, unfamiliar areas gradually acquire a more dangerous reputation, while the same spate of crimes in a familiar area brands only a few corners or blocks as dangerous. If people avoid the dangerous sections, this differential generalization has important implications for the way they use the city. People who live in hazardous environments routinely learn which specific areas are particularly bad, while those who lack this knowledge avoid the entire area, a process Hannerz observed among black ghetto dwellers in Washington (1969).

Dover Square residents use the same strategy. Black residents who drew freehand maps of the entire city, for example, distinguished between sections of Winslow that are particularly dangerous, such as public housing projects, and others that are relatively safe. Whites and Chinese, who do not know Winslow, perceived the entire area as uniformly dangerous. It seemed that those who drew more accurate and detailed maps of both Dover Square and the adjacent neighborhoods were less frightened than those who drew less sophisticated maps.

Questionnaire data on the construction of categorical identities suggest that these concepts are similarly dependent on experience and familiarity. Using a five-point scale, sixty-five individuals (twenty-six Chinese, sixteen blacks, eleven whites, nine Hispanics, and one West Indian) rated the relative danger of social categories defined by age, sex, and ethnicity. The responses differed significantly by ethnic group, and revealed a tendency to see one's own group as safer. For example, 30 percent of the Chinese, 33 percent of the whites, 33 percent of the Hispanics, and only 25 percent of the blacks rated teenage black girls as dangerous, while 25 percent of the blacks, 14 percent of the Hispanics, 9 percent of the whites, and none of the Chinese saw adult Chinese men the same way. Teenage Hispanic boys seemed dangerous to 56 percent of the blacks, 63 percent of the Chinese, 83 percent of the whites, and only 22 percent of the Hispanics. Blacks as a whole seemed less concerned than whites or Chinese about teenagers. Teenage white boys were thought dangerous by 31 percent of blacks, 59 percent of Chinese, 44 percent of Hispanics, and 58 percent of whites (see Table 9).

Age and sex differences produced greater variation than ethnic differences in perceptions of dangers. All groups consistently perceived women and older people as much less dangerous than young people, regardless of ethnicity. Teenage males were considered most dangerous. Teenage black boys seemed dangerous to 56 percent of blacks, 70 percent of Chinese, 55 percent of Hispanics, and 50 percent of whites, while no one considered adult Chinese women dangerous. Overall, 9 percent of the respondents felt that blacks were not dangerous, 12 percent felt the same about both Hispanics and whites, and 23 percent about Chinese, while 19 percent felt that way about teenagers, 29 percent about adults, 46 percent said the same about the elderly, and 27 percent expressed this opinion about children. Twenty-five percent felt that males were not dangerous, and 37 percent said the same about females. Thus, Dover Square residents take age, sex, and ethnicity into account in constructing social categories of dangerous people.

Interpersonal Management and Confrontation

Residents also adopt a variety of offensive, active strategies for managing encounters with potentially dangerous people. One of these is to maintain a determined, businesslike manner: an appearance of self-confidence and strength, and a studied indifference to the safety of pockets or purses where money could be concealed send off signals that a person is a poor choice as a victim. The self-presentation should indicate that this person will resist if attacked. Any indications of fear, timidity, or clutching of purse or pocket communicate the opposite: fear and something to hide. A young black woman was emphatic about this. When she carries home the cash from the laundromat where her mother works, she saunters confidently past the street youths in the playground. "If you walk naturally with your bag, they won't do anything, but if you suddenly clutch it and hold it tight, they will figure you have something to steal and are more likely to take it." George suggests going up to someone who looks as if he is about to rob you and saying "Hello, how are you doing? "What's happening?" or even, "Don't I know you from somewhere? What's your name?" Even if the robber is not conned into thinking he is known, he may pause for a minute, and will probably not finish the robbery. Once he reveals his name, he will certainly not rob the person. George thinks that it is most important to treat the criminal like a person, to smile at him and not be afraid of him. Even if you simply say "Hi!" to him, it startles him for a moment, and he will probably not rob you.

Another offensive strategy is to be wary, suspicious, and distrustful, although not to appear so. One must be careful who one allows into the house and avoid letting in drug addicts, if possible, although it is also risky to let a drug addict know that he is not considered trustworthy. People who have frequent visitors to their homes are regarded as inviting trouble, and if they are victimized, it is assumed that they are partly to blame. I once mentioned to some of the street youths that I was thinking about having a party at my house, and they advised me to be very careful who I let in.

One black woman said that one must be careful who one's friends are and screen everyone who comes into the house. When she is asleep, she locks her door and keeps the key so that her young children will not be able to let anyone in without her knowing it. She also, however, tries to be friendly to those she suspects of being criminals. She described one incident in which a boy she knew came to her house after 6:00 P.M., asking if she could get him his clothes from the dry cleaning shop she managed. He had only a ten-dollar bill. She told him to go to the store and get change and then her daughter would get the clothes. Although she had enough change in the house, she did not want him to know that, and she took her pocketbook upstairs before she let him in. At the same time, she did not want him to think that they did not trust him, nor did she want to make him suspicious, so they invited him in and did what he asked. I asked if he would actually rob her, knowing that she knew him. She said he would if he had been drinking, and since she could tell he had been drinking and probably had some drugs in him, she did not want to take the chance. A white woman pointed out that when she walks around, she is always cautious and aware, although not really scared. She is very conscious of other people and pays attention to what they are doing. She looks carefully to see if they are going to bother her. She thinks she can usually tell, perhaps 80 percent of the time, by the way they look, although she could not be explicit about her criteria, saying it was just something about their expression.

A third strategy emphasizes modes of handling other people who might be dangerous. One should avoid getting such people angry, keep cool, and mind one's own business, and avoid getting involved with other people. As a young white man, native to James Hill, said, "If you don't bother people, they won't bother you. You stay out of trouble, and you won't have trouble." Most blacks said that the best form of protection is to "mind your own business." One should not get involved in other people's lives and not judge others or report them to the police. When people are working, according to one woman, a place is much safer because they do not have time to mind each other's business, which always leads to trouble. She protects herself by not getting too friendly with others and not visiting them in their homes. One of her favorite aphorisms is, "Long visits make short friends."

A black woman emphasized the importance of being able to handle people. She described the problems of a Chinese neighbor who cares about her car very much. The street youths continually harass her and do things to the car. One day she even found some BB holes in the window. The black woman pointed out that since the youths know she cares so much, they delight in tormenting her. If she nicely asked them to leave when they were playing baseball next to it, that would be all right, but when she sits by, tenses up, and looks anguished every time a bike comes near they notice this and harass her by vandalizing the car. Another young man has a friend who killed someone in a fight when he was fourteen. When I asked if he was afraid to be around him, the youth said no, because he is careful not to aggravate him or fight with him.

A fourth offensive strategy is to develop a reputation as a person who is tough, who stands up for himself, and who will retaliate in some fashion if he is abused. Personal confrontations, mobilizing allies who can attack, or even calling the police or using the courts are responses that give a person an image as someone who is "not to be messed with." By acquiring this kind of reputation, a person gains protection not only for himself but for his entire family. Persons who gain such reputations are respected and feel relatively confident that they will not be attacked or victimized in the project except by outsiders.

Those who do not resist at all fare worst. As a young black woman said, "If they find they can do harm to people and get away with it, they will do anything. That gets them bold, and then they do it again." A young man began a career in crime when he discovered how easy it was to steal and get away with it. Although many residents fear that calling the police about the street youths will bring retribution, surprisingly often it does not. In several cases, individuals who called the police, testified against the youths, and helped send them to jail suffered no retaliation. Before a trial, the youths threaten and attempt to scare off witnesses, but once a conviction is final, they abandon the idea of revenge because revenge will not reverse the sentence and only risks further charges. Further, only the people who call the police are resented; those who employ violent retaliation are felt to be acting appropriately.

Violent retaliation is not possible for all Dover Square residents, however. It requires, first, that the victim identify and locate the offender and, second, that he himself can fight or is able to mobilize allies who can. Although the identification of offenders within the same ethnic group is generally possible through extended networks, between ethnic groups it becomes problematic. Several cases in which victims resorted to violence or threats of violence illustrate the critical role of preexisting social contacts across ethnic boundaries in retaliating against offenders in other ethnic groups.

An elderly Chinese woman with failing eyesight, who lived alone in the high-rise section, was robbed by three young blacks whom she mistook for her grandchildren. Her twenty-four-year-old grandson, who lived in the low-rise, was skilled in the martial arts and a member of a Chinatown martial arts club. Since he had attended school with Roscoe, a leader of the street youths and a notorious burglar, he went immediately to Roscoe's grandmother and told her that whether or not her grandson was guilty, he was sure that he was involved. He threatened that if anyone came to bother his grandmother again or if Roscoe appeared in the laundromat, he would kill him. Roscoe and his friends avoided the laundromat for an entire week, and the old lady was not robbed again. It is worth noting, too, that this Chinese youth's mother, who lives with him in Dover Square, is an exceptional Chinese woman in that she does not think the project is particularly dangerous. She feels fairly safe because she knows who the "bad" people are.

In a similar case, some youths robbed a white woman whose husband, unbeknownst to them, was Chinese. As soon as the husband came home from work, he went straight to the playground, demanded the wallet back, and announced that he did not want anyone "messing" with his wife or he would have to answer to him. The youths meekly handed the wallet back and have left the woman alone since then. (As background for these incidents, a major black/Chinese confrontation, to be described below, had convinced the street youths that the Chinese are violent and willing to retaliate.)

In general, whites are more likely than Chinese to retaliate for victimization. A young white man from James Hill, familiar with street life, found his car antenna broken. He found out who did it from some of the neighborhood children and then slashed the tires of the culprit's car. He is not frightened of Dover Square and does not think it is at all dangerous. In contrast, a Chinese man whose car was vandalized was unable to discover who was responsible and felt powerless to protect it. He finds the project quite dangerous. A white woman lives alone, but feels fairly safe because her brother, who is highly proficient in kung fu, told the street youths to leave his sister alone. Another white woman feels that the project is safe for her because her son knows a young neighbor who is an active member of the purse-snatch gang. He told the boy that if his mother was ever robbed or attacked, he would hold him personally responsible and beat him up, even if the boy was not involved himself. The son felt that this boy, if he wanted to, could stop other boys from robbing his mother. A James Hill woman often yells at the street youths to stop a crime or to refrain from riding noisy motorbikes through the project. She feels fairly safe because her twenty-five-year-old son threatened to beat the teenagers up if they bothered her. Although her environment contains many hazards, she does not view it as particularly dangerous for her.

Where misdeeds cross-cut ethnic boundaries and the protagonists do not know one another personally, successful retaliation depends on discovering second- or third-order network links that enable the victim to locate the offender. For example, a white boy, Bill, dated a Chinese girl for several months, during which time she began to take drugs. Her brothers discovered her missing one night when she spent the entire night working as a prostitute. They were furious, and blamed the white boyfriend for turning her to a life of drugs and prostitution. But they did not know where he lived or how to find him. They went first to George's house since he is friendly with some of the Chinese street groups. They knocked on George's door at about one in the morning, but found only Renee at home. She said she had no idea where Bill was. They had to wait for another opportunity to find him in a public place where they could attack him.

Meanwhile, the other members of the street group instructed Bill on techniques for handling Chinese fighters, ways to handle a knife against kung fu experts, and the need for caution and watchfulness at all times "because you cannot see them coming." A day or so later, a Chinese boy, Ho, caught Bill in the playground and pinned him to the ground, saying that he ought to kill him. Although Bill's friends were standing around, they did not intervene. Ho did not kill him, however and, according to Bill, only kicked him in the legs. Both George and Bill feel that Bill escaped lightly only because Ho did not find him that first night when he was angrier and had the assistance of his friends.

Even in a burglary, a crime that typically does not involve personal confrontation, the course of events may be affected by personal relations between the parties:

> The Curran family, a Syrian family from James Hill, was burglarized while the mother was away on vacation, leaving her two adult sons home alone. They reported the burglary of a TV set and other items to the police station, and the police soon caught a young man with a TV set in the back of his car. Since one son, Arthur, identified the TV set as his, the police arrested the suspect with the car. Another burglar who was with the first suspect ran away before the police could arrest him. The boy driving the car was not a regular member of the group who committed the burglary, but someone who had been persuaded to borrow his mother's car for the day. He claimed he was not aware that it was to be used for a crime. The older brother of this boy approached Arthur, whom he had gone to school with, and asked him not to testify that the TV set was his. Arthur refused.

Meanwhile, the police were eager to arrest the burglar who had run away, and pressured their suspect to identify the other members of the group.

A few days later, Arthur was parked in front of his house with his girlfriend when two black members of the gang, also project residents, jumped him pulled him out of the car, and stabbed him in the neck to scare him from testifying against the other suspect. Arthur recovered, organized a group of his friends from the Syrian neighborhood in James Hill, and sought out his assailants to retaliate. They found one of the two and beat him up very badly, then dragged him to the steps of the nearest police station and left him there, advising the police to arrest him. They also found the second, but he managed to escape to the police station on his bike without a beating.

The first suspect was sentenced for burglary; the second was arrested after his attack on Arthur and received a sentence for assault and battery against Arthur, who testified against him. Arthur was able to identify all the boys involved in attacking him because his cousin, who also lived in the project, was good friends with this group. Arthur says that he does not think the project is dangerous.

An effective attack may depend on mobilizing allies. In several cases, the attacker succeeded because of his access to a large group of supporters who were willing and eager to fight. Colson points out that mobilizing a group to help retaliate is a basic technique of defending one's rights in stateless societies (1974). The Dover Square situation suggests that it can also be important in state societies when other effective means of settling disputes are not available. In the cases Colson describes, mobilizing allies requires extensive investment of time and resources, since one must maintain personal relationships with others who can be called on for help. One helps others retaliate in the hope that they will reciprocate, but takes the chance that they will not. In Dover Square, only the young males have the time, resources, and inclination for such a strategy. They invest much time in socializing, perfecting their fighting skills, and strengthening social networks that can be mobilized for retaliation.

A well-known case illustrates the importance of mobilizing allies for violent retaliation, underscores the difficulties of identifying offenders across ethnic boundaries, and provides the background for contemporary conceptions of black and Chinese willingness to retaliate. The case began with the harassment of a school child and escalated into a major confrontation between blacks and Chinese. Individuals joined for their own motives, so that separate "action-sets," sets of allies, combined to produce a confrontation that appeared to be a race riot. The incident occurred in 1971, so my account is a reconstruction based on interviews with numerous black, white, and Chinese witnesses and many of the central participants. Their versions generally agree about the course of events, but disagree in their interpretation of why actors behaved as they did.

A small conflict developed between Chinese and Hispanic children in the poly-ethnic elementary school near Dover Square. Some Chinese children were harassed in school, and one or two were attacked by groups of Puerto Rican and black children as they walked home alone. Chinese community leaders began walking the Chinese children home, but one leader, who ventured, as his friend described it, "too far into James Hill" (into the black and Hispanic section), was attacked and injured by a group of black or Hispanic youths. At approximately the same time, a young black man, Wilbur, who regularly returned from work at the same time every day, entered Dover Square at his regular time through a narrow opening at one corner of the project. A large group of Chinese boys armed with bottles and knives sprang out from behind the fences encircling the trash cans and attacked him, beating him severely and yelling at him, "You took our grandmother's purse!" Few blacks were around, and the only person that Wilbur noticed helping him was a Chinese youth who lived nearby and is a skilled martial arts fighter. He was a good friend of one of Wilbur's friends. George claims that he arrived at the fracas and told the Chinese youths, who had Wilbur on the ground and were beating him up, to desist. Wilbur was hospitalized for two months.

Half an hour after this attack, Roscoe, another black leader in Dover Square, a friend of Wilbur's and George's, and widely believed responsible for many of the Dover Square crimes, was attacked in a lunch room in Chinatown where he was eating with a friend. A group of Chinese youths rushed into the lunch stand and stabbed him. No one in the restaurant made any effort to help him. He was also hospitalized. The black youths were infuriated by these attacks on their friends, which they viewed as unprovoked. Wilbur's family was particularly enraged. A neighbor had recorded the number on the license plate of the car in which Wilbur's attackers escaped. Wilbur's friends and Wilbur's brother believe that this attack was a case of mistaken identity, an effort to repay Wilbur's brother for his crimes. (They agree that Wilbur and his brother look very much alike, and Wilbur's brother is generally blamed for much of the crime in the project.)

During the next three days, periodic scuffles occurred among large groups of black and Chinese youths gathered in Dover Square. The playground was full of armed youths, and residents feared to leave their homes or walk past the groups. The Chinese youths talked of bringing in gangs from New York's Chinatown, believed to be much tougher than the local gangs, and the blacks threatened to call in reinforcements from the black public housing projects in James Hill and Winslow, also considered much more violent than Dover Square blacks. This escalation did not occur, however, although it is not clear why. The police were present, but a variety of theories that have been proposed to account for the end of the conflict do not allude to the role of the police in any way. Chinese community leaders claim that they reached the leaders of the Chinese faction and persuaded them to withdraw from the fight. Eyewitnesses claim that a black community leader walked into the middle of the crowd and somehow managed to quiet down the situation. George boasts that he cooled the fighting since he knows both the blacks and the Chinese personally. Another black leader in Dover Square felt that the fight ended simply because the Chinese youths had won and decided not to continue to fight.

Although this case represents an illustration of successful mobilization and violent retaliation, it appears that the Chinese were unable to identify the culprit precisely, but attacked his look-alike brother instead. Mobilization followed extended networks: the Chinese faction was probably mobilized through the martial arts clubs as fellow members offered to help each other retaliate for crimes against their families. Between ten and thirty club members live in Dover Square. The black faction consisted of local Dover Square blacks and friends from James Hill.

Wilbur and his family tried to take the case to court, but received no satisfaction either from the courts or the police. No one was ever arrested or prosecuted, even though Wilbur identified the leader of the attackers from the license plate and tracked down the shop where the boy's father works in Chinatown. Nor has Wilbur retaliated. He still plans revenge, but is not sure when and how it will happen. The incident is now long past, although not forgotten. This conflict convinced the street youths that all Chinese are skilled martial arts fighters and that they will cooperate to protect all other Chinese. By pretending he knew kung fu, a small Chinese boy was able to repel a group of blacks who were harassing him. Blacks are wary of attacking Chinese people while their Chinese neighbors are home, fearing that they will come to the aid of the Chinese victims.

Yet these black youths are unaware of the divisions and factions within the Chinese community that prevent such unified action. Only a minority of the Chinese youths are connected either with informal street gangs or one of the two more formal martial arts clubs located in Chinatown. Very few families have connections that would enable them to mobilize these groups against non-Chinese criminals, and most established Toishanese families with college-educated children find the Chinese gangs almost as frightening as the black muggers. Although these groups assume some responsibility for retaliating against crime committed in Chinatown, both the leaders and the Chinese residents of Dover Square assume that their jurisdiction does not extend outside Chinatown.

A few cases of retaliation or strong threats can earn someone a reputation as a person who will fight. The street youths, some hustler families, and a few other blacks and whites have earned this reputation. These people say that "everyone" knows them and therefore no one would dare to bother them. The reputation has an umbrella effect for friends and family. A young woman said she was safe anywhere in the project because her brother is known to be tough and able to fight. Another street youth said that not only does he feel safe in Dover Square, but that if his aged grandmother came into the project, she would be safe as well. No one would bother her because they would quickly find out who she was. "Everybody gets to know everyone's family real fast, and they all know who is who." Another young man, also reputed to be a good fighter, told me that if anyone bothered me in the project, I should say that I was on my way to visit him, and I would be left alone.

Simply knowing others in the project and being known to them provides a sense of safety even if one does not have a reputation for violent retaliation. An older black woman, for example, said that the project is not dangerous for her since she knows almost everybody, including the teenagers. Only the outsiders are dangerous to her, those who do not know her and whom she does not know. Another black woman believes that "no one will bother me because everyone knows who I am." By implication, she also knows who everyone else is and can decide whom to trust, whom to avoid, and how to locate who abuses her. One white teenage boy said that the project is dangerous for adults because they don't know the teenagers by name, but it is safe for him since he knows who they are. The playground is dangerous for him only if outsiders are present. When I showed a Hispanic girl two photographs of the playground, one of which was empty and the other occupied by four of the street youths playing basketball, she said that the latter was safe, the former dangerous. When the four boys were present she felt that the playground was safe since she knew all four and knew that they would not hurt her. In contrast, the empty playground was dangerous since anyone else might come there. One young black man said he felt very safe in the project because it is one "big, happy family," and he knows everyone that lives there. He does not in fact know all the residents, but those he encounters are not the kinds of strangers he worries about. In general, blacks whose social networks encompass the street youths say that the project is very safe because they "know everybody."

Yet each form of protection—appearing self-confident, suspiciousness, delicate handling of hazardous persons, retaliation, and the creation of a reputation—operates within a world of known persons and identities. Each extends only as far as gossip about reputations, events, and personal histories spreads. These strategies do not apply to the world of strangers, and only protect Dover Square residents against people who know them. Within the project, inside the sphere of known persons, these strategies do provide a sense of safety. These strategies, however, have no impact on outsiders, people who neither know nor are known by the residents of Dover Square.

Gossip and Informal Sanctions

Gossiping about deviants is a common mode of informal social control in the small-scale societies anthropologists usually study, but, in Dover Square, retaliation by gossip is a strategy of very limited efficacy. Gossip can, however, provide useful information about the identities and activities of people who commit crimes. As Hannerz (1967) points out, gossip performs two rather different functions: it is a way of sharing information and it is used in passing judgment. In Dover Square, information sharing is a useful form of protection since it provides details about reputations. This can become a source of concern if rumors of illegal activities become known to the police, but information sharing is largely restricted to extended networks, which in most cases are circumscribed by ethnic boundaries.

The impact of gossip as judgment has a far more restricted scope. It has little effect beyond intimate networks. For example, a black woman saw a gate that had been stolen from her back fence reposing on the back fence belonging to Mrs. Jones, a black neighbor. She accused Mrs. Jones's son of stealing it, but Mrs. Jones said her son had found it, not stolen it. Although many blacks in Dover Square knew about this incident, the woman's gate was never returned. Neither the son's nor the mother's intimate network condemned the action. Another example involves Renee's mother: infuriated that George had slapped her daughter, she arrived at the playground armed with a harmless aluminum pipe and some devastating gossip about George's sexual predilections. "He does it with little boys, right here in the playground," she announced, thus combining malicious gossip with the threat of violence. Later, she filed a criminal complaint against him. He immediately moved out of the project, leaving all his clothes and furniture behind, but it is difficult to sort out the relative impact of the different measures taken by Renee's mother. George claims he departed only because he was afraid the police would arrest him.

Judgmental gossip fails to prevent deviance in Dover Square because the conditions that would make it an effective deterrent are absent (Merry 1981a). Judgments usually flow within intimate networks in which participants share similar values. In a heterogeneous population, intimate networks are numerous, small, and non-localized, rather than large, all-encompassing, and few in number. Gossip is also a more effective control when there is an institutionalized mechanism—like the youth group in the Welsh village (Peters 1972), or the *vito* in the Spanish village (Pitt-Rivers 1954)—for imposing the community's judgment on the offender. In Dover Square, residents can agree to some extent on who the "bad characters" are, but the social organization of the project makes it impossible to translate this judgment into effective sanctions. Two of the most blatant and persistent perpetrators of crime in the project have a community-wide reputation, known to almost all the blacks and whites, and to about half the Chinese, but this information has not been converted into any actions that impinge upon these young men.

Furthermore, if a person's reputation is poor in someone else's intimate network or in an extended network from which he can easily disengage himself, social pressure is far less effective than if his bad reputation is known to virtually everyone in his permanent social universe. Studies of the relationship between network organization and social control indicate that deviants are more susceptible to pressure when they have more contact with others who can be reached by community opinion (Epstein 1969; Wheeldon 1969). The heterogeneous population of Dover Square and its urban surroundings allows the street youths to create social networks consisting almost exclusively of others who share their values. This insulates them from social contact with most of their neighbors who disapprove of their activities. Even their parents seem willing to sacrifice social contacts in their favor. One man was fired from his job in part because of his son's bad reputation, but continued to defend his son. Most parents deny any wrongdoing, even when this means isolating themselves. Because the community's social life is broken among discrete, ethnically based networks, only the judgmental gossip of the deviant's own ethnic group and normatively similar subgroup will have any deterrent effect on his behavior.

The Police and the Courts

Individuals who know the identities of the local criminals, but are unable to mobilize effective informal sanctions or a direct, violent response, still have recourse to formal sanctions: the police and the courts. If victims know the identities of the offenders, they can call the police and report their misbehavior or can attempt to file criminal charges. Formal sanctions, however, are highly unreliable. Simply reporting that a neighbor appeared to be breaking into one's house hardly guarantees that the neighbor will be arrested, tried, convicted, and sentenced for that transgression. Those who must rely on formal sanctions feel less secure than those who employ violence, threats of violence, or even informal sanctions.

Half the interview respondents felt that the police were not very or not at all effective, and only 13 percent said they thought the police were very or extremely effective. But, the police are useful to a few black women who know the street youths. These women call the police frequently and are able to identify the offenders by name. The police know these women, and consider them model citizens in the project. Two of the women are able to utilize the police more effectively because they have personal connections with members of the force. One woman has a brother who is a policeman; another woman worked for the police department and, in charging her neighbor with criminal activities, was able to enlist the assistance of the man she worked for. Such women develop reputations as people who will call the police, which, even though they invite the wrath of offenders, serve also as protection, since youths are reluctant to commit crimes where they can be seen by these women.

Reporting an offender to the police is far more effective if the identity of the offender is known. Without a firm identification of the offender, the police can do relatively little to find or punish him. In two years in Dover Square, the nine local youths whose arrests I heard about were all arrested in connection with a fight or crime between people who knew one another, even though crimes involving strangers are far more common in the project. One young man was arrested for stealing a bike from a friend because a policeman, observing the altercation between the two, approached the second boy and told him that his opponent was a "known troublemaker." The policeman asked the boy, while he was still angry, if he wished to press charges. Another young man was arrested because his next-door neighbor, with whom he and his sisters had been fighting for years, accused him of breaking into her house and attempting to rape her. He responded by threatening her with a gun if she pressed charges; she, in turn, charged him with intimidating a witness. At the time, she was working as a traffic policeman and was friendly with the police. The young man was brought to trial, but was convicted on previous charges that were pending against him. In a third case, a burglary ring operating in Dover Square stole an electronics van and unloaded it in broad daylight in the middle of the parking lot in Dover Square. One neighbor photographed the entire process from his apartment and another called the police. The ring was disrupted and two members were arrested and convicted. In the case of the Curran family described above, a member of a local burglary ring was convicted for his assault on a witness, not for his burglaries. Another burglar was caught when he made so much noise trying to escape from the laundromat after a burglary that a neighbor who was friendly with the laundromat owner and who knew the burglar, also a project resident, heard the noise and called the police.

One arrest occurred not because the victim knew the robber personally, but because the victim was a community worker in an organization that had close ties to the teenage population in the area. Other members of this organization inquired among their contacts in the teenage social system and were able to learn the identity of her attacker in a matter of hours. This case illustrates the problem of identity manipulation particularly well since the robber told the victim, a nun, as he robbed her at knife point, that he was Joe, a notorious project resident. The nun, however, knew Joe personally from teaching him in school and therefore was certain that the robber was not Joe. Her networks in the school and church revealed the robber to be one of Joe's enemies. As a final example, a young man was forced to give up his profitable enterprise of pimping, not because of the complaint of an aggrieved customer, but because one of his neighbors complained to the police about the activity at his house.

Thus, most of the convictions I heard about in Dover Square occurred, not in conjunction with routine, anonymous burglaries or purse snatches, but in the context of personal relationships in which someone who knew the criminal was angry enough to turn to the court system for redress. One way the police can make arrests is by exploiting personal frictions and animosities within the social networks of the criminal. Since police effectiveness is generally measured by rate of arrest and clearance, not by number of averted crimes (which is impossible to measure) (Furstenberg and

Wellford 1973), it is understandable that the police are not particularly interested in cases that hold little promise of arrest or conviction, cases such as a routine burglary where none of the stolen property is marked or a street robbery in which the victim is unable to identify the assailant. When police show a lack of concern about details in such cases, the average citizen feels, not surprisingly, that the police force can and will do little to protect him.

Another strategy for controlling threatening individuals whose identities are known is to take them to court (Merry 1979). This tactic is used primarily in disputes between ex-friends and neighbors. Blacks and whites in particular attempt to use court decisions to settle interpersonal disputes. Colson argues that a court represents an appealing forum for settling disputes since it frees people from the obligations of mobilizing kinsmen to support their rights and from the onerous task of maintaining these relationships in good repair until they are needed (1974). People unable to mobilize support effectively are more likely to have their rights protected by a court than by unreliable allies. In Dover Square, the residents who most often take their antagonists to court are women and the elderly: people who are unable to fight or to mobilize allies.

The criminal courts, however, are not designed to settle personal disputes in accordance with the norms of the participants, nor is it the criminal court's role to suggest a compromise solution, a pattern typical of courts in some small-scale societies (Nader 1969). American criminal proceedings are designed only to determine whether a law has been violated. Consequently, court decisions are rarely an effective means of settling disputes. Instead the courts become simply another weapon in the individual's arsenal that can be used in attacking his enemies. Judges often throw interpersonal disputes out of court without a decision, if they feel neither side has a good case. For example, when George assaulted Renee, her mother took him to court on charges of assault and battery. Her brother threatened to kill him, and George then charged the brother with assault. The judge decided it was a family fight and threw the case out. He told George he would put the cases on file, which was enough to unsettle George, who did not know what the judge meant. In another case, a twelve-year-old boy started to beat up a seven-year-old girl; the girl's mother objected. This angered the boy's mother. In the fight that ensued between the two women, the girl's mother punched the boy's mother. The boy's mother took the girl's mother to court, charging her with assault and battery. The judge was harsh to the girl's mother, not allowing her to speak, but dismissed the charges. A week later the boy's mother brought someone else in Dover Square before the same judge on the same charge, and the judge responded by asking, "What is wrong with you that you can't get along with your neighbors? I don't want to hear from you again." He again dismissed the charges.

Another case began in the same way. A fourteen-year-old black boy harassed a fourteen-year-old white girl. Her mother, in anger, decided to complain to the boy's grandmother, who was taking care of him. Knowing that she had to go alone to confront the boy's grandmother, who lived a block away in Dover Square, and fearing that blacks would join together and surround a lone white person, the girl's mother took her large German shepherd with her for protection. As she and the dog approached the house, the boy emerged carrying a butcher knife and said that he was going to get the dog. His grandmother restrained him, saying "We will handle this legally." Thus, the grandmother dealt with the conflict by threatening court action, although the white woman then left and the grandmother did not in fact go to court.

Another incident also demonstrates the role of the court as a sanction in interpersonal disputes. An older white man, Fred, lounging in the laundromat, suspected that an elderly Chinese man was about to be robbed since a young black girl, the sister of a youth blamed for some local crimes, was wandering through the laundromat asking for change for a twenty-dollar bill. This elderly Chinese man agreed to make change and pulled out his billfold, revealing a roll of bills worth at least five hundred dollars. She left soon after, and Fred concluded that the request for change was a ruse to identify who had money. He thought the Chinese man, having been so identified, would be robbed on his way home. He went to his house, called the police, and returned to the laundromat with his German shepherd to protect the old man. When the police arrived, they claimed they could not escort the Chinese man home unless he was sick, but with the aid of another Chinese man as translator, the elderly gentleman quickly claimed that he was sick, and was escorted home to his apartment in James Hill. He was a complete stranger to Fred.

The next day, the girl's brother and a friend insulted and threatened Fred. Fred immediately went to the courthouse and took out a warrant against the white boy, charging him with assault. The following day, the boy apologized profusely and said that he had meant no harm. A few days later, the boy's probation officer stopped by to ask Fred if the boy had bothered him again. Thus, in this case the older man was able to use the court system effectively against the boy, not by having a judge render a decision, but by taking advantage of the fact that the boy was already on probation and the court system could easily apply pressure on him directly. Even in this case, however, the criminal justice system could provide relief only because the older man knew the boy personally.

Other incidents reveal other uses that are made of the court. Two young men had a violent fight, using chains and dogs. One was severely injured and hospitalized. He took his opponent to court for attempted murder, while the other man took him to court for assault and battery. The injured man is now attempting to sue his assailant for damages, probably under a statute that entitles victims of violent crimes to reimbursement. A young woman, angry at her boyfriend, took him to court on eight criminal charges, including kidnapping and assault and battery. Another woman charged her daughter's boyfriend, who fathered the daughter's child, with statutory rape.

Thus, people file complaints against one another in criminal court, a procedure that costs nothing, in order to handle personal conflicts that cannot be managed any other way. Taking someone to court is a sanction against perceived infringements of rights. This mechanism requires knowing the identity of the offender, however, and cannot be used to manage relations with strangers. But, by providing an alternative means of redress and by freeing the individual from the burden of maintaining close ties with potential allies who would be willing to defend his rights violently, if necessary, the availability of courts may decrease violence between people who know one another (Merry 1979).

Avoidance and Withdrawal

The majority of Dover Square residents adopt a variety of defensive strategies. They make their homes fortresses by barricading them with expensive locks and elaborate window bars, by stockpiling guns, by learning to live with large guard dogs in small apartments, and by calling the police to report crimes even when they do not know who is responsible. They are always cautious, always stay home at night, and often prefer not to venture outside alone even in the daytime. Eighty-three percent of all families living in the more vulnerable ground-floor apartments have installed heavy iron bars on one or more of their windows. These are the people who feel most afraid and whose lives are most constricted by the fear of crime: the elderly, the residents who speak Chinese only, and those residents who are socially isolated and unconnected. Their mode of defense is escape and retreat, but if the fragile shell of safety around their homes is violated, the loss of a sense of security can be devastating. Unlike those who adopt offensive strategies, who carry their protective armor around with them, the defensive residents are vulnerable any time they leave their homes. This is the image of the typical urbanite, cowering in fear in a barred haven of safety. Yet this represents only one pole on a continuum ranging from those who traverse the city with a sense of self-confidence and ease that springs from their mastery of the urban environment and their extensive knowledge of its locations, its residents, and its cultural patterns, to the newcomer ignorant of the slightest variations in the danger of different places, the nuances of social categories, and the reputations of particularly dangerous people.

Those who adopt defensive postures rarely know who the street youths are, nor are they skilled in identifying those categories of persons and places that are likely to be dangerous. Thus, the proportion of families installing window bars varies significantly between ethnic groups. Of the families who live in ground-floor apartments, 93 percent of the Chinese, 80 percent of the whites, and 78 percent of the blacks have paid for these expensive bars. Further, likelihood of installing window bars is related to familiarity with the street youths, regardless of ethnicity. Of the first-floor families friendly to the youths, 65 percent have bars; of those only acquainted with them, 72 percent have bars; of those who see them as strangers, 92 percent have bars. These correlations do not prove a causal relationship between not knowing the teenagers and installing bars, but do suggest that those who see them as strangers are also those who rely on bars for protection. Although two Dover Square burglars claimed that they can remove the bars without much difficulty, they acknowledged that bars slow them down. About one-third of black and white families have acquired guard dogs, and although few Chinese families have them, many said they would like the protection of a dog, but find them unpleasant to have in the house.

Those relying on defensive strategies are generally far more aware of danger than those adopting offensive ones. Among the eighty-eight questionnaire respondents who answered this question, twenty-nine, or one-third, use offensive approaches and fifty-nine, or two-thirds, use defensive ones. The perceptions of danger of these two groups are significantly different: only two from the first group, or one-fifteenth, think the project is dangerous, while nineteen from the second, about one-third, feel the same way (see Table 10). Those with defensive strategies, however, are in fact slightly better protected against crime. In the victimization survey, roughly three-fourths of the families used defensive approaches and one-fourth offensive ones. Forty percent of the former group experienced a robbery, burglary, or assault after moving into the project, while 50 percent of the second group did.

Those relying on defensive strategies are more frightened, I believe, since they have far less sense of control over their environment. Since they do not know the street youths as individuals and are cut off from channels of communication about their identities and activities, they are unable to retaliate violently, to gossip about them, to report them to the police successfully, or to take them to court. They have no reputations with the street youths that might protect them. Psychological studies support the notion that a lack of control triggers fear (Seligman 1975). Even the illusion of control reduces fear when individuals face unpredictable hazards. Add to this the greater difficulty of predicting the behavior of a stranger than that of a known person, and it becomes easy to explain why those who do not know the youths feel far more helpless and uncertain about managing their hazardous environment than those who are more familiar with street life and know the identities of the threatening individuals.

SOCIAL CONTROL AND URBAN SOCIAL ORGANIZATION

Dover Square appears dangerous to many of its residents because of the massive failure of both informal and formal social control. Yet the absence of effective social control is a function of the social structure of the project itself. Its pattern of social organization contrasts markedly with that of the small-scale societies typically studied by anthropologists, which characteristically have far more extensive systems of informal social control. Comparing these societies with urban villages and Dover Square suggests that two features are critical to achieving effective social control: close-knit and durable social networks and homogeneous norms and values. Although these features primarily affect informal social control, they also impinge on the functioning of formal mechanisms such as the police and the courts.

The ability of a small-scale society to maintain social order depends on the extent to which its members are incorporated into networks of ongoing relationships that they wish to preserve and on the degree to which rules, norms, and customs of behavior are shared. Urban settings characterized by transiency and heterogeneity lack these social characteristics, and consequently have diminished informal social control. Informal social control retains its power only when networks are enduring and values similar. Only in connected social networks can consensus develop concerning individual reputations, and only in normatively homogeneous populations do shared standards of behavior exist in terms of which judgments can be formed. Further, social networks can exert control over their members only if the links are durable. If a sanctioned individual is connected through brittle and easily substitutable ties, he may choose to break off relations rather than conform. The cost of conformity may exceed the rewards of remaining within the group. Clearly, the costs of fleeing a kin network, which is inherently irreplaceable, are far greater than those of leaving superficial friendships. In small-scale societies, the costs of deserting a social network may be very high, consigning the deserter to the unenviable role of stranger and denying him access to lands, hunting territories, and wives. Even in urban villages, kin links can provide important forms of access to housing and jobs (Young and Willmott 1957; Gans 1962a).

The cost of desertion also depends on the external characteristics of a social system. Urbanites encapsulated within rural-based networks that assure their continued survival when their rights to remain in town are uncertain, jobs unreliable, and retirement and sickness benefits lacking desert these networks only at a great cost. For example, Mayer describes the dependence of urban Xhosa migrants in South African cities on networks of "home-boys" in town (1961). They report one another's misdeeds to rural kinsmen and enforce rural norms in the city. Because of the insecurities of influx control and uncertain jobs, these migrants hesitate to desert their country-based networks or ignore the social pressures they impose.

In Dover Square, the structure of social networks, kinship ties, and access to jobs and social services encapsulates individuals within enduring social networks inside their own ethnic groups that constrain them to conform to shared norms and leave them relatively unconcerned about social ties with other ethnic groups or even with individuals in different intimate social networks. Many relationships are fragile and easily substitutable. Further, there is little agreement between these social worlds about standards for appropriate behavior. Even within ethnic groups, substantial differences occur that parallel variations in age, generation, and life style. As Hannerz points out, pressuring an individual to conform to norms he does not believe in is a futile and doomed process (1967). Since Dover Square contains numerous discrete social networks founded on divergent moral codes in an urban context that offers numerous alternative sets of social relationships, the conditions under which effective, community-wide social control emerges are absent.

As we have seen, social control is undermined not only by the structure of social networks but also by the pervasiveness of relations between strangers. In such interactions the implementation of sanctions becomes problematic. For sanctions to serve as effective deterrents to deviance, they must be both powerful and certain of implementation. A sanction that is not severe will have little effect even if its application is certain. But even a severe sanction will have little deterrent effect if the offender feels there is little chance it will be imposed on him. Implementations of sanctions against strangers is problematic because relations with strangers are anonymous and fleeting.

Since a stranger is anonymous, the observer does not know who he is, where he lives, or where he can regularly be found. He is located in a social world of which the observer is totally ignorant. If the observer knew something of his commitments to locations, to sets of social relationships, or to moral definitions of self, he would have some idea where he is vulnerable: what reputation he seeks to preserve, what social relationships he values, and what he would lose if his deviance became public. When these commitments are unknown, a person is correspondingly freer to deviate with impunity.

Further, since relations with strangers are characteristically fleeting and discontinuous, there is no pressure of reciprocity to induce conformity to the normative obligations of such encounters. Jacobson notes that the expectation of continuity is basic to orderly social relationships (1971). It is in relationships in which there is no expectation of a future that rule-breaking is most tempting. For example, a study of migrant workers in the United States found more violence, distrust, and deviance among a group who were strangers to one another before the season and never expected to work together again than among another group consisting of family units that planned to remain together after the picking season (Nelkin 1970). This appears to be a fundamental characteristic of the social life of cities, caused, Gans argues, by the transiency of urban social relationships (1962). Yet, although mobility generally serves to undermine social order by creating discontinuous relationships, Jacobson argues that under certain social conditions even mobile populations find themselves encapsulated within non-localized but enduring social systems that generate an expectation of continuity. "One strategy, therefore, for coping with uncertainty in urban social life is to generate or confirm continuity in social relations" (Jacobson 1971: 630). The strategies Dover Square residents adopt to control their hazardous neighbors, and the points at which these strategies fail, reveal the stark contrast between the difficulty of managing known people and of managing strangers known only in fleeting, anonymous relationships.

CHAPTER 7

Historical
and
Cross-Cultural
Perspectives

Although the problem of urban danger looms large in Dover Square, as in the contemporary American consciousness more generally, it is neither a particularly recent nor a uniquely American phenomenon. Comments from writers in past centuries and in other parts of the world describe a similar unease on urban streets, a familiar sense of the criminal as a ruthless, anonymous, and unpredictable presence in the urban scene, and an analogous concern with the culturally unassimilated, the socially marginal, and the potentially revolutionary segments of society. Eighteenth- and early nineteenth-century London, for example, was often seen as a lawless, disorderly, and dangerous place by its residents. According to Henry Fielding, the writer and a local magistrate, in 1751

> there is not a Street in [Westminister] which doth not swarm all Day with Beggars, and all Night with Thieves. Stop your Coach at what Shop you will, however expeditious the Tradesman is to attend you, a Beggar is commonly beforehand with him; and if you should not directly face his Door, the Tradesman must often turn his Head while you are talking to him, or the same Beggar, or some other Thief at hand, will pay a Visit to his Shop! I omit to speak of the more open and violent Insults which are everyday committed on his Majesty's Subjects in the Streets and Highways. They are enough known, and enough spoken of. The Depredations on Property

are less noticed, particularly those in the Parishes within ten Miles of London. . . . These are however grown to the most deplorable Height, insomuch that the Gentleman is daily, or rather nightly, plundered of his Pleasure, and the Farmer of his Livlihood. . . . The Innocent are put in Terror, affronted and alarmed with Threats and Execrations, endangered with loaded Pistols, beat with Bludgeons and hacked with Cultlasses, of which the Loss of Health, of Limbs, and often of Life, is the Consequence; and all this without any Respect to Age, or Dignity, or Sex. . . .

Street Robberies are generally committed in the dark, the Persons on whom they are committed are often in Chairs and Coaches, and if on Foot, the Attack is usually begun by knocking the Party down, and for the Time depriving him of his Sense. But if the Thief should be less barbarous, he is seldom so incautious as to omit taking every Method to prevent his being known, by flapping the Party's Hat over his Face, and by every other Method which he can invent to avoid Discovery.

Tobias 1967: 23

Other authors confirm the impact of this situation on London residents. In 1775, Jonas Hanway wrote:

I sup with my friend; I cannot return to my home, not even in my chariot, without danger of a pistol being clapt to my breast. I build an elegant villa, ten or twenty miles distant from the capital: I am obliged to provide an armed force to convey me thither, lest I should be attacked on the road with fire and ball.

Tobias 1967: 24

In 1785, the solicitor-general commented on London, "Nobody could feel himself unapprehensive of danger to his person or property if he walked in the street after dark, nor could any man promise himself security in his bed" (Tobias 1967: 33). At the end of the eighteenth century, a well-known treatise on London noted:

The outrages and acts of violence continually committed, more particularly in and near the Metropolis by
lawless ravagers of property, and destroyers of lives, in
disturbing the peaceful mansion, the Castle of every En-
glishman, and also in abridging the liberty of travelling
on the Public Highway.

Tobias 1967: 33

A concern about crime was also a preoccupation of Parisians in the first half of the nineteenth century (Chevalier
1973). Fear of crime lurked not only in the narrow alleys of the
poor, but spread to the broad boulevards of the middle and
wealthier classes as well. One writer commented in 1843:

For the past month the sole topic of conversations
has been the nightly assaults, hold-ups, daring robberies. . . . What is so terrifying about these nocturnal
assaults is the assailants' noble impartiality. They attack
rich and poor alike. . . . They kill at sight, though they
may get the wrong man; but little do they care. At one
time the advantage of being poor was that at least you
were safe; it is so no longer. Paris is much perturbed by
these sinister occurrences. A concern for self-defense
greatly troubles family gatherings especially. Evening
parties all end like the beginning of the fourth act of Les
Huguenots, with the blessing of the daggers. Friends and
relatives are not allowed to go home without a regular
arms inspection.

Chevalier 1973: 3

American cities of this period and somewhat later were
similarly viewed as dangerous places, havens for the "criminal classes" and the "dangerous classes," places of disorder,
vice, prostitution, and crime. Writing of New York in 1872,
Brace described this population as even more dangerous
than that of London (1872: 25):

They are as ignorant as London flash-men or coster-
mongers. They are far more brutal than the peasantry

from whom they descend, and they are much banded together, in associations, such as "Dead Rabbit," "Plug-ugly," and various target companies. They are our enfants perdus, grown up to young manhood. The murder of an unoffending old man, like Mr. Rogers, is nothing to them. They are ready for any offense or crime, however degraded or bloody. . . . They form the "Nineteenth-street Gangs," the young burglars and murderers, the garroters and rioters, the thieves and flash-men, the "repeaters" and ruffians, so well known to all who know this metropolis.

Brace 1872: 27–28

During periods of rapid urban growth in the industrial cities of southern Africa, similar fears of crime were widespread. In the post-war period, Africans in the cities of South Africa lived in terror of the *tsotsis*, urbanized African youths who adopted a particularly violent form of criminality (Mayer 1961; Wilson and Mafeje 1963). To rural African migrants in the city, the *tsotsi* was like a witch, both terribly dangerous and terribly unpredictable. It was impossible to tell who the next innocent victim would be (Mayer 1961: 74–75). In the eyes of country-born Africans in the town of East London, the *tsotsi*'s criminality was boundless:

He knows no inhibitions, no scruples, no remorse. He will do anything to anyone. There are plenty of ordinary criminals who rob because they are poor, or even occasionally assault harmless people on an impulse. But an ordinary criminal, "physically strong and a fast runner, if given a fright while in the act of stealing, will turn his thoughts to escaping. He says to himself, 'My feet!' He is afraid, because he knows he is doing wrong." The genuine *tsotsi* (migrants said) is different, because he is a "criminal with a black heart." "He has never learnt the differences between right and wrong." He is absolutely ruthless. He does not hesitate to use his knife, and to aim where it kills. "He knows where to strike; you are a dead man if you resist him." He is just as merciless to women. "If a *tsotsi* wants a woman, he will take anyone he fancies. Coming up to her in a deserted street, he just points at her and, without a word, signals that she is to follow him. The poor girl, knowing that she is in danger of her life, will follow the *tsotsi* to his room.

Mayer 1961: 74

Tsotsis have no conscience and no shame. They will steal from their own mothers and are impervious to ordinary human appeals. They rob, cheat, and steal mercilessly, not caring if their victims are ruined. Although they represent a threat similar to the rural witch, in town this incarnation of evil is a complete stranger, an anonymous source of evil. To townspeople, however, who are more familiar with the urban environment and who may even have sons who have been tempted into the *tsotsi* life, they cause both fear and sorrow. These people offer more realistic theories for *tsotsi-ism*, speaking of the problems of working mothers, overcrowding, lack of work opportunity for juveniles, the influence of films, and so forth (Mayer 1961: 75).

In these cities, anxiety about crime was broadly defined, focusing not only on crime itself but on all the disruptions of society. In Paris, it was "a terror not related to the problem of crime in the narrow sense of the word but rather to that of crime as a threat to society" (Chevalier 1973: 7). Nineteenth-century Parisians regarded crime as the expression of a sick society, of evils such as pervasive disease and high rates of death, illegitimacy, epidemics of cholera, inadequate sewage and refuse systems, muddy, pestilential streets, the lack of fresh air and sunlight in the narrow, winding alleyways, and the pollution and stench of the air (Chevalier 1973: 48 ff). The city itself appeared a diseased, unhealthy, and noxious environment. The American city of the time was also generally viewed as a place of vice and corruption, where any form of behavior was acceptable and migrants quickly lost the moral virtues common to rural residents. A writer in early twentieth-century America, for example, complained about the dangers of the city of Boston because of its lodging houses, which failed to provide parlors for young men and women to meet, forcing them to socialize in the bedrooms (Wolfe 1913). An examination of crime in nineteenth-century Boston noted the public's preoccupation with vice rather than street crime: the real villain was the rake and the tempster, not the robber or rapist (Lane 1969: 367).

In these examples, striking similarities in notions of danger appear. Nineteenth-century urbanites in Europe and America were anxious about the growing underclass of poor, marginal, and shifting urbanites whom they labeled the "dangerous classes" (Tobias 1967; Chevalier 1973; Monkkonen 1975; Brace 1872; Gurr, Grabosky, and Hula 1977). This was an amalgam of paupers, criminals, drifters, and tramps (Monkkonen 1975: 150–165). Contemporary descriptions of the "dangerous classes" emphasized their immorality, depravity, lack of education and religion, untamed passions, and shiftlessness and unwillingness to work. Their criminal qualities were seen as innate and inherited, transmitted inexorably from parents to children. Thus, this class was inherently and incurably depraved (Gurr, Grabosky, and Hula 1977: 679; Brace 1872: 35). In Sydney, the elite assumed that crime was the natural impulse of the criminal classes (Gurr, Grabosky, and Hula 1977: 347–349). In New York, Brace saw these classes as the product of accident, ignorance, and vice:

Among a million people, such as compose the population of this city and its suburbs, there will always be a great number of misfortunes; fathers die, and leave their children unprovided for; parents drink, and abuse their little ones, and they float away on the currents of the street; step-mothers or step-fathers drive out, by neglect and ill-treatment, their sons from home. Thousands are the children of poor foreigners, who have permitted them to grow up without school, education, or religion. All the neglect and bad education and evil example of a poor class tend to form others, who, as they mature, swell the ranks of ruffians and criminals. So, at length, a great multitude of ignorant, untrained, passionate, irreligious boys and young men are formed, who become the "dangerous class" of our city.

Brace 1872: 28

The dangerous classes included not only the criminals, however, but also the discontented poor:

> tens of thousands, poor, hard-pressed, and depending for daily bread on the day's earnings, swarming in tenement houses, who behold the gilded rewards of toil all about them, but are never permitted to touch them.
>
> All these great masses of destitute, miserable, and criminal persons believe that for ages the rich have had all the good things of life, while to them have been left the evil things. Capital to them is the tyrant.
>
> Let but Law lift its hand from them for a season, or let the civilizing influences of American life fail to reach them, and, if the opportunity offered, we should see an explosion from this class which might leave the city in ashes and blood.
>
> Brace 1872: 29

Solid citizens in nineteenth-century European cities also feared not only the criminality but also the collective violence and revolutionary tendencies of the masses, merging the working classes with the dangerous classes in their fear of urban riots, Luddite mobs, farm riots, and so on (Tilly 1969: 22).

Underlying the notion of the dangerous classes was a deep class cleavage between the wealthy and the desperately poor, a gulf between respectable, affluent society and the "others," the criminals and paupers (Monkkonen 1975). The poor often hated the rich and existing laws and institutions for the indifference and avarice of their class, while the rich feared riot and revolution by the poor (Tobias 1967: 182–184). London criminals formed a separate and distinct social group, inhabiting particular slums and rookeries and dedicated to the notion that stealing was more profitable than working (Tobias 1967: 52–62; Gurr, Grabosky, and Hula 1977: 74). In Paris, the dangerous classes and the upper classes were sharply different, each with its own set of laws, manners, and customs, history, mode of life and death, and location in the city (Chevalier 1973: 69). The world of the criminal was a closed one, alien to the city and to the social world of established Parisians.

In most cities, the criminal class seemed not only morally distinct, but also culturally different. During the period of concern about the Parisian dangerous classes, the city experienced a massive influx of rural immigrants from the provinces of France who brought with them their own way of life and work and their own manners, clothing, and speech, which made their very presence intolerable to the older inhabitants, the established Parisian bourgeoisie (Chevalier 1973: 156). They were viewed as utterly different from the city inhabitants and dangerous to them, savages with roving habits, enemies threatening to overrun and swamp civilization by their numbers and their increase (Chevalier 1973: 359). It is of particular interest that these immigrants were viewed as not only barbarian and savage but as different in race from the established population of Paris (Chevalier 1973: 360). The antagonism between the lower and upper classes was thus biological and moral as well as economic, occupational, and political (Chevalier 1973: 408–409). The belief in the racially distinct character of the dangerous classes complemented contemporary faith in their innate and inherited criminality.

In the same period, England also experienced a massive wave of immigration from the countryside and very rapid growth (Gurr, Grabosky, and Hula 1977: 42). Among the arrivals were large numbers of Irish peasants, who formed settlements of desperate poverty in which they struggled to survive in temporary and poorly paid work. To contemporary writers, these Irish peasants were both inherently criminal and morally dangerous to the English working class (Tobias 1967: 46; Engels 1845: 104–107). The Irish brought a filthy, degraded, and squalid style of life that contemporaries feared they would introduce to the English workers (Engels 1845: 104–107). Among their disreputable habits were the custom of one family living all in the same room, wearing tatters and no shoes, subsisting only on potatoes, throwing garbage and waste right outside the front door, and building pigsties next to the house or allowing the pigs to live right in their homes with them and permitting their children to play with the pigs and wallow in their filth (Engels 1845). Engels bemoaned the

Irish lack of furniture in their homes, their tendency to sleep on straw and rags, and their habits of drink which degraded their English fellow workers as they learned their bad habits, "having to live alongside and compete with the uncivilized Irish" (1845: 107). Other writers of the period observed that the shiftlessness and savagery of the Irish removed them from the ranks of the working class, accusing them of corruption, degradation, and disorganization, even though many English laborers lived the same way (Lees 1969: 359–361). The Irish were widely regarded as particularly criminally inclined (Tobias 1967; Gurr, Grabosky, and Hula 1977: 42).

The notion of the foreign immigrant as a particularly criminal, immoral, and dangerous element in the city was well entrenched in American thought in the late nineteenth and early twentieth centuries, especially in the cities of the North (Higham 1955). In tracing the developing American nativism of the period from the 1880s to the 1920s, Higham documents the recurring theme of the dangerous foreigner. Foreigners threatened political radicalism, labor unrest, anarchism and political violence, and criminality. They were also dangerous because of their failure to assimilate rapidly. Particularly toward the end of the nineteenth century, some American nativists became concerned about their racial differences as well, thundering against the horrors of "race suicide" and "racial mongrelization" resulting from inbreeding with large populations of foreigners from Southern and Eastern Europe (Higham 1955: 131–139). Writers of this school held that traits such as an affinity for freedom and democracy were innate, biological characteristics of Anglo-Saxons. Thus, the infusion of populations without these traits could undermine the American political order. The foreign danger encompassed both their inherited incapacity for self-government and the risks of deterioration in the racial fabric of the country. As early as 1885, Josiah Strong trumpeted the dangers of foreign immigration to American cities, to religion, morality, politics, and class strife (Higham 1955: 39). He accused the immigrants of crime and immorality, of corrupting municipal governments, and of strengthening Catholicism and socialism. The demand for immigration restriction in the

1890s included rhetoric about the dangers of large numbers of illiterates, paupers, criminals, and madmen to American character and American citizenship (Higham 1955: 103).

As in Europe at the same time, this was a period of deepening division between rich and poor, between old American and new immigrant. As the new immigrants crowded into the urban slums, they became associated with fears of foreign discontent, developing class cleavages, collective violence, and disturbances of the peace. These recent arrivals were the least assimilated and the most impoverished of the immigrants. The embers of this fear were fanned by the violence of Haymarket Square in 1883. Here, a peaceful demonstration erupted into a bloody confrontation between labor organizers and the police. Sennett describes the way the reaction of middle-class residents in Chicago merged with anxiety about a rash of local burglaries to become a generalized fear of anarchistic foreigners living on the other side of the city (1973).

As immigration continued, different ethnic groups acquired particular reputations for danger. The Irish, for example, were reputed both to be criminal and to threaten a Catholic takeover of the country (Handlin 1941). During the mid-nineteenth-century flood of Irish to Boston, a Boston mayor noted the common fear that the Irish are "a race that will never be infused into our own but on the contrary will always remain distinct and hostile" (Handlin 1941: 185). In 1837, complaints were voiced in Boston that

> instead of assimilating at once with the customs of the country of their adoption, our foreign population are too much in the habit of retaining their own national usages, of *associating too exclusively with each other*, and living in groups together. These practices serve no good purpose, and tend merely to alienate those among whom they have chosen to reside. *It would be the part of wisdom to* ABANDON AT ONCE ALL USAGES AND ASSOCIATIONS WHICH MARK THEM AS FOREIGNERS, *and to become in feeling and custom, as well as in privileges and rights, citizens of the United States.*
>
> Handlin 1941: 185

American fear of Catholicism, deeply rooted throughout the nineteenth and early twentieth centuries, focused on fear of the pope and a papist uprising. Bostonians thought the Irish were both criminal and subversive, and nineteenth-century matrons feared that their Irish maids were conspiring toward a papal takeover by reporting details of their private lives to the parish priest (Handlin 1941: 186).

Italians were portrayed as quick with their knives and always ready to fight, and as organized criminals (Higham 1955: 160). In 1887 the Chicago *Herald* asserted, "It is not just abject poverty which causes such nasty and cheap living; it is simply an imported habit from Southern Italy" (Nelli 1970: 11). The assistant district attorney of New York County asserted that "a considerable percentage, especially those from the cities, are criminal" (Nelli 1970: 126). The U.S. Immigration Commission noted that "certain kinds of criminality are inherent in the Italian race" (Nelli 1970: 126). Throughout the early 1900s there was much discussion in the media of the Black Hand, a mafia-type organization (Nelli 1970: 130). During Prohibition, Italians and other foreigners were particularly associated with crime, and talk of crime waves blended with concern about foreign lawlessness (Higham 1955: 264–268).

Jews were feared not so much because of their criminality, but because of their alleged immorality, greed, vulgarity and desire for world domination (Higham 1955: 280–281). Henry Ford railed against the dangers of Eastern Jewish bankers, while others pointed to the involvement of Jews in the international community to the detriment of their loyalties to America. Fear of the Chinese, long-established in the United States, focused on their unfamiliar way of life (Miller 1969). According to popular stereotypes of the late nineteenth century, the Chinese were cruel, practiced torture and infanticide, smoked opium constantly, and were cunning, tricky, and untrustworthy. Above all, they were impossible to assimilate (Miller 1969). In 1868, the *New York Times* editorialized, "Although they are patient and reliable laborers, they have characteristics deeply embedded which make them undesirable as a part of our permanent population. Their religion is wholly unlike ours, and they poison and stab" (Miller 1969: 171). Chinese also earned a reputation for sexual perversions and for luring American women into prostitution with the entice-ment of opium (Miller 1969: 198). Chinese laundries were in-famous as dens of vice, and Americans were warned not to let their young girls near them. The fear of the "yellow peril," which coalesced in restrictive immigration legislation in 1882, thus reflected nationwide fears of a population viewed as culturally simply too different, having too many practices in conflict with American life to be absorbed (Miller 1969).

The influx of culturally distinct populations has sparked a concern about danger and criminality in modern Switzer-land as well, where foreign workers from Italy, Spain, Greece, Turkey, and Yugoslavia are believed far more likely to com-mit crimes than the native-born Swiss, although studies sug-gest that they actually commit fewer crimes (Clinard 1978: 136). In a recent study of the Shetland Islands off the coast of Scotland, a crime wave was attributed to the presence of oil-workers from England, even though the crime rate had not in fact increased (Renwanz 1980).

In each of the above cases, danger is associated with the entrance into the society of a culturally and racially distinct population. This group often but not always forms a separate and oppressed class at the bottom of the social hierarchy, huddled into the worst slums, taking the poorest paying jobs, and surviving on a minimum of resources. This largely unas-similated underclass is sharply divided from respectable so-ciety and generally feels considerable hostility toward the dominant population. Since their characteristics are innate and unchangeable, their very presence becomes a danger, not only because of their criminal activities but also because of the threat of social change. The fear of crime blends with the fear of social revolution by an alienated and dissaffected portion of the population, often one that receives a dispro-portionately small share of society's resources. Since these populations are viewed across a large cultural and social di-vide, stereotypes persist unchallenged by the reality of per-sonal contact or accurate information.

In the light of this pattern, the recent American preoc-cupation with crime could be a reaction to rapid social

change and demands for social justice by minority populations as much as to increases in the rate of crime itself. The
1960s and 1970s saw renewed demands for social change
as America suddenly discovered its poor and the federal
government embarked on an unprecedented campaign to
achieve social justice. Race riots in the cities, student demon-
strations against the Vietnam war, a general revolt against pa-
triotism and authority, the coming of age of the 1950s baby
boom with an unusual numerical dominance of the young,
the spread of drug use from ghetto communities to the American middle class, the stresses of an unpopular war vividly
portrayed every night on TV screens across the country, and
new militant and aggressive demands for social equality from
racial and ethnic minorities merged with rising crime rates to
create a sense of danger in American cities. This was also
a period of substantial migration of non-white minorities,
Southern blacks and Hispanics from Mexico and Puerto Rico,
to the major industrial cities of the Northeast and Midwest. In
his analysis of a 1969 Baltimore poll on the fear of crime,
Furstenberg found that those most concerned about crime as
a social issue were also those most upset by rapid social
change and demands for racial equality (1971). National polls
on fluctuations in the public's perception of the amount of
crime from the mid-1960s to the present reveals that concern
about crime rises during periods of racial violence, assassina-
tion, war protest, campus unrest, and increased occurrence
of criminal activities and drops between these crises (Erskine
1974: 131).

It has often been argued that the fear of crime is simply a
way of talking about the fear of blacks in a covert and legitimate way, in which the fear of black violence blends with uneasiness about black demands for social and economic equality. In fact, this survey of attitudes toward crime and danger
suggests that crime does carry overtones of social protest,
both by economically disadvantaged classes and by groups
that feel marginal and excluded. The fear of crime is in part a
response to the perceived hostilities and antagonisms of such
groups, whose discontent and cultural marginality threaten
to disrupt the established social and economic order.

DANGER AND URBAN SOCIAL STRUCTURE

Although a concern about danger appears widespread in cities, is this an inherent and inevitable feature of urban life? Do cities always seem dangerous to their inhabitants? In other words, are there features of the social structure of the city itself that engender a sense of danger? An adequate answer to these questions requires a fuller exploration of the cross-cultural and historical literature on urbanism than is possible within the scope of this book, but on the basis of some preliminary research, it is possible to propose some answers and to develop a theory, quite speculative at this stage, concerning the conditions under which danger blossoms as a major public concern. One limitation of this endeavor, however, is the nature of information available about past times. The historical record primarily provides insight into the opinions of the dominant classes, while the voice of the common people is typically muffled and inarticulate, absent from the published documents of the era.

A brief survey of urban ethnographies and historical studies of cities suggest that danger is an issue only in large, industrial, heterogeneous cities during periods of rapid growth, social change, and deepening class cleavages. During the early years of the industrial revolution in Europe and the United States—the eighteenth and early nineteenth centuries—elites voiced concern about the dangers of the new populations swarming into the cities. Widespread crime was an issue in colonial New York, for example, and citizens were afraid to be out in the evening (Greenberg 1974: 220–223). At the same time, crime rates apparently rose, although the historical data is sketchy (Gurr, Grabosky, and Hula 1977). A similar concern appeared in nineteenth-century Sydney (Gurr, Grabosky, and Hula 1977) and in the cities of southern Africa during the initial phases of urban growth and industrialization. Epstein, for example, describes the danger and disorder of the Copperbelt towns of Zambia during the 1920s and 1930s, their period of initial rapid growth (1958: 26), and we have already noted the fear of crime in South African cities in the 1950s. The post-war era in South Africa saw an unprecedented expansion of industrial capacity, mushroom-

ing cities, and a flood of African migrants from the countryside to man the developing factories and mines (Venter
1962).

During the second half of the nineteenth century in Europe and the early twentieth century in the United States, the
cities gradually began to cope with the new immigrants: city
services and job opportunities improved, and the desperate
poverty of the urban masses was somewhat alleviated. Paris
made progress in sewage and refuse systems, for example,
improving the quality of life in general and combatting the
spread of disease and high death rates among the poor as the
city officials dimly began to perceive their responsibilities for
the urban poor as well as for the elite (Chevalier 1973). In
the same period, as England became richer, London devoted
greater resources to the urban poor, eliminating the worst
housing conditions and providing better street lighting, water, and other services (Tobias 1967: 41). The idea of a city
police department was introduced in 1829 in London and
soon thereafter adopted in Paris and the cities of the United
States. Boston had its first police department in 1837. Standards of order shifted in these cities, as people came to expect more orderly streets, lower rates of crime and violence,
and greater government control over urban life (e.g., Lane
1969).

In London, Stockholm, and Sydney, rates of common
crimes of theft and violence declined from 1850 to 1950,
then climbed dramatically in the post-war period (Gurr, Grabosky, and Hula 1977: 203, 619). Similar long-term reversals
in crime trends were reported in France (Lodhi and Tilly
1973: 300), in Buffalo (Powell 1966), and in Chicago (Gurr,
Grabosky, and Hula 1977: 646). Between 1860 and 1950, the
arrest rates for murder and assault dropped sharply in Boston, with only one-quarter as many assault arrests at the end
of the period as at the beginning (Lane 1969). In Columbus,
Ohio, the murder rate in the city dropped while the rate
of theft by trickery increased (Monkkonen 1975: 36). In
general, urban America witnessed a gradual ebb in crime
throughout the period from 1870 to 1940 (Gurr, Grabosky,
and Hula 1977). In the light of these historical patterns, the
increase in crime that afflicted the industrial cities of America

and Western Europe, particularly Sweden and Germany, in the 1960s and 1970s was not a new phenomenon, but a return to a previous condition. In fact, the crime rate in the United States was abnormally low during the 1930s and 1940s, so that the postwar increases were simply a return to normalcy.

Concern about danger was apparently rare in pre-industrial cities, even when crime was a facet of urban life. Sjoberg, in his overview of pre-industrial urbanism, for example, notes that crime was very common in ancient and non-industrialized cities even though it was usually severely punished (1960: 246–249). The city, however, was often seen as an island of safety in a sea of bandits (Sjoberg 1960: 246). Thirteenth-century England was a place of great violence and frequent homicides, yet this was apparently more common in rural areas than in the cities of London and Bristol (Given 1977: 175). Although the Middle Ages were generally a violent era with frequent fights, murders, and extensive bribery and corruption, according to one historian, "Not only were medieval criminals more numerous than their modern counter-parts, but by reason of their numbers and importance, they elicited much more general sympathy than they do nowadays, and were as a rule dealt with by society in a more lenient manner" (T. F. Tout, quoted in Given 1977: 33). Elizabethan London, in the late sixteenth century, also experienced frequent crime, but primarily pocket picking and cutpursing rather than violent crime (Salgado 1977). Organized fraternities of thieves lived in particular sections of the city. Yet, as in the pre-industrial cities Sjoberg examined, this situation does not appear to have elicited any sense of fear or danger, and in fact thieving was viewed as a skill to be admired and pickpocketing was almost a spectator sport. Widespread prostitution was similarly accepted as normal and not a cause for concern. Other studies of medieval cities make no mention of concern with danger (Roerig 1967; Saalman 1968).

Ethnographic accounts of small, non-industrialized cities similarly indicate that danger is not necessarily an issue even when crime is rife. Timbuktu in 1940, a city of six thousand, was plagued with internal thieving and raiding outside the city such that everyone regularly locked their doors, but Miner mentions nothing of danger or fear of crime (1953: 250–254). In Tripoli in the early 1960s, a city of about two hundred thousand, Gulick notes some liquor and narcotics crimes, smuggling, and prostitution, but again makes no mention of a fear of crime (1967). Other studies of non-industrial cities similarly fail to mention a significant fear of crime (e.g., Bascom 1959; Harris 1956; Fox 1977). Even modern Swiss cities, typically small, homogeneous, and economically based on highly skilled industries and financial and professional services, are not perceived as dangerous despite some crime (Clinard 1978). Although this survey is hardly comprehensive, it is suggestive. Danger may not be characteristic of small, non-industrialized cities in the same way that it dominates major, industrial urban areas.

How can we explain this differential appearance of urban danger? Based on these cross-cultural and historical materials and the theory developed in the study of Dover Square, I will suggest a series of conditions that elicit a sense of danger, acknowledging that this is a first endeavor and is still tentative. Confirmation of these hypotheses demands further research. However, it appears that a concern about danger emerges in response to three sets of conditions, roughly divided into demographic changes, changes in patterns of crime, and changes in the urban social structure.

First, danger becomes an issue during periods of rapid urban growth when the institutions of the city are not yet able to cope with the flood of immigrants. It is unable to provide housing, sufficient jobs, sewage and water systems, street lighting and electricity, and fire, police, court, and prison systems adequate to the new problems of social order. This is generally a temporary phase of urban growth, subsiding as the city begins to invest in providing better services for all its citizens. The issue of danger is more salient when the immigrant stream consists of a population perceived as culturally and racially distinct, one whose way of life, values, dress, speech, and manners are unfamiliar to established urbanites and who must go through some period of assimilation before they no longer stand out as obviously different. Thus, danger appears as an issue at a time of increasing cultural diversity.

Second, a concern about danger reflects changes in the incidence and in the nature of crime. It emerges during periods of rising crime rates, suggesting that it is not the crime rate itself but the perceived increase in crime that engenders fear. The situation appears to be worsening. Equally important, crime seems to shift to a more violent and ruthless form and to take place to a greater extent between strangers. Concern about danger accompanies a shift from perceiving the criminal as a picturesque, even romantic figure engaged primarily in theft, to perceiving him as a more ruthless, violent, faceless menace attacking randomly and impersonally, without reason or cause. Crime becomes less the product of great and romantic criminals and more a widespread movement of the popular masses, a transition that occurred in both nineteenth-century Paris (Chevalier 1973: 77) and London (Tobias 1967) as the fear of crime escalated. The shift in the nature of crime seems to accompany growing class cleavages between criminal and victim, so that crime itself carries with it overtones of ethnic and class animosity and hostility. These antagonisms accompany the growing diversity and deepening stratification of the industrializing city.

Third, increasing concern about crime accompanies major changes in urban social structure. It appears during periods of developing class and cultural cleavages between rich and poor, property owner and worker, native and foreigner. As the gap between these groups widens, the boundaries become more rigid and the social distance wider. The elite begins to believe that the dissaffected population of urban poor, who are demanding improvements in their situation, often employing violence, seek to overturn the social order. The economic distinctness of this population is generally joined with a sense that they are culturally, racially, and ethnically foreign and that they share neither common values nor similar commitment to the existing social order. These are times of shifting political, economic, and moral orders in which continued native elite dominance is threatened. The elite expresses fears of moral decay, a concern with "national deterioration" (Tobias 1967: 32), and uneasiness about fallen women, pervasive theft, and a lack of responsiveness to traditional institutions. The potential disruption arises both from challenges to the economic order and assaults on established cultural traditions.

This is also a period in which urbanites confront large numbers of strangers for whom they have not yet developed adequate cognitive maps. The immigrants themselves are newcomers, ignorant of the cultural skills that enable experienced urbanites to navigate their complex human environment, and are easy prey to con-men, thieves, and wealthy urbanites who exploit their naïveté. Their cognitive maps are rudimentary or non-existent, and they must learn slowly and painfully which persons to trust and which to distrust, which places are safe and which should be avoided, and when a stroll after dark is a hazardous undertaking. On the other hand, the established urbanites also lack familiarity with the new immigrants and have no means of classifying and predicting their behavior. The influx of immigrants threatens to swamp their systems for dealing with strangers, leading to the formation of gross, undifferentiated, and often inaccurate stereotypes of the groups perceived across major social divides. Categorical identities, founded on ethnic and racial criteria, may explain the virulence of hostility toward these new populations.

Thus, the danger of the city is at heart the fear of strangers, but in a complex and multifaceted way. It is the fear of unfamiliar cultural groups, of people who are not committed to the established urbanites' life style or social order, who express their antagonisms in part through crime. For the poor, it is both a mode of survival and a means of expressing hostilities against the rich. Obviously the preponderance of victims will always be those close by and accessible, but those forms of crime that loom largest as sources of danger acquire added virulence and viciousness from underlying class and ethnic antagonisms. As Monkkonen notes in his study of the dangerous classes in nineteenth-century Columbus, Ohio, the criminals are not the very poor, but those who are still resisting poverty, those who are in a sense revolting from their position and attempting to better it (1975). Rather than sliding into crime from poverty, it is those who fail in crime who become paupers. The bulk of the criminal population seems always to be the young, those who are still fighting against a position at the bottom of the social order. Thus, concern about crime masks deeper anxieties about changes in the social and moral order and the specter of revolution by the poor and exploited classes.

I argue that the fear of crime serves as a way of rationalizing and legitimizing increased control of the subordinate populations who are labeled as dangerous. Because of the confounding of anxiety about crime and social unrest, of the fear of crime and the fear of social change, branding a discontented, potentially revolutionary group as criminal builds on existing fears while focusing on only a narrow slice of the total range of dangers that are involved. The effect is increased demands for control, both through the legal system and through legitimate and illegitimate collective violence. The great fear of crime in eighteenth-century London, for example, lead to a staggering increase in the number of capital crimes (Beattie 1974). By the 1820s, between 200 and 220 offenses were punishable by death, including pickpocketing, horse theft, shoplifting, sheep-stealing, and servants' thefts from masters (Cockburn 1977; Beattie 1974). During the 1720s, a period of intense concern about crime, the authorities were particularly apprehensive and more quickly inclined to haul men and women into court for activities that would have been ignored in other times (Beattie 1974: 71). The anxiety about black slaves and the possibility of a slave revolt in colonial New York inspired a host of regulations concerning their rights to carry a weapon of any kind, train a dog, or attend funerals after dark (Greenberg 1974: 44). The nineteenth-century elite of Sydney, assuming that crime was the natural impulse of the criminal classes that made up a substantial portion of the population of this penal colony, enacted restrictive laws preventing freedom of association, the distribution of spirits, access to weapons, and severe punishments for infractions of these rules (Gurr, Grabosky, and Hula 1977: 347–349). Dollard describes fears felt by blacks in the American South of the 1930s who realized that they were subject to vigilante violence not only from whites but also from local law enforcement officers (1937). American ideas about the dangers of foreigners and racial minorities have frequently erupted in vigilante violence and lynchings directed against blacks, Italian communities at the turn of the century (Higham 1955), Chinese in the late nineteenth century (Nee 1974), Catholic convents (Handlin 1941), Jews (Higham 1955), and numerous other groups (Brown 1969a and 1969b).

Some have argued that the concern with law and order pervasive in the United States in the 1960s and 1970s reflected similar demands for increased control over groups that were becoming too militant and too threatening to the social order (Graham 1969). The fears generated by frightening statistics on crime rates provided the political basis for increased investment in law enforcement personnel and institutions to shore up the power of the state to control such threatening populations. Political rhetoric about crime rates thus conceals deeper political purposes of maintaining the status quo and a stable social order. This analysis does not deny that such developments occur only in the context of real increases in crime, but argues that the meaning of crime, its social and political significance, cannot be assessed independently of the social structure and power relations between the groups involved.

CHAPTER 8

Danger and Urban Social Theory

The cross-cultural and historical analysis of the meaning of danger parallels the argument developed in the study of Dover Square: danger has many meanings, including, but extending far beyond, the incidence of crime. Danger encompasses the fear of the stranger, the morally reprehensible, disorderly, or culturally alien person, and the anonymous member of a hostile and threatening social category. In Dover Square as in the large industrializing cities of the nineteenth century, groups appear dangerous not only because they commit crime but also because they are hostile and potentially disruptive. A sense of danger springs from antagonisms between groups that emerge from both class and cultural differences. The historical examples portray danger arising primarily from class conflicts, but in each case the class antagonisms are reinforced by cultural differences. In Dover Square, group conflicts stem primarily from cultural differences, but are buttressed by economic rivalry such as that the whites and blacks feel toward the economically more successful Chinese.

Both in Dover Square and in industrial cities more generally, dangerous experiences include insult, humiliation, loss of community, and the erosion of a position of dominance as well as the risk of criminal attack. Further, it is not all crimes that seem dangerous, but primarily random and unpredictable actions by strangers. Danger is a cognitive assessment of a situation: it is part of the learned and shared cultural repertoire by which urbanites negotiate and manage their hazardous environment.

Chapter 1 discussed the widely accepted hypothesis that the fear of crime undermines neighborhood social cohesion, atomizes the community, prevents the formation of social ties, and reduces informal social control and the inclination to intervene in crime incidents. Several efforts to test this hypothesis have so far been inconclusive (Yancey 1971; Conklin 1975; Hartnagel 1979). My research suggests that this theory is overly simple. The fear of crime affects different social relationships differently. It has virtually no impact on relationships with friends, family, and neighbors who are known and trusted. It impinges to a greater extent on relations with acquaintances. The major burden, however, is on relations with strangers. Thus, the effect of the fear of crime on a local community depends on the kinds of relationship that prevail between residents. Where most know one another and are interconnected through dense ties of kinship and friendship, even a high crime rate will probably have little impact within the neighborhood. On the other hand, where neighbors are strangers, as in Dover Square, fear of crime will lead to avoidance, reluctance to initiate social contact, and the perpetuation of social boundaries.

DOVER SQUARE IN THE CONTEXT OF URBAN ETHNOGRAPHY

Although they describe different kinds of communities, other ethnographies of low-income American neighborhoods report striking similarities in the ways residents perceive and manage danger. In his study of Pruitt-Igoe, a large housing project in St. Louis, Rainwater found black families to be continually concerned about the dangers of their environment, both physical and moral (1966, 1970). They felt unable to protect their children from the hazards of their deteriorating housing, from the violence of other children, the humiliation and degradation of encounters with caretakers and employers, and the temptations of an exciting and gratifying street life drawing them away from respectable family roles. Children learned early about the nature of adult life, the dangers of interpersonal violence and conflict, lack of respect for others, and omnipresent risks to one's self-respect. They discovered that they could not avoid these dangers and had to learn to manipulate them and even to seek out risks and engage in "bad" behavior (Rainwater 1970: 222–226). One woman described how she used to hit her children when they came home beaten by other children and was pleased to find that they had learned to beat up the other children first, even if the police said they were bad (Rainwater 1970: 193). Although Valentine did not address the issue of danger directly, she also described a low-income black community in which violence and sudden death were familiar occurrences (1978).

In the low-income black neighborhood in Washington, D.C., described by Hannerz, trouble was also a preoccupation of local residents (1969). They discussed who was likely to do what, which streets and streetcorners should be avoided, and what times of day and seasons of the year were particularly dangerous. Residents appeared to adopt two strategies for coping. One was the use of cognitive maps similar to those used by Dover Square residents. The other was "minding your own business," not meddling in other peoples' affairs (Hannerz 1969: 65–66). This latter strategy, also adopted by black and white inhabitants of Dover Square, emphasized the management of interpersonal relationships, rather than simple withdrawal into a fortress of bars and locks. As in Dover Square, "mainstream" or working-class black parents endeavored, usually without much success, to insulate their children from the temptations of the street and the activities of more street-life–oriented youths in the neighborhood.

Suttles' study of a multi-ethnic low-income neighborhood in Chicago described a community much more like Dover Square than either Pruitt-Igoe or the Washington neighborhood, except that each ethnic group occupied its own territory (1968). He was particularly interested in how residents of an area that was defined as a slum, and in which the other residents were labeled untrustworthy and dangerous, found ways to establish relations based on trust. He argued that they formed a provincial morality, distinct from the public morality that regulates relations between individuals in non-slum communities. First, residents restrict their social relationships to the safest ones, withdrawing into their households or small territorial groupings where they encounter only people they know. They construct cognitive maps of places that they define as safe and that are protected by local gangs, areas Suttles referred to as "defended neighborhoods" (1972). Second, they trust only those whom they know personally. The process of establishing trust is one of exchanging details of personal history so that one can be known as an individual. Suttles argued that Addams-area residents also organized themselves into corporate groups that facilitated the identification and location of strangers in social space. For example, he suggested that teenagers form gangs with names and corporate identities in order to facilitate identifying and coping with strange teenagers on local streets.

More generally, Jacobson suggests that the formation of relationships with an expectation of continuity is essential to the creation of trusting relationships in the city (1971). The hope of maintaining the relationship in the future, as well as the obligation to conform to normative expectations in order to avoid future sanctions, provides the basis for social order in such relationships. Individuals create and maintain such ties when they become enmeshed in ongoing social networks, although these are not necessarily locally based. In his research in Uganda, Jacobson observed the formation of ongoing relationships between civil servants in a provincial town (1973). Since they were regularly circulated through the country on relatively short tours of duty, they expected in the future to encounter their friends from one town at some other post. Even if they did not meet the same people, they were at least likely to find friends of friends. This expectation of continuity in the future maintained and solidified these relationships (see also Cohen 1969; Roberts 1973).

In each of these cultural contexts, the bedrock of urban social order is the creation of personal relationships from transient, anonymous ones. Even if the information available about a person is simply that he is a drug addict and cannot be trusted, this knowledge facilitates prediction of his behavior and makes possible a strategy of careful avoidance. Discontinuous, transient relationships create the unease and indeterminacy of urban life. Such relationships, of course, also make possible the city's oft-noted freedom and tolerance: its

openness of expression, acceptance of deviance, and opportunities for creativity and self-fulfillment unentangled by the
webs of small-town and village gossip. This freedom is the flip
side of the anonymity and uncertainty caused by omnipresent strangers in the city.

My study of Dover Square differs significantly from other
urban ethnographies on low-income American communities
in one regard, however. While Rainwater, Hannerz, and Suttles emphasized the danger of the environments they examined, I found, in a similar setting, urbanites who appeared unconcerned. The difference, however, is more apparent than
real. The three earlier studies implicitly compared their communities with middle-income communities. They ignored
variations between residents within a neighborhood. I, on the
other hand, emphasized the range of opinions among residents, but did not contrast this community with other, less
crime-ridden areas. All residents were aware that their environment contains hazards, but some were more concerned
than others. Even among blacks, some were as worried as the
people Hannerz, Suttles, and Rainwater described, while others felt confident of managing their environment and claimed
it was not at all dangerous.

Territory and Social Order

Dover Square residents have managed to create small social
worlds within which they feel safe, but their strategies have
not provided any overarching social order for the neighborhood. In this sense, Dover Square has evolved quite differently from the neighborhood Suttles studied (1968). Addams-
area residents organized into structurally equivalent ethnic
and territorial groups, which coalesced or split depending on
the situation. Yet a reexamination of his data in light of the
very different pattern in Dover Square suggests that the social
order he observed was actually founded on the territorial
dominance of a single, cohesive ethnic group.

The Addams area was originally Italian, but in the few
years prior to Suttles' study gained a large number of black,
Mexican, and Puerto Rican residents. At the time of Suttles'
study, the Italians were one-third of the total population; one-

quarter were Mexican, 17 percent black, and 8 percent Puerto Rican (1968: 22). Each occupied a distinct territory. In spite of this ethnic diversity, groupings of similar age, sex, ethnicity, and territory coalesced along regular lines in situations of conflict, a pattern Suttles termed "ordered segmentation." A minor fracas might engage groups of one age, ethnic group, and territory against others of the same age and ethnicity from a different area. As the conflict escalated, additional people would be drawn into it in predictable ways. Individuals of all ages in one ethnic group and territory would join against individuals of all ages of that ethnic group in another territory. Thus, the Italians of the Addams area would unite against the Italians "over on Western" (Suttles 1968: 32). If a conflict continued, it would reach a third level: the opposition of all residents of one territory to all those of another territory, regardless of ethnicity. Such events rarely happened, however, and the third level of organization generally did not progress beyond rumor and the apprehension that other territories might forge such a coalition.

There were many indications that the Italians dominated the area. It was once totally under Italian control, and the Italians were the only group that ever predominated in the whole area (Suttles 1968: 16). All ethnic groups generally perceived the area as one that "belonged" to the Italians, who were thought to have "prior rights" to the territory, and who, most residents believed, comprised the majority of the population (Suttles 1968: 20). The surrounding city considered the Italians responsible for whatever happened there, since the area was viewed as an Italian neighborhood. Italians controlled most of the retail businesses and political connections to city government: the political and economic power of the neighborhood. The Italians were the only group in which adolescent street-corner groups persisted as adult social clubs, so only among the Italians were the adults able to control the adolescent street groups (Suttles 1968: 117). The only church that united a local ethnic group as a whole was the Italian Catholic church; the other groups either attended outside-run churches as "guests" or belonged to many small churches. The role of the Italian Catholic church in maintaining order was illustrated by a case in which two Italian boys robbed two Mexican boys (Suttles 1968: 45). Some Mexican men made vague threats to the Italian priest about what they would do if the wallets were not returned. The priest, with the aid of the precinct captain, was able to locate and return the wallets. The Mexican community, however, had no equivalent organization that could provide recourse to an Italian in the same situation. The stability of the Italian neighborhood fostered dense social networks, which reduced anonymity and increased the control of members over one another.

Given these conditions, it seems unreasonable to argue that the basis for order in the Addams area was simply the regular combination and recombination of structurally equivalent segments. A more accurate model is that the order derived from the organization and cohesion of the Italians, whose members felt the area belonged to them and that they were responsible for it. Territory is an important factor in maintaining urban social order when neighborhoods are under the unambiguous control of a single group. Substantial numbers of non-members can then be accommodated within the order provided by the dominant group. Street-corner gangs may have controlled territory in the way Suttles describes, but their activities did not necessarily extend to the protection of other residents.

In Dover Square, the lack of order seems related to ambiguity about which group, if any, is dominant in and has responsibility for public areas in the neighborhood. Although Chinese residents are statistically the majority of the population, many people in the project feel the Chinese do not "belong." Several Chinese respondents believed that they represented only 25 percent of the project population and, as a minority, had neither the right nor the responsibility to exercise control over events in the neighborhood. They were very conscious of the fact that they are not in Chinatown and that Chinatown organizations do not extend their jurisdiction to Dover Square. In a similar housing project on the other side of the expressway, however, Chinese residents play a very different role. It is 60 percent Chinese, but, in this Chinatown project, they are the dominant group. Chinese residents run the tenants' association, notice and question intruders, and call the police, the project management, or intervene in some other way when the project is invaded by outsiders. Five hundred yards away in Dover Square, the Chinese residents do none of this.

To some extent, black residents of Dover Square do act as a dominant ethnic group that exercises control over the territory. They are aware of intruders, warning their friends when suspicous outsiders appear. When a neighborhood youth was attacked by roving gangs of white boys, older neighborhood boys retaliated, then mounted a watch at one end of the project in case the whites returned. One young black man felt that he "owned" the project and, when he was sent to jail, passed on his "control" to his partner. This control is acknowledged by other black residents. For example, an adult black woman referred to the partner as the "manager" of the project, when she introduced him to an elderly lady, and asked him to protect her elderly friend. Adult black women also exert effective control over behavior in the public areas of the development. Many watch the streets and, when they see behavior of which they disapprove, either call out to the youths to stop or telephone the police.

Surveillance and control by black residents affects nonblack residents as well. When some local blacks observed outsiders attempting to rob the homes and steal the cars of their white neighbors, they told them to stop. Both a white and an Hispanic young woman complained that the local black boys always harass and beat them but noted that these same boys protect them from outsiders who come into the project and bother them. A few Chinese and white residents felt particularly safe because their black neighbors promised to look out for them. In general, blacks perceive the project as a safe area in which they have some responsibility for activity in the streets. On the other hand, it is the whites who dominate connections with the management and local politicians, and, as we have seen, there are no local businesses or neighborhood organizations to provide unity for the whole neighborhood.

Thus, social order in a neighborhood depends on the presence of a dominant group that perceives itself as responsible for public areas. To effectively control public behavior, this group must possess organizational structure and internal cohesion. The group need not be ethnic, but it must be sufficiently homogeneous to construct extensive social networks within the neighborhood and generate some consensus about standards for behavior. Two conditions can prevent the formation of a dominant group. First, if a neighborhood is experiencing ethnic transition, dominance may become uncertain (Molotch 1972). Second, if a neighborhood is administratively integrated so that no group is predominant or has prior rights over the territory, as occurred in Dover Square, the majority population will probably be unorganized and will probably not perceive itself to be responsible for order in the streets. Under these conditions, neighborhoods are likely to consist of frightened, alienated individuals and are likely to be characterized by increased tension, conflict, and fear. This was, in fact, the case in Dover Square.

Territory and Defensible Space

The importance of territorial dominance has implications for "defensible space," the notion that architectural design can prevent crime (Newman 1973). Based on a study of crime in New York City housing projects, Newman found that buildings where residents must share with strangers public space close to their homes have higher crime rates than buildings, housing similar populations, where shared space is small enough to allow residents to become personally acquainted. Further, when public areas are more clearly demarcated and linked to particular apartments, residents are more likely to exercise surveillance and intervene in incidents of crime and disorder. Residents of large high-rise buildings are unable to identify intruders and rarely cooperate with their neighbors to control crime in the impersonal hallways, staircases, and undifferentiated expanses of project grounds. To decrease crime, Newman advocated the creation of real and symbolic boundaries between the area of a particular social group and the outside, strongly defined areas of influence, and adequate windows for surveillance. Together, these design features produce "defensible space," areas that residents feel they control and can defend against intruders or criminals.

Newman's insights are clearly validated by one element

of the design of Dover Square. In its narrow, dark passageways, far from any residential cluster and immune to regular surveillance, crime is rife. But crime also is rife, and intervention by residents also rarely occurs, in other spaces that are defensible by virtue of their design. The courtyards, for example, are surrounded by low-rise buildings that open onto small sections of sidewalk and parking area and include a porch and stairwell shared by only four families. Yet residents often fail to evict intruders or intervene in crimes in these spaces, and roughly half the robberies whose location I could determine occurred in these spaces.

Residents fail to intervene in these areas, despite their defensible space, for at least two reasons. First, the social fragmentation of the project often makes it difficult for residents to distinguish intruders from their neighbors' visitors. If their neighbor belongs to another ethnic group and is a stranger, residents cannot know whether an outsider they observe is a dinner guest or a thief. One Chinese family, for example, assumed that the man they saw going upstairs intended to visit the black family who lived in an upper apartment. Only later did they discover that he had burglarized the other apartment. The design of the stairwell demarcated the space as semi-private, but social heterogeneity thwarted effective intervention.

A second problem with defensible space is choosing a viable strategy for intervention. Many people observe incidents yet fail to act because they feel there is little they can do. Often, their inability to speak English leaves Chinese residents unable to call the police, or their fear that a phone call will implicate them in prolonged court proceedings and cost them days of lost wages makes them unwilling. Some shy away from American judicial institutions altogether, a legacy of generations of illegal immigration to this country. In all ethnic groups, residents fear retribution that may result from involving the police, and several have experienced retaliatory burglaries. One woman, who called and identified by name the burglars she observed, was threatened by these youths and, fearing for the safety of her three young children, refused to testify. Few people have the courage to rush into the street and physically accost a criminal, unless they feel certain that their neighbors will join in the chase. For all the reasons described above, those who give chase frequently find themselves alone.

Newman's claim was that "through the manipulation of building and spatial configurations, one can create areas for which people will adopt concern" (1973: 206). My evidence indicates that, for this to happen, architecture is necessary, but not by itself sufficient. Design can provide preconditions for effective control, but it cannot create such control if the social fabric of the community is fragmented and ethnically divided, and territorial dominance is ambiguous. In Dover Square, more than half the residents feel they are outsiders and therefore not responsible for the public spaces around them. Many Chinese and white residents see the project as a "no man's land" in which they are simply a small and helpless minority. Of the fifteen instances of intervention in crimes or disorders that I either observed or heard about, only four involved a Chinese resident, although the Chinese comprise half the population; over half (eight) involved blacks, despite their one-fourth representation in the community; and one-fifth (three) involved whites, although only one-tenth of all residents are white. Since the architectural design has the same impact on all ethnic groups, it appears that willingness to defend public spaces around the home depends not only on physical features but also on cultural definitions of territorial dominance, the ability to identify intruders, and the availability of effective modes of intervention (Merry 1981b).

SOCIAL BOUNDARIES AND URBAN SOCIAL THEORY

In his imaginative essay on the nature of social life in cities, distilling the ideas of two decades of work by the Chicago School of urban sociology, Wirth argued that ecological conditions of size, density, permanency, and heterogeneity create a social world of impersonal, superficial relationships in which individuals are unhitched from close ties to social groups, such as community and family, and freed from the reins of social control (1938). Neighborhood and family connections atrophy, acquaintanceships replace friendships, and secondary contacts proliferate over primary ones. The result is an increase in anomie: a sense of normlessness, a lack of attachment to any moral code at the individual level, and a loss of consensus at the societal level. Wirth paints an image of the urbanite living a fragmented life. He is no longer anchored in the primary ties of family, kinship, or neighborhood, but develops a "schizoid" personality from playing separate roles in different worlds simultaneously.

This increasingly superficial social environment makes the urbanite blasé, both because he has few intimate relationships and because he must insulate himself from the myriad of unknown people he confronts daily. Ultimately this process results in freedom from informal controls, the loss of spontaneous self-expression, and an absence of direct participation and involvement in common concerns inherent in an integrated society. The urbanite becomes Park's "marginal man," who interacts mostly with strangers. The price is lost intimacy, anonymity, and the social void, anomie. Anomie contributes to personality disruption and breakdown, crime, corruption, and suicide since it encourages individual relationships based on mutual exploitation and self-aggrandizement rather than intimacy. The city increasingly falls prey to social disorganization (see also Smith 1979; Hannerz 1980).

Despite Wirth's gloomy vision of urban life, he also acknowledged the existence of small social worlds in the city, viewing it as a mosaic. His own research described in detail life in a Jewish ghetto (1928), one of these worlds, and other ethnographies produced by the Chicago School explored the miniature social systems of hoboes (Anderson 1923), taxi-dance-hall girls (Cressey 1932), rooming-house districts, and the leisured Chicago elite (Zorbaugh 1929; see generally, Hannerz 1980). Park also acknowledged the existence of these small social worlds:

> The processes of segregation establish moral distances which make the city a mosaic of little worlds which touch but do not interpenetrate. This makes it possible for individuals to pass quickly and easily from one moral milieu to another, and encourages the fascinating but dangerous experiment of living at the same time in sev-

eral different contiguous but otherwise widely separated worlds.

1952: 47

Yet, neither Wirth nor the other Chicago sociologists examined how these separate worlds articulated with one another
or the implications of the co-residence of several ethnic and
social enclaves in close proximity.

Several aspects of Wirth's vision of the city have been
severely criticized in the last four decades. First, criticism has
focused on the social characteristics Wirth described as typically urban, arguing that these characteristics are in fact
found only in large, industrialized cities, and that Wirth con-
founded the differing impacts of urbanism and industrialization (Gans 1962b; Sjoberg 1960). Traditional Yoruba cities,
for example, are large, dense settlements with none of the
anomie, impersonality, superficiality of relationships, or disorder of Wirth's model (Bascom 1959; see also Krapf-Askari
1969). Miner's study of Timbuktu also revealed urban form
without the "urban way of life" (1953). In Fox's useful typol-
ogy, cities exhibit a wide range of social patterns, only a few
of which conform to Wirth's city (1977). On the other hand,
the conditions Wirth described as typically urban do appear
in rural proletariats organized according to industrial modes
of production (e.g., Nelkin 1970). In small towns populated
by non-agricultural elites, social lives may be organized
around a pattern based on that of the distant city (Harris
1956). Wirth's views were, in fact, heavily influenced by
his experience in the 1930s in Chicago, a growing, heterogeneous, industrializing metropolis that, some claim, has assumed the same role in urban sociology that the middle-class
Viennese family has played in Freudian psychology.

A second thrust of criticism concerns Wirth's failure to
place adequate emphasis on the existence of urban villages,
small enclaves within cities, characterized by ongoing, intimate relations of kinship and friendship. In these stable, often
ethnically homogeneous settlements, relationships are lasting and personal, individuals endure the social pressures of
friends and family, and the disorder of the city rarely pene-

trates (e.g., Whyte 1943; Young and Willmott 1957; Gans 1962a; Suttles 1968; Hannerz 1969). Such communities are geographically based and emerge when housing and economic conditions permit continued residence in the same location over generations. They may also emerge when an immigrant minority, either because of insecurity in the city or lack of commitment to the new way of life, tries to maintain close ties to its homeland by creating an encapsulated social world that replicates the world of the village (Mayer 1961; Lewis 1972; Jacobson 1973; Nee 1974).

A third set of criticisms concern Wirth's neglect of new structures of social order that emerge in cities and are often overlooked by scholars seeking the traditional units of neighborhood and family. Yet, as the territorial urban community crumbles, other shapes of community arise. Sociologists and anthropologists have delineated a wide range of "nongroups" that structure urban social life, such as social networks, action-sets, coalitions, and factions (Boissevain 1968). Wirth expected voluntary associations to play a critical role in the emerging urban social order (1938: 81), but this expectation has not been realized, at least in American cities. On the other hand, the social network, in a variety of forms, has become one of the predominant patterns of urban social organization (Bott 1957; Mitchell 1966, 1969; Boissevain 1974).

Networks can serve as the basis for urban social groups even if they are neither geographically based nor permanent. In a penetrating essay, Jacobson argues that urbanites often construct social worlds of non-localized social networks (1971). Others note that networks may be enduring but intermittently activated (Mayer 1966; Boswell 1969; Jacobson 1976). In elections in Indian cities, for example, each candidate generates a network that becomes involved only during campaigns, but remains latent at other times (Mayer 1966). Mayer calls this temporary, goal-directed social network an "action-set." Action-sets, periodically reactivated, become "quasi-groups." Thus, urban social life consists of intricate webs of latent social ties that can be mobilized or ignored depending on the exigencies of the situation.

The benefits of Wirth's insights may be lost, however, in

this barrage of well-founded criticism. Wirth's vision was not wrong, but partial. In fact, much of his portrayal of the anonymity and superficiality of social relationships, the prevalence of social disorganization and anomie, resonates with the modern urbanite's experience. Primary and intimate relationships exist within urban villages and social networks, but the problematic interactions that are the focus of Wirth's analysis lurk in the gaps between these worlds. In our eagerness to dispel the inaccuracy of his image as a description of the totality of urban life, we may neglect the importance of the kinds of relationships he describes.

This returns us to the problem Wirth hinted at but ignored: the relationships between the pieces of the urban social mosaic. These pieces may be geographically based communities or non-localized social networks. Several non-localized networks may occupy the same space, as they do in Dover Square. Whatever their configuration, the question of how these networks articulate with one another is, as Jacobson suggests, a critical problem for urban anthropology (1971). It is here that Wirth's urban way of life appears, and here that the breakdown of social control is greatest. Yet this question has received relatively little attention from anthropologists, who have tended to focus on enduring ties. For a full understanding of urban social life, it is essential to examine the nature of social boundaries, the processes by which they are created and maintained, and their implications for enduring social groups.

Wirth argued, for example, that individuals who are detached from organizations and groups pose the greatest threat to social order because they are not controlled by any social group or moral code (1938: 76). However, as the case study of Dover Square illustrates, it is not those who are detached, but those who appear detached, who are responsible for crime, disorder, and fear. It is these individuals who are least susceptible to social control. Although they are firmly anchored in an existing social group or network, their social moorings are unknown to the observer, who sees them as apparently "detached" persons. Criminals in Dover Square actively foster their appearance of anonymity, of detachment, in order to escape punishment from their victims. Thus, it is the separation between social worlds, as much as the detachment of individuals, that produces anomie and social disorder.

The social relationships among the pieces of the urban mosaic assume significance for at least three reasons. First, when urbanites fear attack or other harm, it is the absence of relationships across social boundaries that creates a sense of danger. Second, these cracks in the surface of social life are the source of racial and ethnic conflicts. Confrontations over school busing, neighborhood transition, gang warfare, equal work opportunities, and integration of housing all reflect the underlying friction between ethnic and social enclaves. Crime also can be seen as another facet of intergroup conflict. Third, urbanites categorize individuals across social boundaries in terms of race, ethnic background, and class, which strengthens and perpetuates social boundaries. The cognitive models of each ethnic group in Dover Square warn against social interaction with other ethnic groups and thus reinforce the social boundaries themselves.

Cultural Distance and Ethnic Boundaries

This analysis suggests a rethinking of Barth's notion of the nature of ethnic boundaries (1969). He focuses on ethnic groups as organizations or interacting populations rather than as bearers of cultural traditions. However, although his suggestion to study "the ethnic boundary that defines the group, not the cultural stuff it encloses" (1969: 15), has been very productive for research on ethnicity, his assumption that culture is epiphenomenal may lead to a fundamental misunderstanding of the function of ethnic boundaries, at least in urban neighborhoods. In heterogeneous cities in which fear of strangers is common, cultural differences are essential to the formation and maintenance of boundaries. In Barth's view, only a limited set of cultural differences are relevant to the maintenance of an ethnic boundary: the symbols or signs that enable individuals to identify others of the same group, and the standards by which behavior is judged. However, in Dover Square, the degree of cultural difference assumes a critical role as individuals develop cognitive categories and strategies of avoidance to minimize the hazards they face.

The greater cultural gap between the Chinese population and the black and white populations contributes to the sharper cleavage in social interaction between these groups. Earlier chapters described the great differences in family patterns, occupations, social mobility, norms of male and female behavior, and familiarity with "street life" that divide the two groups. In spite of the long tradition of hostility between black and white in the U.S., and the pervasive racial hostility in other parts of its surrounding city, Dover Square blacks and whites are more likely to participate in the same institutions and share public spaces with each other than either is with the Chinese. Few social ties bridge the gap between Chinese-speakers and English-speakers, even though most of the younger Chinese residents speak fluent English. Despite the equal residential proximity of all ethnic groups, more friendships occur between blacks and whites. Those social ties that do develop across ethnic boundaries are founded on shared interests, values, and ideas about proper behavior.

Because individuals cope with hazardous environments by withdrawing into spheres of social relationships that are perceived as safe and by avoiding interactions that seem unpredictable and uncertain, people whose behavior is alien and unfamiliar because of their adherence to a distinct cultural system will seem dangerous, and interactions with them will be avoided. Under these conditions, cultural differences are not irrelevant, but fundamental to the formation of ethnic boundaries.

IMPLICATIONS FOR URBAN POLICY

Reducing the Fear of Crime

Contrary to frequent claims by researchers and law enforcement personnel, this study suggests that a moderate reduction in the crime rate will not reduce fear of crime. Only changes that alter the nature of relations between the small social worlds that constitute the city, that improve communication between these worlds, that refine cognitive categories, and that decrease anonymity will reduce the uncertainty urbanites feel in coping with individuals outside their own social enclave. The reaction of Dover Square residents to a substantial drop in the crime rate during the last six months of my research is instructive. Few residents realized that there was less crime. Many of the local youths active in crime were temporarily in jail, but only those residents connected to the social networks of these youths knew that they were gone and that crime had diminished. Others, ignorant of the absence of some of the most active criminals, felt as frightened as before.

When a sense of danger is exacerbated by sharp cultural differences, improved communication could reduce fear. It is difficult, however, to create settings in which such communication will occur. People, in Dover Square and elsewhere, prefer to interact in settings that they find predictable and orderly, that emit cues of safety rather than danger. These settings tend to be staffed by members of their own ethnic group and attended primarily by others of their group. As one black resident said, she does not want to go to a meeting unless she knows that other blacks will be there; she does not want to feel out of place. A multi-ethnic staff or team of organizers sensitive to these issues is essential. One incident illustrates this clearly. In an attempt to provide more recreational services to city children, the mayor's office sponsored mobile recreation programs in local neighborhoods. When the game center, staffed by an enthusiastic group of young blacks and whites, appeared in the playground of Dover Square one hot summer day, both black and white children participated eagerly and boisterously. Only one Chinese mother brought her children, however, and she stayed only a few minutes. Others were quickly ushered past the playground by their parents, for whom this setting did not signal safety. A ring of small Chinese faces peeked sadly from behind fences and curtains.

Not only must a group attempting to induce interethnic communication provide a setting perceived as safe, it must also satisfy the immediate, instrumental goals of the participants. The two successful interethnic organizations in the project are an infant care center and a day care program for older children, both of which are essential for working mothers. People who work long hours are probably less inclined to devote time to organizations that satisfy only diffuse community needs or purely social or recreational ends if these organizations appear to be at all unsafe or uncomfortable.

The solution to urbanites' and suburbanites' fear of the city is not the adoption of more locks, bars, and guard dogs, or an enhanced police presence, but greater knowledge of the city and its residents. If suburbanites and urbanites knew the city more intimately, they could draw finer distinctions between areas they consider safe and those they think are dangerous. Areas that are unknown can more easily acquire a reputation for danger. If a person hears of a crime occurring in a familiar area, he may decide that the corner, block, or immediate area where the incident occurred is dangerous, but will not extend that attitude to the entire neighborhood. Hearing of a similar incident in an unfamiliar area, however, he is likely to generalize his sense of danger to the whole district since he cannot pinpoint a particular corner or street he should avoid. Through this process of generalization, unfamiliar areas come to be considered more dangerous than familiar areas. For persons unfamiliar with most areas in the city, the implication of this process of generalization is clear: the whole city becomes a dangerous place that should be avoided as much as possible.

Integrating Residential Environments

This research also has implications for efforts to integrate housing (Merry 1980). Foes of school busing often advocate residential integration as a more preferable way to increase social contact between racial groups and bring about social and economic equality. Advocates of housing integration have two goals. One is to provide good housing. Given the political realities of the United States, the only way minority groups may be able to acquire decent, low-cost housing may be through integration with whites, who have greater political influence. In this light, Dover Square is a success: it provides minority populations good housing at a reasonable price.

The second goal of advocates of housing integration is to facilitate social interaction and communication between ethnic groups and thereby enhance understanding and tolerance. To some extent, this has occurred in Dover Square. Black and white youths, in particular, are more accepting of one another than are their parents, who did not grow up in this environment, and are generally more tolerant than many of the other residents of the city. One black woman feels that Dover Square blacks are more tolerant of Chinese people than ghetto blacks, for example, who perceive all Chinese as the enemy in Vietnam. On the other hand, integrated housing is not a panacea. Co-residence does not inevitably break down barriers between ethnic groups and may even intensify hostility, if anger against inconsiderate neighbors is interpreted in ethnic terms. Some residents are unwilling to think in ethnic terms and are open to communication and contact with all individuals, but others find that the multi-ethnic residential situation simply aggravates their prejudices. A few instances of interethnic friendship have emerged between people who share significant values, life styles, and attitudes, such as educated whites and Chinese, black and white youths active in street life, and working-class blacks and whites committed to work, church, and family. Overall, however, there has been little interethnic sharing or development of neighborly sociability.

If social services that accommodated cultural differences were available to facilitate communication and deal with conflicts between ethnic groups, a setting that is now difficult for many residents could become an attractive situation that could foster a new generation of more tolerant individuals. Homogeneity is not the only solution to urban danger; another possibility is communication, so that differences could be appreciated as variations, not strange and frightening forms of behavior.

Where boundaries between social groups are sharp and bridged by few social ties or shared memberships in organizations, even a moderate crime rate will generate fear, which then further exacerbates the boundaries within the neighborhood. If the problem of urban danger is to be resolved without increased state monitoring and control of subordinate, dangerous groups, a greater understanding of how to facilitate intercultural communication and diminish the uncertainty of managing strangers, both within local neighborhoods and in the city as a whole, is essential.

Appendix

TABLES

Table 1

Perceptions of Danger Compared to Rate of Victimization

| Ethnic group | Perception of Dover Square | | | | | | | | Rate of victimization | | | | | |
| | Extremely-very dangerous | | Fairly dangerous | | Not very dangerous | | Not at all dangerous | | Never victimized | | Victimized once* | | Victimized more than once | |
	No.	%	No.	%	No.	%	No.	%	No.	%	No.	%	No.	%
Chinese	3	8	9	23	21	53	7	18	44	40	52	47	15	14
Black	1	4	2	9	5	22	15	65	15	35	22	51	6	14
White	2	11	6	33	4	22	6	33	6	20	15	50	9	30
Hispanic	0	0	0	0	6	46	7	54	6	43	8	57	0	0
Total	6	6	17	18	36	38	35	37	71	36	97	49	30	15

* Primarily robberies, burglaries, or assaults.

Source: Perceptions of danger based on author's survey of a selected sample of 101 residents of Dover Square, of which 94 belonged to one of four ethnic groups as follows: 40 Chinese, 23 blacks, 18 whites, 13 Hispanics. Seven others were excluded from the analysis.

Rate of victimization based on author's survey of a selected sample of 201 households in Dover Square, of which 198 belonged to one of four ethnic groups as follows: 111 Chinese households, 43 black households, 30 white households, 14 Hispanic households. Three others were excluded from the analysis.

Table 2

Perceptions of Danger Related to Social Ties to Street Youths

| | Relationship to street youths* | | | | | |
| Perception of Dover Square | Does not know street youths (N = 41) | | Knows street youths (N = 55) | | Total (N = 96) | |
	No.	%	No.	%	No.	%
Extremely-very dangerous	5	12	2	4	7	7
Fairly dangerous	7	17	10	18	17	18
Not very dangerous	20	14	17	31	37	39
Not at all dangerous	9	22	26	47	35	36

*Lambda (asymmetric) = 0.153. Chi square significance = 0.037.
Source: Author's survey of a selected sample of 101 residents of Dover Square, excluding 5 missing cases.

Table 3

Perceptions of Danger, Controlling for Victimization

	Experience of respondent											
	Never victimized*				Victimized once or twice†				Victimized three or more times‡			
	Does not know street youths		Knows street youths		Does not know street youths		Knows street youths		Does not know street youths		Knows street youths	
Perception of Dover Square	No.	%	No.	%	No.	%	No.	%	No.	%	No.	%
Extremely dangerous	0	0	0	0	2	11	0	0	1	10	0	0
Very dangerous	0	0	0	0	3	11	1	4	0	0	1	6
Fairly dangerous	0	0	1	8	6	32	4	15	1	10	5	31
Not very dangerous	8	67	2	17	6	32	9	33	6	60	6	38
Not at all dangerous	4	33	9	75	3	16	13	48	2	20	4	25

*Chi square significance = 0.038. Kendall's Tau B significance = 0.044.
†Chi square significance = 0.077 Kendall's Tau B significance = 0.0027.
‡Chi square significance = 0.383. Kendall's Tau B significance = 0.379.
Source: Author's survey of a selected sample of 101 residents of Dover Square, excluding 5 missing cases.

Table 4

Perceptions of Danger in Relation to Other Variables

Variable	Significance (chi square)	Degree of association (lambda asymmetric)
High association		
Frightened if alone at night	0.00*	0.316
Expects to be victimized	0.00*	0.293
Ethnicity	0.00*	0.288
Good street fighter	0.00*	0.271
Number of precautions taken	0.00*	0.200
Familiarity with "street youths"	0.03†	0.153
Number of years living in project	0.00*	0.153
Thinks Dover Square is a safe place to live	0.00*	0.153
Expects help if victimized	0.00*	0.127
Low association		
Expects to remain in project	0.40	0.109
Sex	0.36	0.068
Frightened if alone in the daytime	0.00*	0.052
Number of times victimized in last year	0.18	0.051
Number of victimizations of household	0.25	0.051
More afraid than in former residence	0.01†	0.021
Personal connections with police	0.91	0.019
Most of friends live in project	0.29	0.000
Age	0.18	0.000

*Significance ≥ 0.01.
†Significance ≥ 0.05.
Source: Author's survey of a selected sample of 101 residents of Dover Square.

Table 5

Fear in Dover Square Compared to Fear in Previous Place of Residence

Perception of Dover Square	Degree of fear felt by respondent*							
	More fearful in Dover Square (N = 34)		Not more fearful in Dover Square (N = 62)		Not sure (N = 1)		Total (N = 97)	
	No.	%	No.	%	No.	%	No.	%
Extremely dangerous	1	3	0	0	0	0	1	1
Very dangerous	6	18	0	0	0	0	6	6
Fairly dangerous	7	21	4	7	0	0	11	11
Not very dangerous	11	32	14	23	0	0	25	26
Not at all dangerous	9	27	44	71	1	100	54	56

*Chi square significance = 0.001.

Source: Author's survey of a selected sample of 101 residents of Dover Square, excluding 4 missing cases.

Table 6

Robbery Locations and Perceptions of Dangerous Places

| | Robberies | | Chinese* | | | | Black* | | | |
| | | | Dangerous | | Safe | | Dangerous | | Safe | |
Place	No.	%‡	No.	%	No.	%	No.	%	No.	%
Area around house	37	61	2	10	18	90	1	4	22	96
Laundromat	2	3	6	100	0	0	17	65	9	35
Grocery store	4	7	1	50	1	50	14	74	5	26
Square	3	5	9	47	10	53	3	43	4	57
Playground	1	2	15	94	1	6	8	60	6	40
Dark, narrow alleys	14	23	21	100	0	0	8	72	3	27
Parking garage	0	0	17	100	0	0	23	96	1	4

*Figures represent those respondents who expressed an opinion.
†Includes other residents besides Chinese, blacks, and whites.
‡Percentage of robberies commited in Dover Square as reported in author's survey of 201 households.
Source: Robberies from survey of victimization experience of selected sample of 201 households in Dover Square; figures include robberies reported by witnesses as well as by victims. Perceptions of danger based on maps drawn for author by selected sample of 90 residents of Dover Square: 41 Chinese, 30 blacks, 12 whites, 2 Hispanics, 5 others.

Place	White[*]				Total sample[†]					
	Dangerous		Safe		No opinion		Dangerous		Safe	
	No.	%	No.	%	No.	%	No.	%	No.	%
Area around house	1	11	8	89	35	39	4	5	51	57
Laundromat	4	100	0	0	51	57	29	32	10	11
Grocery store	1	50	1	50	65	72	7	8	18	20
Square	0	0	4	100	59	66	12	12	19	22
Playground	5	58	3	42	49	55	30	33	11	12
Dark, narrow alleys	11	92	1	8	44	49	42	46	4	4
Parking garage	10	100	0	0	36	39	53	59	1	1

Table 7

Social Ties to Street Youths and Perceptions of Dangerous Places

Place	Friend (N = 13)				Acquaintance (N = 34)				Stranger (N = 43)			
	Dangerous		Safe		Dangerous		Safe		Dangerous		Safe	
	No.	%	No.	%	No.	%	No.	%	No.	%	No.	%
Hustler hangouts												
Playground	1	11	8	89	10	67	5	33	24	100	0	0
Laundromat	2	25	6	75	15	79	4	21	9	100	0	0
Front of laundromat	0	0	9	100	8	67	4	33	8	100	0	0
Square	1	25	3	75	2	25	6	75	11	48	22	52
Grocery store	4	50	4	50	13	81	3	19	2	67	1	33
Narrow, dark alleys	2	100	0	0	11	100	0	0	8	100	0	0
James Hill Avenue*	3	75	1	25	3	43	4	57	10	71	4	29
Dover Street*	2	50	2	50	3	27	8	73	5	38	8	62

*Streets bordering Dover Square.
Source: Maps drawn for author by sample of 90 residents of Dover Square.

Table 8

Reports of Crime, 1972–1976

	Victimization survey		Police reports	
Type of crime	No. reported (× 3)*	Average annual rate per 1,000 population	No. reported	Average Annual rate per 1,000 population
Burglaries	267	28.7	40	4.5
Robberies, purse snatches, and attempted robberies[†]	150	16.1	117	13.1
Assaults	30	3.2	7	0.8
Larceny	57	6.1	103	11.6
Auto theft	126	13.5	98	11.1

*To be comparable with police reporting area, which has three times as many households as were covered in author's survey.

[†]Actual number of robberies, etc., reported in victimization survey (N = 50) is smaller than number in Table 9 (N = 61) because number reported here excludes reports by witnesses.

Source: Author's survey of victimization experience of 201 households, 244 individuals, and calls to the police to report crimes.

Table 9

Ethnic Background Related to Perception of Social Categories

Social category	% rating social category dangerous*				
	Chinese (N = 26)	Black (N = 16)	White (N = 11)	Hispanic (N = 9)	Other (N = 1)
Children					
Chinese	4	18	0	0	0
Black	25	38	17	22	0
White	8	13	8	0	0
Hispanic	9	38	42	22	0
Teenage boys					
Chinese	35	25	36	11	0
Black	70	56	50	55	0
White	59	31	58	44	100
Hispanic	63	56	83	22	0
Teenage girls					
Chinese	4	6	17	11	0
Black	30	25	33	33	0
White	15	7	17	11	0
Hispanic	17	19	33	25	0
Adult men					
Chinese	0	25	9	14	0
Black	47	44	17	43	0
White	31	38	8	14	0
Hispanic	27	44	42	43	0
Adult women					
Chinese	0	0	0	0	0
Black	11	19	17	43	0
White	8	6	0	14	0
Hispanic	8	6	0	0	0
Elderly men					
Chinese	0	6	0	0	0
Black	11	19	0	0	0
White	0	19	0	0	0
Hispanic					

| Social category | % rating social category dangerous* | | | | |
	Chinese (N = 26)	Black (N = 16)	White (N = 11)	Hispanic (N = 9)	Other (N = 1)
Elderly women					
Chinese	0	12	0	0	0
Black	0	12	0	0	0
White	8	6	0	0	0
Hispanic					
Drunks	29	29	18	56	0

*Percentage calculated by summing responses of "extremely," "very," and "fairly" dangerous.

Source: Author's survey of a selected sample of 101 residents of Dover Square, excluding 38 missing cases.

Table 10

Perceptions of Danger Related to Strategy for Managing Danger

| Strategy | Population using strategy | | Perception of Dover Square | | | | | | | | | |
	No.	%	Extremely dangerous No.	%	Very dangerous No.	%	Fairly dangerous No.	%	Not very dangerous No.	%	Not at all dangerous No.	%
Offensive												
Chinese	1	3									1	100
Black	20	77					2	10	5	25	13	65
White	5	25							2	40	3	60
Hispanic	3	30									3	100
Other	0	0										
Total	29	33					2	7	7	24	20	69
Defensive												
Chinese	29	97			2	7	7	24	15	52	5	17
Black	6	23			1	17			2	33	3	50
White	15	75	1	7	1	7	6	40	3	20	4	27
Hispanic	7	70							4	57	3	43
Other	2	100	1	50					1	50		
Total	59	67	2	3	4	7	13	22	25	42	15	25

Source: Author's survey of a selected sample of 101 residents of Dover Square, excluding 13 missing cases.

Bibliography
and Index

BIBLIOGRAPHY

Anderson, Nels. 1923. *The Hobo: The Sociology of the Homeless Man*. Chicago: University of Chicago Press.

Bailey, F. G. 1969. *Stratagems and Spoils: A Social Anthropology of Politics*. New York: Schocken Books, Pavilion Series.

Barnes, J. A. 1954. "Class and Committees in a Norwegian Island Parish." *Human Relations* 7:39–58.

Barth, Frederik, ed. 1969. *Ethnic Groups and Boundaries: The Social Organization of Culture Difference*. Boston: Little, Brown and Co.

Bascom, William. 1959. "Urbanism as a Traditional African Pattern." *Sociological Review* 7:29–43.

Beattie, J. M. 1974. "The Pattern of Crime in England 1660–1800." *Past and Present* 62:47–95.

Beck, Robert (Iceberg Slim). 1967. *Pimp: The Story of My Life*. Los Angeles: Holloway House.

Bell, Colin, and Howard Newby. 1971. *Community Studies: An Introduction to the Sociology of the Local Community*. New York: Praeger.

Biderman, Albert, and Albert Reiss. 1967. "On Exploring the 'Dark Figure' of Crime." *Annals of the American Academy of Political and Social Science* 374:1–15.

Boggs, Sarah L. 1965. "Urban Crime Patterns." *American Sociological Review* 30:899–908.

———. 1971. "Formal and Informal Crime Control." *Sociological Quarterly* 12:319–327.

Boissevain, Jeremy. 1968. "The Place of Non-Groups in the Social Sciences." *Man* 3:542–556.

————. 1974. *Friends of Friends: Networks, Manipulators and Coalitions*. New York: St. Martin's Press.

Boswell, D. M. 1969. "Personal Crises and the Mobilization of the Social Network." In *Social Networks in Urban Situations: Analyses of Personal Relationships in Central African Towns*, ed. J. Clyde Mitchell, pp. 245–297. Manchester: University of Manchester Press.

Bott, Elizabeth. 1957. *Family and Social Network: Roles, Norms, and External Relationships in Ordinary Urban Families*. London: Tavistock.

Brace, Charles Loring. 1872. *The Dangerous Classes of New York and Twenty Years's Work among Them*. New York: Wynkoop and Hallenbeck.

Brown, Richard Maxwell. 1969a. "Historical Patterns of Violence in America." In *Violence in America: Historical and Comparative Perspectives*, vol. 2, ed. Hugh Davis Graham and Ted Robert Gurr, pp. 35–65. Washington, D.C.: U.S. Government Printing Office.

————. 1969b. "The American Vigilante Tradition." In *Violence in America: Historical and Comparative Perspectives*, vol. 2, ed. Hugh Davis Graham and Ted Robert Gurr, pp. 121–171. Washington, D.C.: U.S. Government Printing Office.

Chevalier, Louis. 1973. *The Laboring Classes and the Dangerous Classes in Paris during the First Half of the Nineteenth Century*. Trans. Frank Jellinek. New York: Howard Fertig.

Clark, Ramsey. 1970. *Crime in America*. New York: Pocket Books.

Clay, Phillip L. 1972. *A Safe Place to Live: Security in Multi-Family Housing*. Roxbury, Mass.: Lower Roxbury Community Corporation.

Clinard, Marshall B. 1978. *Cities with Little Crime: The Case of Switzerland*. Cambridge, England: Cambridge University Press.

Cockburn, J. S., ed. 1977. *Crime in England, 1550–1800*. Princeton: Princeton University Press.

Cohen, Abner. 1969. *Custom and Politics in Urban Africa: A Study of Hausa Migrants in Yoruba Towns*. Berkeley: University of California Press.

Colson, Elizabeth. 1974. *Tradition and Contract: The Problem of Order*. Chicago: Aldine.

Conklin, John E. 1975. *The Impact of Crime*. New York: Macmillan.

Cressey, Paul G. 1969. *The Taxi-Dance Hall*. Chicago: University of Chicago Press.

Dollard, John. 1937. *Caste and Class in a Southern Town*. 3rd ed., 1949. New York: Doubleday.

Douglas, Mary. 1966. *Purity and Danger: An Analysis of Concepts of Pollution and Taboo*. Harmondsworth, England: Penguin Books, Pelican.

Downs, Roger M., and David Stea, eds. 1973. *Image and Environment: Cognitive Mapping and Spatial Behavior*. Chicago: Aldine.

DuBow, Fred, Edward McCabe, and Gail Kaplan. 1979. *Reactions to Crime: A Critical Review of the Literature*. Washington, D.C.: U.S. Department of Justice.

Engels, Friedrich. 1845. *The Condition of the Working Class in England*. Trans. and ed. W. O. Henderson and W. H. Chaloner, 1958. Palo Alto: Stanford University Press.

Epstein, A. L. 1961. "The Network and Urban Social Organization." *Rhodes-Livingstone Institute Journal* 29:29–61. Rpt. in *Social Networks in Urban Situations: Analyses of Personal Relationships in Central African Towns*. Ed. J. Clyde Mitchell, pp. 77–116. Manchester: Manchester University Press, 1969.

————. 1969. "Gossip, Norms, and Social Network." In *Social Networks in Urban Situations: Analyses of Personal Relationships in Central African Towns*. Ed. J. Clyde Mitchell. Manchester: Manchester University Press.

Erskine, Hazel. 1974. "The Polls: Fear of Violence and Crime." *Public Opinion Quarterly* 38:131–145.

Evans-Pritchard, E. E. 1937. *Witchcraft, Oracles, and Magic among the Azande*. Abr. ed. Oxford: Clarendon Press, 1976.

Foster, George M., and Robert V. Kemper, eds. 1974. *Anthropologists in Cities*. Boston: Little, Brown and Co.

Fowler, Floyd J., and Thomas W. Mangione. 1974. "The Nature of Fear." Mimeographed. Boston: Survey Research Program of University of Massachusetts-Boston and the

Joint Center for Urban Studies of MIT and Harvard University.

Fox, Richard. 1977. *Urban Anthropology: Cities in Their Cultural Settings*. Englewood Cliffs, N.J.: Prentice-Hall.

Furstenberg, Frank F. 1971. "Public Reaction to Crime in the Streets," *The American Scholar* 40:601–610.

————, and Charles F. Wellford. 1973. "Calling the Police: The Evaluation of Police Service." *Law and Society Review* 7 (Spring):393–406.

Gans, Herbert J. 1962a. *The Urban Villagers: Group and Class in the Life of Italian Americans*. New York: Free Press.

————. 1962b. "Urbanism and Suburbanism as Ways of Life: A Re-evaluation of Definitions." In *Human Behavior and Social Processes*, ed. Arnold M. Rose. Boston: Houghton Mifflin Company.

Given, James Buchanan. 1977. *Society and Homicide in Thirteenth-Century England*. Palo Alto: Stanford University Press.

Gould, Peter, and R. White. 1974. *Mental Maps*. Harmondsworth, England: Penguin.

Graham, Fred P. 1969. "A Contemporary History of American Crime." In *Violence in America: Historical and Comparative Perspectives*, vol. 2, ed. Hugh Davis Graham and Ted Robert Gurr, pp. 371–387. Washington, D.C.: U.S. Government Printing Office.

Greenberg, Douglas. 1974. *Crime and Law Enforcement in the Colony of New York 1691–1776*. Ithaca, N.Y.: Cornell University Press.

Greifer, J. 1945. "Attitudes toward the Stranger: A Study of the Attitudes of Primitive Society and Early Hebrew Culture." *American Sociological Review* 6:739–745.

Gulick, John. 1967. *Tripoli: A Modern Arab City*. Cambridge, Mass.: Harvard University Press.

Gurr, Ted Robert, Peter N. Grabosky, and Richard C. Hula. 1977. *The Politics of Crime and Conflict*. Beverly Hills: Sage.

Hallowell, A. Irving. 1938. "Fear and Anxiety as Cultural and Individual Variables in a Primitive Society." *Journal of Social Psychology* 9:25–47. Rpt. in *Culture and Expe-*

rience, by A. Irving Hallowell, pp. 250–265. New York: Schocken, 1955.

Handlin, Oscar. 1941. *Boston's Immigrants*. Cambridge, Mass.: Harvard University Press, 1959.

Hannerz, Ulf. 1967. "Gossip, Networks, and Culture in a Black American Ghetto." *Ethnos* 32:35–60.

————. 1969. *Soulside: Inquiries into Ghetto Culture and Community*. New York: Columbia University Press.

————. 1970. "The Management of Danger." Paper presented at the Conference on the Anthropology of Cities, 1970. In *Exploring the City*, by Ulf Hannerz. New York: Columbia University Press, 1980.

————. 1980. *Exploring the City*. New York: Columbia University Press.

Harris, Marvin. 1956. *Town and Country in Brazil*. New York: Columbia University Press.

Hartnagel, Timothy F. 1979. "The Perception and Fear of Crime: Implications for Neighborhood Cohesion, Social Activity, and Community Affect." *Social Forces* 58:176–193.

Higham, John. 1955. *Strangers in the Land: Patterns of American Nativism, 1860–1925*. New Brunswick, N.J.: Rutgers University Press.

Hindelang, Michael J. 1974. "Public Opinion Regarding Crime, Criminal Justice, and Related Topics." *Journal of Research in Crime and Delinquency* 11:101–116.

————, Christopher S. Dunn, L. Paul Sutton, and Alison L. Aumick. 1973. *Sourcebook of Criminal Justice Statistics*. Washington, D.C.: U.S. Government Printing Office.

Jacobs, Jane. 1961. *The Death and Life of Great American Cities*. New York: Random House, Vintage Books.

Jacobson, David. 1971. "Mobility, Continuity, and Urban Social Organization." *Man* 6:630–645.

————. 1973. *Itinerant Townsmen: Friendship and Social Order in Urban Uganda*. Menlo Park, Calif.: Cummings.

————. 1976. "Fair-weather Friend: Label and Context in Middle-Class Friendships." In *The American Dimension: Cultural Myths and Social Realities*, ed. W. Arens and Susan P. Montague, pp. 149–161. Port Washington, N.Y.: Alfred.

Kingston, Maxine Hong. 1976. *The Woman Warrior: Memoirs of a Girlhood among Ghosts*. New York: Alfred A. Knopf.

Krapf-Askari, Eva. 1969. *Yoruba Towns and Cities: An Enquiry into the Nature of Urban Social Phenomena*. London: Oxford University Press.

Lane, Roger. 1969. "Urbanization and Criminal Violence in the Nineteenth Century: Massachusetts as a Test Case." In *Violence in America: Historical and Comparative Perspectives*, vol. 2, ed. Hugh Davis Graham and Ted Robert Gurr, pp. 359–371. Washington, D.C.: U.S. Government Printing Office.

Lee, Rose Hum. 1960. *The Chinese in the United States of America*. London: Oxford University Press.

Lees, Lynn H. 1969. "Patterns of Lower-Class Life: Irish Slum Communities in Nineteenth-Century London." In *Nineteenth-Century Cities: Essays in the New Urban History*, ed. S. Thernstrom and R. Sennett, pp. 359–385. New Haven: Yale University Press.

LeVine, Donald N. 1979. "Simmel at a Distance: On the History and Systematics of the Sociology of the Stranger." In *Strangers in African Societies*, ed. William A. Shack and Elliot P. Skinner, pp. 21–37. Berkeley: University of California Press.

Lewis, Oscar. 1972. "Urbanization without Breakdown: A Case Study." *Scientific Monthly* 75:31–41.

Liebow, Elliot. 1967. *Tally's Corner: A Study of Negro Streetcorner Men*. Boston: Little, Brown and Co.

Lodhi, Abdul Qaiyum, and Charles Tilly. 1973. "Urbanization, Crime, and Collective Violence in Nineteenth-Century France." *American Journal of Sociology* 79:296–318.

Lofland, Lyn H. 1973. *A World of Strangers: Order and Action in Urban Public Space*. New York: Basic Books.

Lynch, Kevin. 1960. *The Image of the City*. Cambridge, Mass.: Technology Press.

Mayer, Adrian C. 1966. "The Significance of Quasi-Groups in the Study of Complex Societies." In *The Social Anthropology of Complex Societies*, Association of Social Anthropologists, Monograph No. 4, ed. Michael Banton, pp. 97–123. London: Tavistock.

Mayer, Philip. 1961. *Townsmen or Tribesmen: Conservatism and the Process of Urbanization in a South African City*. 2nd ed. Cape Town: Oxford University Press, 1971.

McIntyre, Jennie. 1967. "Public Attitudes toward Crime and Law Enforcement." *Annals of the American Academy of Political and Social Science* 374:34–47.

McLemore, S. Dale. 1970. "Simmel's 'Stranger': A Critique of the Concept." *Pacific Sociological Review* 13:86–94.

Merry, Sally Engle. 1979. "Going to Court: Strategies of Dispute Management in an American Urban Neighborhood." *Law and Society Review* 13:891–925.

————. 1980. "Racial Integration in an Urban Neighborhood: The Social Organization of Strangers." *Human Organization* 39:59–69.

————. 1981a. "Toward a General Theory of Gossip and Scandal." In *Toward a General Theory of Social Control*, ed. Donald Black. New York: Academic Press (forthcoming).

————. 1981b. "Defensible Space Undefended: Social Factors in Crime Control through Environmental Design." *Urban Affairs Quarterly* 16: in prep.

Milgram, Stanley. 1970. "The Experience of Living in Cities: A Psychological Analysis." *Science* 167:1461–68.

Miller, Stuart Creighton. 1969. *The Unwelcome Immigrant: The American Image of the Chinese, 1785–1882*. Berkeley: University of California Press.

Miner, Horace. 1953. *The Primitive City of Timbuctoo*. Princeton: Princeton University Press.

Mitchell, J. Clyde. 1956. "The Kalela Dance: Aspects of Social Relationships Among Urban Africans in Northern Rhodesia." *Rhodes-Livingstone Papers*, No. 27. Manchester: Manchester University Press.

————. 1966. "Theoretical Orientations in African Urban Studies." In *The Social Anthropology of Complex Societies*, Association of Social Anthropologists, Monograph No. 4, ed. Michael Banton. London: Tavistock.

————. 1969. "The Concept and Use of Social Networks." In *Social Networks in Urban Situations: Analyses of Personal Relationships in Central African Towns*, ed. Mitchell. Manchester: Manchester University Press for the Institute for African Studies, University of Zambia.

Molotch, Harvey. 1972. *Managed Integration: Dilemmas of Doing Good in the City*. Berkeley: University of California Press.

Monkkonen, Eric H. 1975. *The Dangerous Classes: Crime and Poverty in Columbus, Ohio, 1860–1885*. Cambridge, Mass.: Harvard University Press.

Nader, Laura. 1969. "Styles of Court Procedure: To Make the Balance." In *Law in Culture and Society*, ed. Nader. Chicago: Aldine.

National Crime Commission: U.S. President's Commission on Law Enforcement and the Administration of Justice. 1967. *Task Force Report: Crime and its Impact—An Assessment*. Washington, D.C.: U.S. Government Printing Office.

————. 1968. *The Challenge of Crime in a Free Society*. New York: Avon.

Nee, Victor, and Brett de Bary Nee. 1974. *Longtime Californ': A Documentary Study of an American Chinatown*. Boston: Houghton Mifflin Company, Sentry Edition.

Needham, Rodney. 1979. *Symbolic Classification*. Santa Monica, Calif.: Goodyear.

Nelkin, Dorothy. 1970. "Unpredictability and Life Style in a Migrant Labor Camp." *Social Problems* 17:472–487.

Nelli, Humbert S. 1970. *The Italians in Chicago, 1880–1930*. New York: Oxford University Press.

Newman, Oscar. 1973. *Defensible Space: Crime Prevention through Urban Design*. New York: Macmillan, Collier Books.

Orshansky, Mollie. 1965. "Counting the Poor: Another Look at the Poverty Profile." *Social Security Bulletin* 28 (Jan.):3–29.

Park, Robert E. 1952. *Human Communities*. Glencoe, Ill.: The Free Press.

Pepinsky, Harold. 1980. *Crime Control Strategies: An Introduction to the Study of Crime*. New York: Oxford University Press.

Peters, E. Lloyd. 1972. "Aspects of the Control of Moral Ambiguities: A Comparative Analysis of Two Culturally Disparate Modes of Social Control." In *The Allocation of Responsibility*, ed. Max Gluckman. Manchester: Manchester University Press.

Pitt-Rivers, Julian A. 1954. *The People of the Sierra*. 2nd ed. Chicago: University of Chicago Press, 1971.

Pitts, Jesse R. 1968. "Social Control: The Concept." In *International Encyclopedia of the Social Sciences*, vol. 14. New York: Macmillan.

Powell, Elwin H. 1966. "Crime as a Function of Anomie." *Journal of Criminal Law, Criminology, and Police Science* 57:161–171.

Proshansky, Harold M., William H. Ittelson, and Leanee G. Rivlin, eds. 1976. *Environmental Psychology: People and Their Physical Settings*. 2nd ed. New York: Holt, Rinehart, and Winston.

Rainwater, Lee. 1966. "Fear and the House-as-Haven in the Lower Class." *Journal of the American Institute of Planners* 32:23–31.

———. 1970. *Behind Ghetto Walls: Black Family Life in a Federal Slum*. Chicago: Aldine.

Renwanz, Marsha. 1980. "Crime and Ethnicity in the Shetland Islands." *Newsletter of the Association for Political and Legal Anthropology* 3:28–33.

Roberts, Bryan. 1973. *Organizing Strangers*. Austin and London: University of Texas Press.

Rörig, Fritz. 1967. *The Medieval Town*. Berkeley: University of California Press.

Saalman, Howard. 1968. *Medieval Cities*. New York: George Braziller.

Salgado, Gamini. 1977. *The Elizabethan Underworld*. London: J. M. Dent and Sons.

Sansom, Basil. 1972. "When Witches Are Not Named." In *The Allocation of Responsibility*, ed. Max Gluckman. Manchester: Manchester University Press.

Scheibe, Karl E. 1974. "Legitimized Aggression and the Assignment of Evil." *The American Scholar* 43:576–592.

Schuetz, Alfred. 1944. "The Stranger: An Essay in Social Psychology." *American Journal of Sociology* 49:499–507.

Seligman, Martin E. P. 1975. *Helplessness: On Depression, Development, and Death*. San Francisco: W. H. Freeman and Co.

Sennett, Richard. 1973. "Middle Class Families and Urban Violence: The Experience of a Chicago Community in the Nineteenth Century." In *The American Family in Social-Historical Perspective*, ed. Michael Gordon. New York: St. Martin's Press.

Shack, William A., and Elliott P. Skinner, eds. 1979. *Strangers in African Societies*. Berkeley: University of California Press.

Silberman, Charles E. 1978. *Criminal Violence, Criminal Justice*. New York: Random House.

Simmel, Georg. 1950. *The Sociology of Georg Simmel*. Trans. and ed. Kurt H. Wolff. Glencoe, Ill.: Free Press.

Siu, P. C. P. 1952. "The Sojourner." *American Journal of Sociology* 58:34–44.

Sjoberg, Gideon. 1960. *The Preindustrial City*. New York: Free Press.

Smith, Michael P. 1979. *The City and Social Theory*. New York: St. Martin's Press.

Stack, Carol B. 1974. *All Our Kin: Strategies for Survival in a Black Community*. New York: Harper and Row.

Sung, Betty Lee. 1967. *Mountain of Gold: The Story of the Chinese in America*. New York: Macmillan.

Survey Research Center, Institute for Social Research. 1975. "Quality of Life in the Detroit Metropolitan Area: Public Safety." Ann Arbor, Mich.: Survey Research Center, University of Michigan.

Suttles, Gerald D. 1968. *The Social Order of the Slum*. Chicago: University of Chicago Press.

———. 1972. *The Social Construction of Communities*. Chicago: University of Chicago Press.

Tilly, Charles. 1969. "Collective Violence in European Perspective." In *Violence in America: Historical and Comparative Perspectives*, vol. 2, ed. Hugh Davis Graham and Ted Robert Gurr, pp. 5–35.

Tobias, J. J. 1967. *Urban Crime in Victorian England*. New York: Schocken Books.

Turner, V. W. 1967. *The Forest of Symbols: Aspects of Ndembu Ritual*. Ithaca, N.Y.: Cornell University Press.

―――. 1969. *The Ritual Process: Structure and Anti-Structure*. Chicago: Aldine.

U.S. Bureau of the Census. 1967. *Statistical Abstract of the United States, 1967*. 88th ed. Edwin D. Goldfield, Director. Washington, D.C.: U.S. Government Printing Office.

U.S. Department of Justice, Federal Bureau of Investigation. *Uniform Crime Reports for the United States, 1975*. Washington, D.C.: U.S. Government Printing Office, 1976.

U.S. Department of Justice, National Criminal Justice Information and Statistics Service. *Criminal Victimization Surveys in Thirteen American Cities*. Washington, D.C.: U.S. Government Printing Office, 1975.

Valentine, Bettylou. 1978. *Hustling and Other Hard Work: Life Styles in the Ghetto*. New York: Free Press.

Venter, Herman J. 1962. "Urbanization and Industrialization as Criminogenic Factors in the Republic of South Africa." *International Review of Criminal Policy* 20: 59–71.

Wheeldon, P. D. 1969. "The Operation of Voluntary Associations and Personal Networks in the Political Processes of an Inter-Ethnic Community." In *Social Networks in Urban Situations*, ed. J. Clyde Mitchell. Manchester: Manchester University Press.

Whyte, William F. 1943. *Street-Corner Society: The Social Structure of an Italian Slum*. Chicago: University of Chicago Press.

Wilson, James Q. 1966. "Crime in the Streets." *The Public Interest* 5:26–35.

―――. 1975. *Thinking About Crime*. New York: Basic Books.

Wilson, Monica, and A. Mafeje. 1963. *Langa: A Study of Social Groups in An African Township*. London: Oxford University Press.

Wirth, Louis. 1928. *The Ghetto*. Chicago: University of Chicago Press.

―――. 1938. "Urbanism as a Way of Life." *American Journal of Sociology* 44:1–24.

Wolfe, Albert Benedict. 1913. *The Lodging House Problem in Boston*. Published from the income of the William H. Baldwin, Jr., 1885 Fund. Cambridge, Mass.: Harvard University Press.

Wolfgang, Marvin E. 1967. "Urban Crime." In *The Metropolitan Enigma: Inquiries into the Nature and Dimensions of America's Urban Crisis*, ed. James Q. Wilson. Washington, D.C.: Chamber of Commerce of the United States.

Wood, Margaret M. 1934. *The Stranger: A Study in Social Relationships*. New York: Columbia University Press.

Yancey, William L. 1971. "Architecture, Interaction, and Social Control: The Case of a Large-Scale Public Housing Project." *Environment and Behavior* 3:3–21.

Yngvesson, Barbara. 1976. "Responses to Grievance Behavior: Extended Cases in a Fishing Community." *American Ethnologist* 3:353–373.

Young, Michael and Peter Willmott. 1957. *Family and Kinship in East London*. London: Routledge and Kegan Paul.

Zorbaugh, Harvey F. 1929. *The Gold Coast and the Slum*. Chicago: University of Chicago Press.

INDEX